INTELLECTUAL PROPERTY PROTECT

INTELLECTUAL PROPERTY PROTECT

BUSINESS-ALIGNED IP STRATEGY

CHERYL MILONE ESQ, BSEE

LIONCREST PUBLISHING

COPYRIGHT © 2024 #IP2IP, CHERYL MILONE, ESQ., BSEE
All rights reserved.

INTELLECTUAL PROPERTY PROTECT
Business-Aligned IP Strategy

FIRST EDITION

ISBN 978-1-5445-4459-5 *Hardcover*
      978-1-5445-4457-1 *Paperback*
      978-1-5445-4458-8 *Ebook*

*For Rebecca, Jason, Mom, Dad, Cynthia, Emily and Hershey,
and my wonderful family, with honor, respect and humility.*

CONTENTS

FOREWORD 13
By Julie Mar-Spinola

INTRODUCTION 17
Simplified Execution

PART I: EXECUTION

1. MISSION QUALITY 29
   *Intellectual Property (IP) Strategy Starts
   and Succeeds with Quality*

2. #IP2IP PATENTS: OPPORTUNITY AND ANALYSIS 55
   Win the Race to Patent

   Opportunities 58
   Analysis 75

3. #IP2IP PATENTS: RISKS 93
   Planning for Prevention

   > Patent Uncertainty under 101 Dominates in a Descent
   > Down the Alice Rabbit Hole
   > By Robert Rando 97

4. #IP2IP PATENTS: YOUR FUTURE SUCCESS 117
   Innovating the Patent System

   > Strive for Quality Patents and Additional IP
   > By Julie Mar-Spinola 124

   > Monetization for SMEs to Enterprises
   > By Erich Spangenberg, with Jonas Block 127

   > Value-Driven IP Portfolio Management
   > By Ruud Peters 130

5. #IP2IP COPYRIGHTS 137
   It's All in the Writing
   Co-Author, J. Christopher Lynch

   > Opportunities 141
   > Analysis 144
   > Risks 153

6. #IP2IP TRADE SECRETS 159
   The Trade Secret Program You Didn't Know You Had

   > Opportunities 161
   > Analysis 166
   > Risks 184

7. #IP2IP TRADEMARKS AND DESIGN PATENTS............... 191
   Make Your Mark and Succeed by Design
   Co-Author, J. Christopher Lynch

   Opportunities 193
   Analysis 221
   Risks 223

PART II: OBJECTIVE

8. IP HONOR 229
   Honor the Individual

PART III: SYSTEMS

9. COST 245
   $60 and a Dream

10. #IP2IP CHECKLIST 273
    Do Business in the Bullseye
    Co-Author, J. Christopher Lynch

    CONCLUSION 285
    A Smile Goes a Mile

    ACKNOWLEDGMENTS 293
    ABOUT THE AUTHOR 299
    REFERENCED INDIVIDUALS (LINKEDIN) 301
    NOTES 303

*"We are what we repeatedly do.
Excellence then is not an act but a habit."*

—WILLIAM DURANT, AN AMERICAN WRITER,
BASED ON HIS INTERPRETATION
OF ARISTOTLE'S WORK

FOREWORD

BY JULIE MAR-SPINOLA

Cheryl Milone and I walked the intellectual property (IP) path of patents together since the early 2000s, but on opposite coasts. Despite the geography, we became dear friends and colleagues. Though we worked in different industries, Cheryl and I set our sights on the same target—urging, supporting, and creating ways to ensure IP assets, particularly patents, are valid, valuable, and available to all innovators.

Living on the East Coast, Cheryl's IP expertise was honed by her engagement with the financial industry in funding her startup dedicated to empowering the US patent system. As a new patent attorney in 2006, she invented processes and practices for ensuring strong and enforceable patents through social means, by founding her nationally lauded Article One Partners, which offers a crowdsourced IP research platform to vet quality patent assets. She's been doing great things in the IP space since then, optimizing IP strategy across electronics and mechanical industries, and from other startup founders through to Fortune 100 companies, most recently as a managing director and global head of IP strategy in engineering at a leading investment bank. As a result, Cheryl is well qualified to write this book; we are fortunate she has.

Patents are complex creatures for even the most experienced patent practitioners, holders and monetizers. Less-experienced stakeholders—the casual problem solver or tinkerer who accidentally creates something new and useful for the masses, the corporate engineer or scientist assigned to beat their competitors' competing products or find a cure for some trending disease, the supervising professor and student researcher with their unexpected findings on a given thesis—often reach crossroads for how best to preserve and protect their inventions with limited knowledge and budgets on the next steps of protecting and perhaps monetizing their inventions. Some will hand off their inventions to in-house counsel or university technology offices to handle, and some will find attorneys who offer their services for lower fees (and less experience) to file applications for patents. All are fine, but as I learned growing up in our family's restaurant business, the thriving businesses are those with owners who can cook in the kitchen. You should know enough about how to protect your inventions and innovations.

This book, *Intellectual Property Protect: Business-Aligned IP Strategy*, is Cheryl's latest outreach to the innovating community. The mission I believe Cheryl fulfills is to cut a clear, viable path for those looking to adequately protect their inventions on quality principles and ensure these valuable assets are aligned to support a thriving business through tried-and-true best patent practices. In fact, for entrepreneurial readers, developing corresponding trademarks, trade secret portfolios and appropriate copyright protections can serve as a fortress against would-be opponents and solidify the value of your enterprise multifold. In addition, this book can at least boost the reader's level of sophistication in patents and the other forms of IP if they know (and can ask pointed questions about) what is needed to ensure their IP assets are well described and well vetted, to survive future enforcement challenges. It will not surprise me if this book becomes a valuable resource to its readers, akin to having an impactful mentor sitting by your side and cheering you on with action, strength and clarity.

INTRODUCTION

SIMPLIFIED EXECUTION

My father, a doctor himself and always one to exceed expectations, began his convalescence after brain surgery by talking with the surgical staff in the recovery room. A few days later, he was ready to leave the hospital.

There were papers to sign and bottles of prescription medications to deal with. A diligent nurse gave us detailed instructions for administering each pill—how many, taken in the morning or night, with or without food. Did it have to be so complicated?

"I appreciate your help," I said. "But for all these medications on the chart, will any hurt him or be less effective if he takes them *with* food? I'm trying to make this as simple as possible." The nurse met my eyes and smiled. She understood my goal.

"Yes—" she said after a careful review of the chart "—each of these can be taken with food."

I turned to Dad and said, "We'll make two sets of pills to take at breakfast and dinner to make this easy." With the wonderful nurse's expertise, I could simplify that one task so my father could focus on the more difficult ones for his full recovery.

Long off those medications, Dad still remarks on my endless quest for simplicity in execution wherever I can find it. That is a goal that I apply not only during health emergencies but also for the law.

After all, patent law isn't brain surgery.

Once experts simplify execution, they succeed in making a subject accessible, so the audience has the information to make informed decisions.

I offer this book with the same objective in mind—to simplify the execution of intellectual property (IP) and enable rational business decisions. IP protects innovation, giving its owner a valuable competitive advantage in the market. However, the topic traditionally elicits a sense of cost and complexity. Business is better understood with well-defined strategies.

By bringing IP into the ordinary course of business, you can build your IP strategy based on business planning, budgeting and accountability. Business-aligned IP strategy then simplifies execution.

Author. The information I present derives from my twenty-four years as an intellectual property attorney, supporting companies from startups (including my own) to Fortune 50 companies. My legal practice focused on patent and trade secrets. I also am fortunate to be an inventor, entrepreneur and technology business owner, enabling me to sit in the seat of business owners and experience the stress of financials and business priorities as a context for IP. This book is written from the mindset of a business owner, with legal principles as necessary tools.

Intended Audience. While multiple audiences can benefit from this book, it is targeted at small and medium enterprises (SMEs) and individual inventors. SMEs and individual inventors are often new to IP and navigating its complexity. They may also have limited access to funding. Therefore, simplified execution of IP strategy is highly impactful. Larger enterprises also can benefit from a focus on business-aligned IP strategy, even within their relatively greater experience with IP.

While written primarily for business executives, the information presented is still relevant to attorneys and patent agents as IP professionals. I welcome IP professionals and have incorporated into this book outstanding insights and feedback from IP visionaries (see acknowledgments). Business-minded IP professionals will find value for their individual or corporate clients as in-house or outside professionals.

Intended Technologies and US Geography. This book addresses the technology areas of electronics, whether implemented in hardware and/or software (generally referenced as computer-implemented technology) or in mechanical devices for IP protection in the United States. These technologies and the geography are covered by my experience in both counseling clients and executing IP strategy in my own startup.

Other technology and scientific areas, notably biochemical

innovations, are beyond the scope of this book. IP subject matter is specialized, with patent professionals generally working in either electrical and mechanical areas or biochemical fields. Those with biochemical innovations are best served by experts in those subjects. Similarly, international geographies require professionals with expertise in each relevant jurisdiction.

Muses. Thank you to my son, Jason, for designing the cover, applying his artistic talent to my attempt at playing chess, and giving me my favorite part of this book. To my daughter, Rebecca, my inspiration to start writing in the first place—watching you at age ten write your first book in pencil—you have my appreciation and admiration.

Co-Author and Contributors. I have also been fortunate to have leading IP experts as colleagues and contributors to this book, including **J. Christopher Lynch, Julie Mar-Spinola, Ruud Peters, Rob Rando, Erich Spangenberg and Jonas Block.** This book builds upon the brilliant insights and inspiration of these and many other outstanding IP leaders, highlighted throughout, using their cited published works and advocacy for strong US patent rights.

THE INTELLECTUAL PROPERTY SPECTRUM

Many companies are founded upon a single good idea. Growing those companies requires protection across IP along the *intellectual property spectrum*. It includes patents, copyrights, trade secrets, trademarks and design patents. The process of building IP involves identifying and refining that good idea and honoring the inventors and creators as the sources of it.

INTELLECTUAL PROPERTY: PROTECT THEN PROFIT

While I'm formally educated as an electrical engineer and lawyer, my heart has always been in applying my expertise to create business value. This requires more than filing for and managing IP. It requires IP protection of innovation with high-quality, cost-efficient and timely IP assets aligned with business objectives. Once protected as assets, IP can drive profits. First, you protect. Then, you profit.

My expertise is weighted toward the protection side, as reflected in the book's focus and title, *Intellectual Property Protect*. However, protection is pursued with the end in mind. *Business-Aligned IP Strategy* explains business planning and budgeting to optimize IP protection. The main objective of business is profit. Getting protection correct places you in the best position to profit.

Let's showcase it this way: *invest in protection to increase profit*—or #ip2ip with my penchant to shorten phrases in pursuit of simplified execution. You can expect to see **#ip2ip** throughout this book and even in a closer look at the cover background.

> INVEST IN PROTECTION TO
> INCREASE PROFIT = #IP2IP

#IP2IP WALK-THROUGH

Speaking of execution, the book has three parts: Execution, Objective and Systems, with each chapter beginning with actions, or "ACTions." My mission extends beyond education to prompt ACTion with the highest and best use of your valuable time and resources. As you read more, you'll see "*Top-10*

Takeaways" and instructions to pause on reading and complete IP filings. Execution is front and center, with these approaches to simplify it.

IP assets derive from your creations and inventions. You honor them by protecting them and, in doing so, recognizing their inventors and creators. I will have succeeded if this book prompts that protection.

Part I: Execution. Building on this introduction, Part I focuses on Execution with ACTions. Chapter 1 presents the **Mission** for IP protection—in a word, **Quality**—as our overall action of *IP Strategy Starts and Succeeds with Quality*. Patent and IP quality expands beyond a historic showcase of patent quantity, or patent arsenals, as a value driver. The IP spectrum also is introduced, along with tackling the first question for every innovator: How much is it going to cost?

In Chapters 2 through 7, you'll learn how to jump-start IP strategy based on exploring three sections—Opportunities, Analysis and Risks—for the IP spectrum: **Patents** (*Win the Race to Patent*, *Planning for Prevention* and learn from the most successful historic patent monetizers for a glimpse into profit in *Your Future Success*), **Copyrights** (*It's All in the Writing*), **Trade Secrets** (*The Trade Secret Program You Didn't Know You Had*) and **Trademarks and Designs** (*Make Your Mark and Succeed by Design*).

Part II: Objective. Chapter 8 introduces my career-long passion: **IP Honor** (*Honor the Individual*), which is about the heart of patents and intellectual property: people.

Part III: Systems. I step off my evangelism box to discuss the pragmatic topics of cost and checklists. As showcased in Chapter 9: Cost, our precious US patent system reflects optimism in supporting new inventors with an economic incentive of *$60 and a Dream*. I contribute by providing the life cycle cost and sample annual budgets for US patent grants from one to twelve patents.

Chapter 10 rounds out #ip2ip with a system to operationalize IP strategy, in an all-too-familiar approach to organization—a **checklist**. While common in business, it's uncommon for IP strategy. So I built my own with an objective of simplifying execution to take ACTion for both offense and defense and to *Do Business in the Bullseye*.

Finally, to avoid leaving you with a cold, hard checklist, I close on a personal note, *A Smile Goes a Mile*. It's about having a positive attitude, a powerful tool I was fortunate to learn from my family. I would like to pass it on to you, and if you are so inspired, for you to pass it along to others as a way of honoring them and their infinite potential.

Style. Before forging on to obligatory legal disclaimers, let's pause for a style break. I invoke style choices below that filter throughout #ip2ip. I've made these choices to lighten, due to legal topics, what inevitably becomes complicated and weighty. I strive to avoid complexity, and instead invite readers to the topic and honor their knowledge and business objectives rather than mine. My role is in service of innovators who seek to live the dream of invention.

My style choices take a few forms:

- *Italics.* Like many specialties, intellectual property law has specialized terms, called *legal terms of art.* Some redefine known words or phrases, and others are likely new to the reader. Putting them in italics sets this out from the start (noting that chapter taglines also are in italics as another use of italics in #ip2ip).

- *The Lawyerly Litany.* With due respect to the law and its practitioners, and an acknowledgment that #ip2ip is founded in the law, the legal analysis is secondary to its application to business strategy. The "Lawyerly Litany" sections are intended to provide a minimalist approach to teaching US law and its application, commending you to the abundance of excellent treatises instead. This approach should empower executives and innovators to avoid being weighed down with legal analysis and instead to execute.

- *Insider Lawball.* Sections labeled and boxed with this title represent a deeper treatment of a subject, added to either provide the cutting edge of strategy or an insider's view. A visual is a judge asking attorneys for an insider discussion at the bench. Feel free to join or skip to return to the topic at hand.

- *Commas.* I have a minimalist approach to the use of commas. For grammarians, the only solace I can offer is that when the grammar of commas adapts yet again, perhaps my approach will conform.

THE FIRST LAWYERLY LITANY

Disclaimer. Lastly before we begin our journey together, as the first Lawyerly Litany, I am obliged to specify disclaimers, as authors are sometimes sued for their books. So these are formal disclaimers: Please do not rely on this book as legal advice, nor me as your attorney. I would have to be formally engaged with a signed "engagement letter" as your attorney (including passing a conflict check to ensure I can represent you) for you to rely on the information in this book as legal advice or to present me as your attorney. Purchasing this book does not establish any legal relationship—it is for informational purposes only. Please consult a legal professional to determine the best plan of action for you individually or your company.

Importantly, the views and opinions expressed in this book are those of the author and do not reflect the position, policy or endorsement of any other person or entity. The content by the co-author or contributors similarly do not reflect any endorsement of the book, and similarly do not reflect the position, policy or endorsement of any other person or entity.

#ip2ip Is Current through October 2023. I present this specific timing because, of course, the law changes and will do so in some minor and major respects after the content is locked. You'll also see dates specified throughout #ip2ip. Acknowledging this reality, it is my job to present IP strategy with a timeless foundation that remains relevant within legal developments. I advocate following trends and creating your own, along with formal legal counseling from IP professionals, to ensure that your application of #ip2ip is optimal at the time applied.

Your initial ACTion: take full advantage of your time with

#ip2ip. With honor and excitement to spend this time with you, let's begin.

PART I

EXECUTION

CHAPTER 1

MISSION QUALITY

INTELLECTUAL PROPERTY (IP) STRATEGY STARTS AND SUCCEEDS WITH QUALITY

ACTions

1.1 Prioritize quality over quantity.
1.2 Think beyond patents and across the intellectual property spectrum.
1.3 Showcase crown jewel IP assets aligned with their line of business.
1.4 Be intentional about IP strategy to optimize patent value and reduce risk.

Intellectual property is about creation and work, two noble and pure pursuits. It is the product of human intellect—"knowledge, truths ascertained, conceptions, and ideas," and as many view, real property.[1] Hence the phrase *intellectual property*, as an IP spectrum of rights governed by US laws to help companies protect their innovations and creations. This IP spectrum encompasses the familiar types of patents, copyrights, trade secrets and trademarks.

INTELLECTUAL PROPERTY ASSETS

Some companies are built around a single good idea. But every big company gets big by growing ideas (ideally protected by *patents* and *trade secrets*); presenting inspiring and creative company and product names (*trademarks*), designs (*trade dress* and *design patents*) and content (*copyrights*) to entice customers; fortifying their treasured competitive advantages (*trade secrets*) for market capture; and building brands and goodwill (*trademarks*) along their path to success. The best big companies have assets across the spectrum of intellectual property and adapt and expand their IP assets with growth—even if founded upon a single good idea.

IP is deserving of being incentivized in society, and once achieved, protected. Protection should include fair compensation when these works are copied by others without the owner's permission. The laws governing intellectual property do just that. They convert original creations and works into legal assets, incentivizing inventors and creators to produce works for the benefit of the public.

While IP use by global brands is well known, its benefits for small and medium enterprises (or SMEs) are borne out in research. As the United States Patent and Trademark Office (referred to as USPTO, PTO or the Office) director, the Honorable Kathi Vidal, presented in 2022: "[w]e know that startup companies are far more likely to be successful in raising funds for new product development...than those that have not secured [IP] protection."[2] Similarly, the Honorable Andrei Iancu as a former PTO director in 2020 commented: "[p]atents are primarily for SMEs" because "SMEs have few other tools to win…they do not have economies of scale, for example. If you want competition, if you want to prevent monopolistic behavior, and you want to give the little guy a shot at winning, you want patents for SMEs…"[3]

An Economic Engine. On a macroeconomic level, IP accumulates to the economic strength of national economies. The US legacy of leading global innovation and economic power derives from our IP system. The free world has largely modeled its IP laws around the United States' system, and US intellectual property is open to inventors and creators globally.

The fruits of our intellectual property system have lifted standards of living across the globe, providing broader access to new developments. An investment in the protection of IP and a recognition of its value provides a catalyst for innovation. A third noble and pure pursuit.

Protecting Markets by Stopping or Excluding Copiers. Intellectual property enables owners to prohibit others from copying or using protected rights. This ability to stop copying (or *right to exclude*) creates value in the protected concepts as true, intangible assets.

Stopping others from copying does not mean a right to take action. Rather, the right to exclude protects the owners' market for their offering, giving it a chance to build with competition temporarily held at bay. However, commercializing the offering may be prohibited by the IP rights of others. Often, when the parties in litigation are competitors, they countersue each other to determine the winner regarding competing IP.

THE IP SPECTRUM

The IP spectrum of patents, copyrights, trade secrets and trademarks is founded upon the right to exclude. This right is a government-granted *monopoly*. As with any other right, it is limited, with each type having a differing limitation boundary.

- *Patents* protect inventions for new real-world solutions to problems that you or your company invented before anyone else. Patents explain how an innovation works or *functions* (called *utility* patents) and are published to educate others and advance knowledge. Many innovations are inventions, but not all inventions are patentable. To become a patent, an invention must be new, nonobvious, useful and *eligible* (for example, as opposed to *abstract ideas* or *laws of nature*). The US Patent and Trademark Office administers patents by evaluating applications to determine whether to grant them as patents. Once granted, they last for twenty years from the start date of the patenting process. There are patents for designs, too, called *design patents*, as well as *plant patents*.

- *Copyright* applies the moment your content is memorialized, such as a pen or brush to paper, or a talk or song to a recording—this sentence is copyrighted, for example. Formally, copyright arises when an original work of authorship is part of a tangible medium. Copyright covers works that are expressions of creative ideas, such as writings, art, music, computer software code, databases, data models and digital works, rather than the ideas themselves. Registering copyrights with the United States Copyright Office (Copyright Office or USCO) is not required to take advantage of these rights, but there are critical benefits in doing so.

- *Trade secrets* encompass quite a lot. Inventions can be kept secret rather than pursuing patents for them, in which the invention would be published. You also might be surprised at how many daily business materials can be trade secrets. If your organization doesn't want the competition to know something because it gives you an edge, and if this information is not revealed to the public and there are procedures such as confidentiality agreements in place to protect it, then it's likely considered a trade secret. One might fear there is no way to register a trade secret without revealing the secret. However, copyright registration can obscure portions of filings which contain trade secrets.

- *Trademarks* protect distinctive aspects of a company's name, logo, taglines, phrases, devices and symbols, so long as they identify to the market who made the goods or services (*source identifier*). Trademarks must not confuse the market with the source of goods and services of others. *Trade dress*, or the appearance of products, is another form of trademark and overlaps with *design patents*. Registration for key marks is a must, as well as maintenance of those registrations.

While IP laws are best known for protection against copying by others, for some rights they also include overlapping uses by third parties that are not intentionally copied but are still identical. Two of the four intellectual property rights, patent and trademark, also prohibit this unintended copying. As a result, these rights are broader in scope than copyrights and trade secrets.

THE BIRTH OF INTELLECTUAL PROPERTY IN THE US CONSTITUTION

The concept of modern global intellectual property was born in the United States Constitution. While most laws derive from the authorization of Congress to enact them in the law of our land, protection of IP is specified in these few precious words. Article 1, Section 8, Clause 8, known as the *Limited Times* clause, provides:

> [Congress shall have the power to] promote the progress of science and the useful arts, by securing for limited times to authors and inventors the exclusive right to their respective writings and discoveries.

President Washington's first State of the Union similarly devoted an entire seventy-seven-word paragraph, within a mere 1,096-word speech, to patents. The Patent Act of 1790 was the third law ever passed by Congress, reflecting the importance of IP laws from our country's inception.[4]

INTELLECTUAL PROPERTY BY THE SUCCESS NUMBERS

Numerous studies present the success of IP for startups, which is especially impactful given that SMEs "[create] nearly two-thirds of all new jobs."[5] Once a patent is achieved, statistics provided in 2022 by USPTO Director Vidal are as follows:[6]

> When used as collateral, a patent increases venture capital funding by 76% over three years, and increases funding from an initial public offering by 128%... After five years, a new company with a patent increase its sales by a cumulative 80% more than companies that do not have a patent.

Former Director Iancu of the USPTO said in 2018:[7]

> Approval of a startup's first patent application increases its employment growth over the next five years by 36 percentage points on average.

History also reinforces IP value through game-changing emerging innovations, such as those prompted by the COVID-19 global pandemic:

> IP assets such as brand names, customer data, and trademarks gain value as COVID-19 upends traditional business models.[8]

This is borne out in today's digital revolution, as well as the continuous pace of the next innovation through history. For example, after a shift from manufacturing to a service-based economy in the 1970s, information technology exploded in the 1980s. The US economy transitioned to an information-based economy in which physical assets such as property, plant and equipment (PP&E) declined in importance. These assets were replaced by intangible assets, which now dominate corporate market value at 84 percent of the S&P 500® companies' balance sheets. The ascension of e-commerce companies Apple®, Alphabet®, Microsoft®, Amazon® and Meta® by 2018 as the five largest global companies by market cap leading the S&P 500® demonstrates this shift.[9]

TANGIBLE ASSETS VS. INTANGIBLE ASSETS FOR S&P 500 COMPANIES, 1975-2018

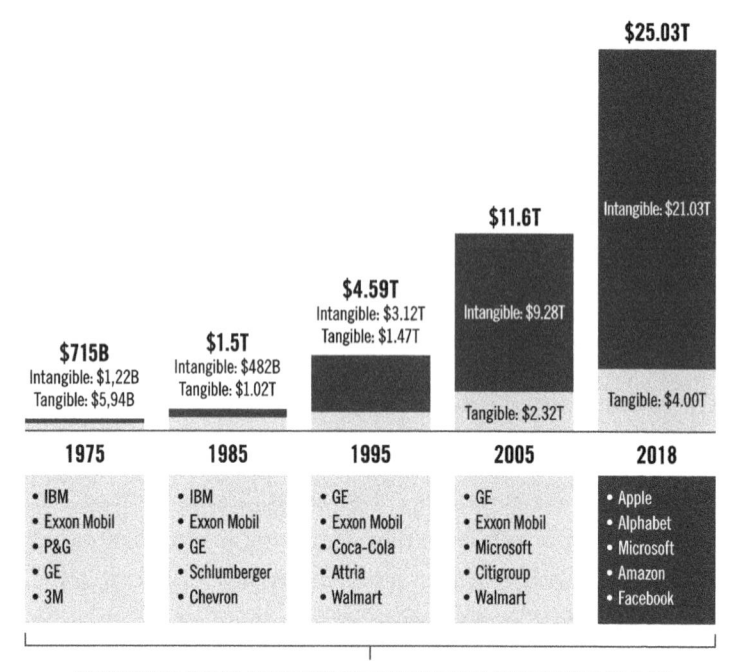

	1975	1985	1995	2005	2018
Total	$715B	$1.5T	$4.59T	$11.6T	$25.03T
Intangible	$1.22B	$482B	$3.12T	$9.28T	$21.03T
Tangible	$5.94B	$1.02T	$1.47T	$2.32T	$4.00T

Five largest global companies by market cap as of December 31, 2018

- 1975: IBM, Exxon Mobil, P&G, GE, 3M
- 1985: IBM, Exxon Mobil, GE, Schlumberger, Chevron
- 1995: GE, Exxon Mobil, Coca-Cola, Attria, Walmart
- 2005: GE, Exxon Mobil, Microsoft, Citigroup, Walmart
- 2018: Apple, Alphabet, Microsoft, Amazon, Facebook

TANGIBLE ASSETS
- Easy to value
- Thick and efficient secondary markets
- Insurable

INTANGIBLE ASSETS
- Difficult to value
- Thin and inefficient secondary markets
- Difficult to Insure

"Copyright Aon plc 2019," of the graph in "2019 Intangible Assets Financial Statement Impact Comparison Report."[10]

While the makeup of intangible assets and their contribution to market cap can be nuanced, depending on the size and type of company, industry and lines of business, this statistic demonstrates that IP can be capitalized as assets on the balance sheet.

There is also global recognition of the importance of intangible assets, with the European Union presenting the following:

> Intangible assets such as inventions, cultural creations, brands, software, know-how, and data are the cornerstone of today's economy.[11]

The ascension of intangible assets (as well as assets which IP facilitates, such as know-how, brand and goodwill) supports managing IP holistically. By doing so, synergies and cost-benefit analyses can be applied in selecting IP assets to maximize protection for innovations.

IP ASSETS ARE DESIGNED FOR COST-EFFICIENCY

The concept of IP is to incentivize innovation so that inventors and creators will bring the innovation to market to benefit society. Then, when the limited monopoly right expires, society can use the innovation free from its economic cost.

Another facet of these rights is the *cost efficiency* of procuring IP. Before you react with rising financial emotions, cost efficiency focuses on getting IP assets—IP protect—and not profit. Profit understandably raises the potential of high-cost litigation. However, litigation can occur whether or not you have IP if you are sued for infringement. Therefore, arming yourself with IP assets and the attendant education of defensive use warrants at least exploring the opportunity and its costs.

In addition, an article about fundamental startup costs states that on average an owner should expect to pay between $1,000 and $5,000 annually on professional consulting fees and $1,200 on insurance.[12] Annually! In contrast, IP investments afford protection over decades and even on an unlimited basis. For example, a utility patent at the highest IP investment is in force for twenty years from the application filing date, and protection of trade secrets and trademarks are potentially unlimited.

Procurement costs can be distributed over years. Additionally, as the statistics for SMEs with even one patent show, benefits can be achieved by elevating quality over quantity. Similarly, where litigation is prompted based on third-party copying or for defense against a competitor lawsuit, how many patents are optimal to assert in litigation? One study about competitor patent litigation from case law decisions in 2011 found that plaintiffs assert on average 2.2 patents per case.[13] Courts also limit the number of patents or numbered inventions as the key property right description in the patent, called *claims*, that can be adjudicated, accumulating to a single-digit number of patents on average.[14]

Compared to other business operational costs, and with uncertainty about litigation costs, whether or not you pursue IP, cost-efficient IP investment is economically rational.

On this basis, I present all-in costs *and* the time period over which they apply. All-in includes attorney, service, and administrative costs, plus USPTO formal fees on an annual budget. Second, costs are based on attorneys, but with deference to selecting instead the excellent resource of patent agents at generally lower costs than attorneys.[15]

Disclaimer. With costs changing over time, the data below is estimated as of September 2023 (as discussed in Chapter 9: Cost).[16] In addition, costs are impacted by the complexity of the subject matter and the acuity of your professional and the PTO patent representatives, among other factors. Therefore, these costs are for general information only and are not a guarantee nor offer for legal services generally or at the presented reference costs.

- *Patents* (for utility) are granted 56 percent of the time after a complicated and expensive filing process with the United States Patent and Trademark Office, compared to other IP assets. The estimated cost (including attorney, administrative and PTO fees) can be **as low as $60 initially, followed by $17,500 to $20,000 spread out over the next two to three years**. The timing is based on a $60 investment to secure up to one year to start the formal patenting process of a utility filing, followed by an average of 25.9 months for the PTO decision. Granted, patents generally afford protection for twenty years from filing (with maintenance fees). **A design patent estimated cost is less than $4,000 over 21.3 months.**

- *Copyrights*, while automatically arising "from the fixation of an original work," should be registered to maximize enforcement potential, as the most cost-effective IP investment at less than $100 DIY registration using free US Copyright Office resources. With professional support, **the estimated cost is between $750 and $1,500.** Copyrights have a much longer duration than patents, generally expiring after the "life of the author plus seventy years."

- *Trade secrets*, once developed under a program to retain their secrecy, do not have to be registered. Their only required costs are the investments in human resource agreements and maintaining their secrecy, but identifying trade secrets in summary form at the timing of pursuing patents and copyright is advised. Where they are documented with copyrights, their **estimated cost equates to that for copyrights, plus fees for redacting evidence** with add-ons for redacted files to protect secrecy. They remain protected during their period of secrecy internally and where competitors fail to independently uncover them.

- *Trademarks* come into being without formal registration because they exist from use in commerce as common law rights. Even so, registering them with the US Patent and Trademark Office can reap additional statutory benefits, cost-efficiently deter infringers and maximize enforcement potential, at less than $500 DIY for a single-class federal application using free USPTO resources, or with professional support at **an estimated cost of less than $3,000 over 11.2 months where registration is successful.** Trademarks remain in force as long as trademark use continues and registrations are maintained, actively monitored and addressed where copying is found.

INTELLECTUAL PROPERTY STRATEGY

Technology owners ideally fund operations through revenues, but potentially attract investors to seed launches or grow operations. Other factors command operational focus, with needs increasing as the company grows.

IP is Optional. Enter stage left—*intellectual property*—as an optional undertaking. Given the demands on business owners with limited resources, optional IP is easily deprioritized and sometimes bumped off the business planning list entirely.

Where IP is pursued, companies typically follow a standard approach to IP strategy: an invention should be *patented* and anything written *copyrighted*. But beyond that framework, the entire area for many new to IP spells C-O-S-T, complexity and interacting with lawyers and professionals, adding yet more cost.

IP strategy is hard to come by, often simply focused on maximizing patent arsenals. In an article citing 2015 data, titled "Why IP Strategy Matters," Johanna Dwyer of QipWorks® posits that "[a]n effective [IP] strategy is an integral component in the business models of successful technology companies and is often their key source of competitive advantage. Yet, a surprising number of companies have no IP strategy at all. Of those that do, most have IP strategies…written independently from their business strategy, focusing solely on the number of inventions and patent grant percentages."[17]

A need for IP strategy also flows from competitors. Plato's *Crito* teaches us that we are obliged to a system that provides us with rights. The rights of others will prompt obligations for you. Analyzing IP assets includes understanding how they might be used against you. Even high-quality IP assets are subject to potentially high-quality assets of others. They also are impacted by market and competitive data and other factors that may reduce the value of IP assets (or even render them worthless). Declining these obligations, on the other hand, may result in learning from competitors via seven-figure litigation costs. Therefore, IP strategy optimizes not only offensive but also defensive considerations.

If risk is your primary motivator to explore IP, then look at your obligations also as a means of fully unlocking IP. As an executive responsible for maximizing investment returns, meeting your obligations for IP defense can create opportunities for IP protection of your offerings. This transforms an obligation into an opportunity to capitalize on IP protection and support your business objectives and ultimately, your success.

MISSION QUALITY: QUALITY IS THE NEW QUANTITY

Historically, the bellwether of innovation has been represented by a scorecard of the quantity of patents in *patent portfolios* owned by worldwide companies. Companies like IBM® and Toshiba® are indicative of this legacy. Fifty companies alone were found to account for about 30 percent of all patents in 2018, with many patent owners simply touting their growing stockpile.[18] Some companies also purchase patent portfolios to trigger a stepwise presence in their ownership relative to their peers. IP other than patents, while valuable, do not garner the same level of press and industry attention.

Even today, the most common question asked in intellectual property discussions is, "How many patents do you have?" Patent portfolio size is a ready way to demonstrate valuable assets within the arsenal and to measure next to competitors. The quantity approach is generally the purview of larger companies, with the need to build the portfolio over time requiring significant resources. For SMEs, I respectfully submit that even on the path to an arsenal, a portfolio needs to be built. So we'll focus on that building process.

The number of patents a company holds is the beginning of the discussion for IP strategy. Questions like "How many patents do I need and why?," "What do my patents cover?" and "What do I do next?" encompass quality as a measure of value. Given that IP represents 84 percent of corporate value in intangible assets, unlocking greater value can significantly impact corporate valuation. For SMEs, too, where large portfolios are unattainable within funding constraints, the more pressing need is to justify the investment and return on IP assets.

Quality Is the Mission. Webster defines "quality" as "a degree of excellence" and "superiority in kind."[19] Add superiority in substance and process to the traditional quantity approach for IP. In doing so, we elevate our attention and resources to controllables.

An absence of strategy or inaction can be overwhelmed by variables outside of our control, which distracts us from pursuing value. I call this *Mission Quality* and I propose that it be contemplated as part of intentional decision-making in every aspect of IP strategy. Quality *is* the mission, and simplified execution enables us to keep quality first-place.

Measuring Quality. Quality has been determined based on publicly available data about IP value, dominated by the binary outcome of patent litigation. Did the patent owner win? Then the patent is quality.

As described above, success in patent litigation is an indicator of quality for the company's portfolio as the company would select its highest quality patents to assert. Studies show the average number of patents per litigation ranges from 2.2 to generally less than twelve. Therefore, a relatively small number of patents can support the quality of portfolio.[20]

Over the late 1990s and 2000s, there was a marked increase in the number of patents found to be invalid in litigation, leading commentators to proclaim that patents were of low quality.[21] The industry reacted with a number of changes to address patent quality. Nevertheless, patent quality today remains uncertain. To understand what happened, let's explore several trends which shine a spotlight on patent quality.

COMPUTER-IMPLEMENTED INVENTIONS CREATE A DIGITAL REVOLUTION AND PATENT UNCERTAINTY

The 1950s introduced computers to business users. By the 1980s, computer hardware and software dominated the corporate landscape, further fueled by the 1991 emergence of the internet. Software appeared as part of computer offerings, and with it came a tsunami of new inventions that most readers cannot envision a world without.

Back in the day, as with any period of technology transformation, companies chased market dominance. Battle lines were drawn, with legal protection as a weapon. Even before patent protection for computer-implemented inventions was introduced, copyright protection initially was in the balance.[22] Computers performing *functions* (recall utility patents are about function) brought these inventions squarely within the purview of patents. A landmark 1981 case by the United States Supreme Court

(SCOTUS) declared that software is patentable.[23] But since, other cases have in turn declined patent protection for certain computer innovations because they allegedly are too *abstract* to be true inventions. And so began a pendulum swing to hold computer-implemented inventions *ineligible* for patenting.

The USPTO's Oversight of Computer-Implemented Inventions. With the initial allowance of patents for computer-implemented inventions, the floodgates opened at the USPTO to seek patent protection. Using new computer technology itself to determine their quality, the Patent Office's resources were stressed. Patents as a result were granted on some questionable computer inventions. On the heels of being granted, some of these lower-quality patents were presented in litigation, as we are about to see.

PATENTS AS LOTTERY TICKETS

As computer and software patent acquisitions and litigation became commonplace, patents were described as "lottery tickets." There were large-scale acquisitions of patent portfolios with financial sums in the billions. Global litigations called the "smartphone wars" started in 2010, lasted a decade, and added to the notoriety, brought on by a "circular firing squad" of worldwide brands such as Apple®, Microsoft® and Samsung®, to determine the winner of the emerging smartphone market with billions at risk. At the same time, individuals who purchased patents asserted them against companies large and small. Litigation and patent lotteries got a lot of attention (and not all good). Let's take a closer look at these factors, as they have reshaped the US patent system itself and patents' stature in the IP spectrum.

Insider Lawball

A Troll Is as a Troll Does

In the 1990s, patent commentators decried a new breed of patent owners which licensed patents to assert in litigation rather than "practicing" them to commercialize offerings, called *nonpracticing entities* (NPEs). This in and of itself is not malfeasance.

In fact, it ignores a critical aspect of the US patent system: a patent grant does not require that the owner commercialize her invention. Some groundbreaking inventors cannot afford to build their inventions. Prominent 19th century American inventors (such as Thomas Alva Edison, who spurred the industrial revolution) were NPEs who sometimes licensed their patents to others to be commercialized. The ability to license without commercializing was key to the design of the US patent system as an improvement over older legal frameworks (such as that of Great Britain).[24]

Our US patent law approach was proven right in the overwhelming success of the US patent system, with inventors having the ingenuity to invent and work with third parties to license patents and drive the US legacy in leading global innovation and wealth.

What then is the problem with NPEs? Patent litigation brought by an NPE, in contrast to a competitor, impacts resolution dynamics. Patent lawsuits between competitors often involve both parties as patent owners, and therefore a settlement incentive of the accused (or *defendant*) brings its own patent litigation, called a *countersuit*, against the filing party (or *plaintiff*). Both parties then face similar defense costs and potential damages, encouraging resolution. As NPEs do not make, use or sell offerings, countersuits are not available. Companies which commercialize have greater risk in NPE versus competitor litigation.

Some NPEs also have been the industries' own worst enemy, threatening lawsuits with monetary demands at amounts far below the cost to defend the litigation. Recipients of lawsuits often settled to avoid the burden of defending themselves, even where lawsuits were questionable. This tactic gained cries of foul from companies large and small, and even charities, giving rise to the more pejorative label of "patent troll."[25]

A Troll Is as a Troll Does. Blanket labeling of NPEs as patent trolls misses the mark. It is not this use of patents that triggers malfeasance. It is the misuse of our legal system represented by plaintiffs seeking settlements below the cost of litigating, not the asset as the subject of litigation. Indeed, this conduct is not limited to patents, with "ambulance chaser" commonly describing some plaintiffs in civil suits. So too here. I propose instead of patents receiving a bad name based on bad actors—a troll is as a troll does!

Moreover, patents need not be devalued based on the conduct of some bad-acting owners. Judges have ample remedies to assess conduct and to curb bad actors and meritless litigation.[26] Extortion settlements motivate bad actors. Attention to economic consequences for bad actors curbs the behavior, and over time reduces dockets overwhelmed by a failure to disincentivize misuse. All upright stakeholders, including our judicial system, benefit from judicial action.

Patents were put under a microscope, with the 2008 economic downturn contributing to the problem by making myriad patents from bankrupt startups easy to scoop up and add to the lottery. Many of these patents then asserted in litigation were found invalid. The takeaway is that many NPE patents to computer-implemented inventions were substantively tested under the scales of justice and deemed to be low quality.[27]

An increase in NPE litigation in parallel with invalidity outcomes was a perfect storm; mud was thrown not only at NPEs but patents, and it stuck. Congress became involved to correct perceived litigation abuses and low-quality patents by passing sweeping patent law changes in the 2011 America Invents Act (AIA). These included paths to make it easier to challenge the quality of patents at the USPTO.

The battle is still raging when it comes to patent *eligibility* as we'll explore in the next chapter (with debate expanded beyond computers).[28] As a result, the state of the US patent system based on the US patent-eligibility standard is a risk to the value of patents.

THE OPPORTUNITY FOR MISSION QUALITY
BUSINESS-ALIGNED IP STRATEGY

This foray into the history of patents for computer-implemented invention as an emerging technology demonstrates patent dynamics and the perceived value of assets.

Societal circumstances can also affect new laws. Witness for trade secrets, the impact of security breaches in the 2020s, inspired a first-of-its-kind US federal trade secret law to support the prosecution of agents committing theft of American innovation. Another extreme for enforcement in 2021 was the Biden administration's proposal to grant royalty-free licenses to countries for use of COVID-19-related patents in making their own vaccines under a waiver of IP rights within a global trade agreement, the Trade-Related Aspects of IP Rights (or TRIPS).[29] I put my stake in the ground alongside outstanding IP leaders and state simply that undermining patent rights damages innovation, leaving the eloquent support to myriad articles.

Within this pace of technology today, IP quality plays a much larger role than the historic quantity of patents, suggesting that *quality is the new quantity*. Of course, some larger enterprises will continue to seek a leading spot in the size of their patent portfolios, showcasing quantity. For smaller companies with limited budgets, this book presents quality as the primary driver of IP strategy.

Let's start with three recommended approaches for achieving quality for intellectual property assets: (1) quality substance and process, (2) crown jewel IP assets and (3) business-aligned IP strategy.

QUALITY SUBSTANCE AND PROCESS

IP assets arise from the original works of their creators and inventors. The ability to get patent rights is dependent upon the timely filing of patent applications at the USPTO. Additional IP assets of copyrights and trademarks have optimal statutory benefits based on the timeliness of registration with their respective agencies. The timing of filing therefore is both an opportunity and a risk. The filing processes and interactions with agencies that administer IP rights require specialized planning and resources.

Quality in is a condition precedent for quality out—so, too, for IP protection. The path to finding value begins and succeeds with an up-front focus on quality. By doing so, mistakes or distracting issues are minimized. The overall cost throughout the asset life cycle is reduced, and the return on investment is increased.

At a higher aspirational level, intellectual property advances art, science, and technology. You honor the gift of patents and other IP rights by meeting the statutory obligations to validate and strengthen the IP assets supporting your business. You lead by example for a strong US intellectual property system.

CROWN JEWEL IP ASSETS

Identifying and valuing IP assets is required at certain corporate milestones, including: (1) planning for IP litigation or defending against it; (2) due diligence in transactions with asset valuation (such as a funding round, acquisition or IP-backed lending using IP as collateral); and (3) in the unfortunate circumstance of bankruptcy. Often, legal professionals including lawyers and financial professionals lead these activities, delivering analytics and opinions about individual assets, albeit at a high cost.

Additionally, IP companies (IPwe® and Parola® being outstanding examples) devoted to data and artificial intelligence (AI) and machine learning (ML) analytics, particularly for patent portfolios, can provide critical and cost-effective insights into the makeup and value of patent portfolios. Taking advantage of these services will offer you a baseline level of insights about patents, including patent ratings.

The focus on quality in substance and process for individual assets ideally increases the value of each asset. A holistic, quality-based approach to the IP spectrum supports assessing not just the intrinsic quality of each asset, but their mutually reinforcing value.

For corporate technology owners getting started in IP or those who answer, "How many patents do I need and why?," "What do my patents cover?" and "What do I do next?" for present and future patenting—the use of *crown jewels* is a simple and elegant IP strategy.

Insider Lawball

What Are Crown Jewel IP Assets?
Crown jewel IP assets are a definable set of IP assets aligned with key commercial innovations and features of the line of business they support.

Introducing the notion of "crown jewels" to IP strategy itself can be game-changing. The metaphor for something treasured and worthy of protection creates a curious mindset to understand the *why* of IP assets rather than just the *how many*.

The Starting Point for Crown Jewels is Business Strategy. Here is a framework for simplified execution within existing business strategies for defining crown jewel IP assets. You may add existing efforts to rate patents to the framework, but this concept is decidedly a business exercise.

A core business function for planning, execution and measurement of ROI is to identify the key commercial innovations and features of each line of business that provide value. Fundamental business strategy involves prioritizing those features and then managing corporate investments to optimize their value. IP is one of the potential investments.

The easiest way to get started is to ask the right stakeholders—namely leaders from technology, business and legal functions—this question: "What are our key commercial innovations and how important are they in protecting our market share?" The top three to five commercial innovations or features for market protection can be designated as crown jewels.

Key Commercial Innovations or Features Are Matched to IP Assets. Each key commercial feature then can be matched with potential or existing protection along the IP spectrum. Starting with key commercial innovations or features makes it easier to consider IP assets holistically, driving cost efficiencies and mutual reinforcement of IP protection.

The top three to five IP assets per line of business can be designated as crown jewel IP assets. Crown jewels in this way are not simply an identification of quality IP assets, but rather are assessed based on their contribution to their related offering.

Crown Jewel IP Assets are the New Patent List. Instead of a patent tally, imagine an executive with a well-defined set of crown jewel IP assets per line of business tucked under her arm, along with a presentation of their value. Executives can then evaluate the prioritized IP assets within familiar business fundamentals. With a greater understanding and connection of crown jewel IP assets to key commercial innovations or features, executives will be more willing to work with these assets in realizing value. Adding the IP assets to business strategy ensures that they are included in every stage of offerings, including planning, R & D, production, growth, revenue, measurement and end-of-life planning.

Summary

The Big Opportunity: Recognize that Patents and IP Support Business. The prime objective of business is business performance. Companies invest in IP to support their performance. After all, IP supports business rather than business supporting IP. If this resonates with you, then act on it by bringing patents and IP into business meetings where they belong, with the timing based on business rather than legal planning. This shifts IP strategy from being outside of business strategy to being part of the ordinary course of business. Business-minded legal professionals also may view this approach as an opportunity to directly contribute to business strategy, endorsing the value of the IP they represent. Chapters 2 through 7 (IP assets) explore each IP asset individually to uncover opportunities to optimize quality and value, followed by cost-efficiency in Chapter 9: Cost.

CHAPTER 2

#IP2IP PATENTS: OPPORTUNITY AND ANALYSIS

WIN THE RACE TO PATENT

ACTions

2.1 **Apply for patent rights before an innovation is made available to anyone outside of the company.** *Top-10 Takeaway.*

2.2 **Apply as early as possible upon creation of an invention.** *Top-10 Takeaway.*

When the general public thinks of innovation, patents spring to mind. Rightly so; they are credited with the historic source of global economic wealth and prosperity, based on the US patent system leading the charge with the American dream of invention.

Inventions are new real-world solutions to problems. Patents are legal instruments for inventions that a patent office approves. In order to obtain a patent, you have to apply to a patent office and undergo an assessment of whether your invention is new, useful and nonobvious.

THE MOST POWERFUL IDEA IN THE WORLD: THE AMERICAN DREAM OF INVENTION

Patent Rights Should Scarcely Be Questioned. Recall that patents (and copyrights) are codified in the US Constitution as "securing for limited times to…inventors…the exclusive rights to their respective…discoveries," or the *Limited Times* clause. When written, as now, patents represented something new and valuable that could spark a journey toward living the American dream. James Madison expressed that the clause "will scarcely be questioned" because patents beget more innovation. Patents can be thought of as stories of technology, much like books. As the US Patent and Trademark Office carefully organizes patents under the US *patent classification* and publishes them, they are available for everyone to learn from. They pass on information that in turn spurs further advancements. Patents are the incentive society is willing to offer in exchange for educating the public about the invention.

An Invention but Not a Patent. Whereas an invention already has been made available to the public, as in other patents or publications before seeking patent rights, a new patent is not warranted. Some inventors decline to seek patents because of the required public availability, opting for trade secrets instead.[30]

The Patent Prize to the First Inventor. Where multiple inventors pursue a patent on overlapping inventions, just one inventor receives a patent—the first inventor. The patent story of technology—again, like a book—is set out as of the date the inventor files her patent application with the Office. The PTO then assesses whether the application contains the first public mention of the story, among other criteria. Eighteen months after filing, the Office generally publishes the pending application, giving the public the knowledge.

Patents or applications by others dated earlier than the subject application have already educated the public about innovation. The PTO also researches an enormous body of publicly available material, whether written, visual or audio, sometimes even based on activities such as sales or use of inventions—known as *prior art*—to determine the public's prior access to an invention. When a patent application is the first source of an invention in light of the prior art, and additional legal criteria are met, the Patent Office deems the invention *patentable* and grants a patent.

PATENT BENEFITS

A technology owner armed with a patent can ask a US federal court (or the International Trade Commission [ITC], regarding imports) to stop third parties from commercializing or importing her patented invention, by bringing *patent litigation* accusing a defendant of copying her patent. There are two primary issues in patent litigation: *infringement* and *validity*. Infringement tests whether the accused infringer sells an offering which is covered by the *patent claims*, or the numbered inventions at the end of the patent, which are the key property right. The defendant commonly argues that the asserted patent is invalid in court and also asks the Patent Office to review the patent in post-grant proceedings (as described in Chapter 3: Patents: Risks). Previously granted patents can be later invalidated because an improperly granted patent does not merit monopoly pricing to bring the technology to the public. Where a court finds infringement, the patent owner is entitled to damages and other relief.

As innovators in an industry are working to improve the same technologies, there are likely overlapping features of offerings covered by different patent owners. This is demonstrated in patent litigation between competitors. Often a company sued for infringement by a competitor responds by asserting its own patents. This dynamic is part of economic incentives in litigation where competing allegations and their adjudicatory costs drive settlement. It also reflects the broader dynamics of victory and defeat in competition, with patents representing one potentially critical tool in the outcome. As with NPEs, the litigation dynamics differ when the patent owner does not engage in commercial activity.

OPPORTUNITIES

Patents are strategic and competitive business tools. Those who understand and leverage these rights can reap significant rewards.

Utility Patents. This chapter focuses on a common type of patent called a *utility* patent, which covers products or processes across technology areas such as machines, computer inventions, electronics and some methods of doing business as the technology areas for #ip2ip. Utility patents relate to the *function or structure* of inventions (while design patents encompass visual look-and-feel innovations and are described in Chapter 7: Design Patents).

Patents Connect People and Companies to Opportunity. Multiple people strive to solve overlapping problems. Consider two different people working on the same problem and converging on the same solution. As described above, while both truly deserve the moniker of inventor, patent law governs that only the first inventor can be granted a patent on the solution.

THE EDISON AND TESLA STORIES OF TECHNOLOGY

Patents Illuminate a Path to Succeed Against the Competition. History is replete with stories demonstrating the opportunity of our US patent system. One example embodies the very symbol of ideas and patents today: the light bulb is arguably the world's most powerful image; universally, the shape stands for an idea. The image is inspired by Thomas Alva Edison, one of the world's great inventors and the creator of the modern-day equivalent of an R & D factory. Edison was awarded over one thousand US and international patents. He inspired generations of inventors. Edison did not come to the patent system with wealth. Rather, his wealth was created through the opportunities afforded by patents.

One is hard pressed to find another at Edison's level of achievement. However, at least in one instance, for one technology covered by hundreds of patents from competing inventors, another inventor won. The competition was not limited to a race for patents but to a key principle of this book—aligning patents with business objectives to beat the competition. You can read about the subject of the folklore in the fabled "War of the Currents" at any hour of the day or night because of the invention itself, the transmission of electricity from its source to a load for, say, powering light bulbs.[31]

The Edison and Tesla "Race" to Commercial Success of Their Inventions. In the 1870s–80s, Edison set his sights on problem solving for electrical transmission using direct current (DC). A former Edison employee, Nikola Tesla, pursued a competing solution in alternating current (AC). Their battle spanned decades, expanding beyond patent litigation and vicious business tactics to a display of AC in illuminating the 1893 World's Fair, and even in the use of electricity for a criminal execution.[32] In this particular race, Tesla was victorious, given our modern-day use of AC. However, history's long ray of light still shines upon Edison, who is known as the most prolific US patent owner of all time.

Tesla Is Commemorated by Elon Musk. After all, Elon Musk's Tesla® car company's trademark pays tribute to Nikola.[33] Interestingly, Elon chose to donate his company's patents to accelerate innovation for electric cars as one basis, but with an underlying brilliance of IP-aligned business strategy.

Transformative inventions and competition are not just left to posterity. Let's jump to two modern-day stories of success and defeat. For the success of patents, Dr. Gary K. Michelson (inducted into the National Inventors Hall of Fame in 2011). He was granted over 950 patents on devices, implants, and procedures that have revolutionized the field of spinal surgery. On the defeated side is yours truly and one of my handful of inventions for my 2008 startup, Article One Partners (AOP).

Dr. Michelson's Patent Journey. Dr. Michelson was dissatisfied with the medical procedures he encountered as a spinal surgeon, often leaving patients with unaddressed severe pain due to partial fixes of difficult-to-access surgical sites and risk of spinal damage. He started first by designing new instruments, recognized in the medical profession as "Michelson Devices." His devices drew other doctors and eventually medical device manufacturers to him and led him to patents, amassed in today's leading global spinal treatment patent portfolio.

Dr. Michelson represents a modern-day example of transforming an idea into the American dream of invention with the sale of his patents for $1.35 billion. His story highlights the impact an inventor can have and a patent system that reflects these opportunities. Dr. Michelson also founded an organization to educate and respect patent rights.[34] Among many resources sponsored by Dr. Michelson is a book by my dear and brilliant former colleague, David Kline (a war correspondent who found his passion in the economics of the patent system), titled *The Intangible Advantage*. I commend it to you for an outstanding pedagogy of US IP laws.

My Personal Journey. My journey with one of my inventions as my big idea for my first startup, AOP or Article One Partners, is an example of the defeated side of the patent coin.[35] It illustrates that some inventions will fail to receive a patent grant due to a competitor's earlier filing date in the race for patents.

AOP was all about how to do prior art research and was based on my exposure to the problem during my time as a junior legal associate. In the late 1990s, hunting for prior art involved flipping through hard copy patents at the USPTO headquarters, in addition to computer searching. Historically, copies of patents were organized at the Office by area of technology in actual shoe boxes, giving rise to the name "patent shoes." To pick the right shoes, a researcher first went to a monolith-sized tome to find the patent *classifications* assigned to the technology area of interest. I'm not exaggerating when I call the book a monolith; it measured two feet by two feet by one foot. After identifying the right *class* as well as *subclass*, one would march off to a long room filled with rows of dusty shelves, find the designated shoe, and flip through the patents it contained. Sometimes patents were missing; other times they were smudged. Weeks turned into months pulling shoes and shuffling through patents. The whole process was, in a word, inefficient. Like many inventors, I thought, *There has to be a better way.*

AOP Crowdsourcing. My idea was to pull a few sentences from a patent I was researching and socialize the description to a community by posting it on the internet and inviting the public (those with an interest, anyway) to respond. I honored people who took a leap of faith and worked with my company with compensation. I ended up inventing a model of researching the quality of patents using a method that was in its infancy. In fact, I was not even aware of its moniker at the time—*crowdsourcing.*

With a filed patent application in hand, I set out to write a business plan and seek investors. At the time, there was buzz around a litigation about the validity or quality of Jeff Bezos's "1-click" patent. I listed Amazon at the top of my outreach for potential investors and developed a tagline for the business, enlisting this metaphor:

> INSTEAD OF LOOKING FOR A NEEDLE
> IN THE HAYSTACK, ASK EACH PIECE
> OF HAY IF IT'S THE NEEDLE.

Tangled Taglines. One day, a colleague put a press release on my desk from a new company, BountyQuest, which had launched a website with investor Bezos to enable prior art research by a community. That got my attention, but the company tagline nearly had me fall off my office chair: *"Instead of looking for a needle in the haystack, ask each piece of hay if it's the needle."* My initial reaction? Shock and disappointment that someone else beat me to the idea. On its heels, though, came a feeling of validation. The idea was commercialized and backed by Amazon. The same tagline demonstrated the truism that many innovators are identifying and solving problems, hence the race to the patent office.

Rising from the Tagline Ashes. What happened next commonly defines the entrepreneurial mindset: pivoting to a business opportunity. Bucking up, finding the contact information for the new company, and reaching for my phone, I decided to prioritize my idea over who launched it. Within the hour, I introduced myself to the company founder, saying, "I have a pending US patent application on this exact idea. Your press release says you do too. What's your filing date?" He paused for a moment, then told me. My turn for a longer pause. "You beat me," I said. "Can I work for you?"

That loss was for only one invention among others for which I was granted patents, as part of my founding and leading AOP—one of the highlights of my career. (As a postscript for BountyQuest, the founder brought me on board, but it was hit in the 2008 economic downturn and closed.)

AOP was about improving the patent system and honoring the individual, and it was based on quality. I was fortunate to be its founder and am proud of its many successes, including its continued operations after purchase by a UK public company in 2015. Note too that defeat is part of the legacy of many business victories. There is an accepted (and even celebrated) statistic by entrepreneurs: 90 percent of all new businesses fail in their first three years. In fact, many entrepreneurs pride themselves on past failures preceding later success.

That early experience could have put me off patents. Instead, it reinforced the predicate dynamic of the system. If the shoe (pun intended) had been on the other foot and I had had the earlier date, I would have had the advantage. It also ingrained in me as an inventor firm respect for the power of patents to protect innovation.

PATENTS THROUGH HISTORY AND NOW

With this backdrop about patent opportunities and stories of their impact, let's take a moment to look at two examples of utility patents. Generally, a patent as a legal instrument has formal language and presentation which, despite honoring innovation, hasn't changed much over time from the first patent laws. This stylized language may, at first glance, bar further review. Please overcome that reaction and take this overview walk with me. To lighten the exercise, we'll use patents for leisure-time games.

Outsized Success with Water Balloons (US Pat. No. 9,051,066). An outstanding solo inventor who volunteers his time today to fight for the rights of patent owners, Joshua Malone exploded onto the toy scene with a revolutionary way to fill bunches of balloons (as the namesake of his company, Bunch O Balloons) with water for, well, exploding them.[36] His patent is the diminutively titled "System and Method for Filling Containers with Fluids." Title aside, the outcome of this patent is outsized because Josh succeeded in a patent settlement of $31 million after expensive litigation.[37] How fortunate the patent system is that Josh chooses to spend his time helping other solo inventors.

Innovating A Classic (US Pat. No. 4,082,285). The second is my favorite pastime of chess in a patent which combines both the physical aspects of the game and an implementation in electronics (this patent is from 1978, and hence it is now expired).[38]

The two parts of the patent are the *specification* and the *claims*. Together they make up what I refer to informally as a *story of technology*. Here is the cover page for each patent, presenting the start of the specification with summary data, the abstract and a representative figure:

(12) United States Patent
Malone

(10) Patent No.: **US 9,051,066 B1**
(45) Date of Patent: **Jun. 9, 2015**

(54) SYSTEM AND METHOD FOR FILLING CONTAINERS WITH FLUIDS

(71) Applicant: TINNUS ENTERPRISES, LLC, Plano, TX (US)

(72) Inventor: Joshua Malone, Plano, TX (US)

(73) Assignee: TINNUS ENTERPRISES, LLC, Plano, TX (US)

(*) Notice: Subject to any disclaimer, the term of this patent is extended or adjusted under 35 U.S.C. 154(b) by 0 days.

(21) Appl. No.: 14/492,487

(22) Filed: Sep. 22, 2014

Related U.S. Application Data

(60) Provisional application No. 61/942,193, filed on Feb. 20, 2014, provisional application No. 61/937,083, filed on Feb. 7, 2014.

(51) Int. Cl.
B65B 3/04 (2006.01)
B65B 3/28 (2006.01)
A63H 27/10 (2006.01)

(52) U.S. Cl.
CPC ... **B65B 3/04** (2013.01); **B65B 3/28** (2013.01); A63H 2027/1041 (2013.01); A63H 27/10 (2013.01)

(58) Field of Classification Search
CPC A63H 27/10; A63H 2027/1041; A63H 2027/105; A63H 2027/1033; B65B 3/04; B65B 3/28
USPC 141/234, 248, 10, 114, 383/3, 71; 446/220–226
See application file for complete search history.

(56) **References Cited**

U.S. PATENT DOCUMENTS

262,517 A	*	8/1882	Hendrie		446/220
1,098,286 A	*	5/1914	Herbert		446/222
1,166,690 A	*	1/1916	Miller		446/222
1,350,935 A	*	8/1920	Frank Pastor		446/222
1,478,757 A	*	12/1923	O'Conner		446/222
1,484,575 A	*	3/1924	Shulin		239/602
1,703,463 A	*	2/1929	Weigel		446/186
2,027,225 A	*	1/1936	Gill		446/226
2,161,274 A	*	6/1939	Behrend		446/224
2,553,941 A	*	5/1951	Rash		446/186

(Continued)

FOREIGN PATENT DOCUMENTS

FR	2911512	*	7/2008
GB	294273		7/1928

(Continued)

OTHER PUBLICATIONS

Balloon Powered Boat, May 17, 2011, http://alittlelearningfortwo.blogspot.com.*

(Continued)

Primary Examiner — Kevin P Shaver
Assistant Examiner — Andrew Stclair

(57) **ABSTRACT**

An example embodiment of an apparatus includes a housing with an opening at a first end and a plurality of holes at a second end, a plurality of hollow tubes attached to the plurality of holes, a plurality of containers removably attached to the hollow tubes, and a plurality of elastic fasteners, each elastic fastener clamping each container to a corresponding hollow tube, such that when the containers are filled with fluid and detached from the corresponding hollow tubes, each elastic fastener seals each container with the fluid inside.

14 Claims, 6 Drawing Sheets

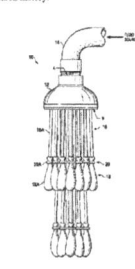

United States Patent [19]
Bathurst

[11] 4,082,285
[45] Apr. 4, 1978

[54] ELECTRONIC CHESS GAME
[76] Inventor: David B. Bathurst, 19857 Susan Ct., Mount Clemens, Mich. 48043
[21] Appl. No.: 741,787
[22] Filed: Nov. 15, 1976
[51] Int. Cl.² A63F 3/02
[52] U.S. Cl. .... 273/237; 340/323 R
[58] Field of Search .... 273/1 E, 85 R, 130 AB, 273/131 A, 136 A, DIG. 28; 340/323 R

[56] References Cited
U.S. PATENT DOCUMENTS

3,654,392	4/1972	Beinhocker et al.	273/136 A X
3,843,132	10/1974	Ferguson	273/136 A
3,888,491	6/1975	Bernard et al.	273/136 A
4,019,745	4/1977	Mustelier	273/136 A

FOREIGN PATENT DOCUMENTS
500,803 5/1976 U.S.S.R. .... 273/136 A

OTHER PUBLICATIONS
Popular Science; "Games Computers Play"; vol. 197, No. 4, Oct. 1970; p. 44.

Primary Examiner—Richard C. Pinkham
Assistant Examiner—Vance Y. Hum

Attorney, Agent, or Firm—Basile and Weintraub

[57] ABSTRACT

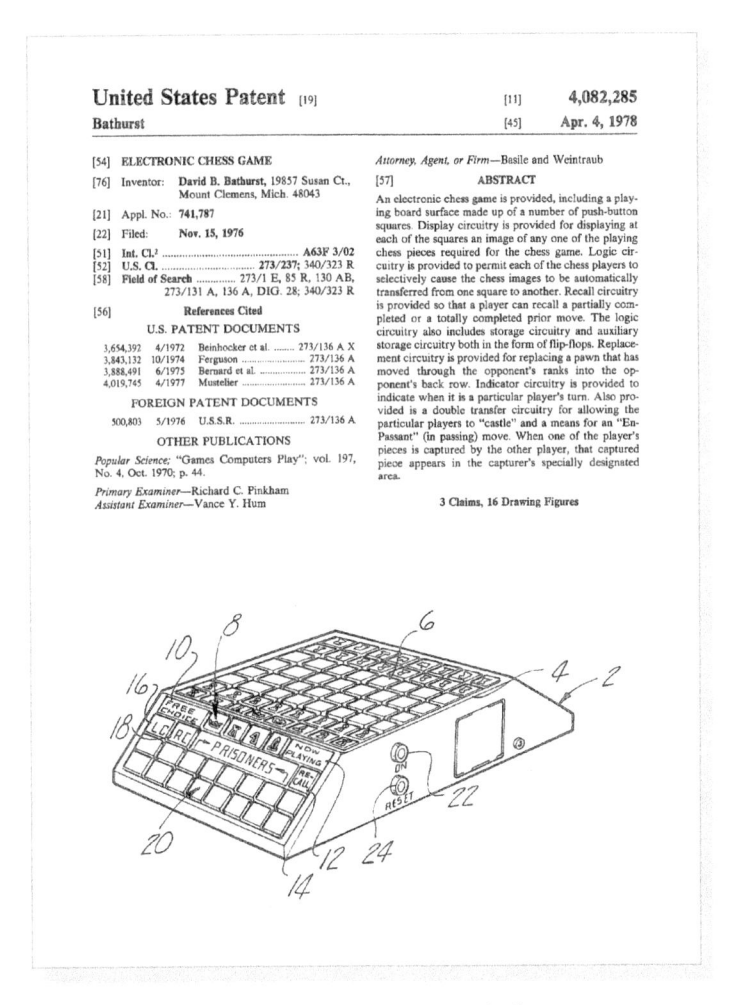

An electronic chess game is provided, including a playing board surface made up of a number of push-button squares. Display circuitry is provided for displaying at each of the squares an image of any one of the playing chess pieces required for the chess game. Logic circuitry is provided to permit each of the chess players to selectively cause the chess images to be automatically transferred from one square to another. Recall circuitry is provided so that a player can recall a partially completed or a totally completed prior move. The logic circuitry also includes storage circuitry and auxiliary storage circuitry both in the form of flip-flops. Replacement circuitry is provided for replacing a pawn that has moved through the opponent's ranks into the opponent's back row. Indicator circuitry is provided to indicate when it is a particular player's turn. Also provided is a double transfer circuitry for allowing the particular players to "castle" and a means for an "En-Passant" (in passing) move. When one of the player's pieces is captured by the other player, that captured piece appears in the capturer's specially designated area.

3 Claims, 16 Drawing Figures

US Pat. Nos. 9,051,066 and 4,082,285, Cover Pages with Representative Figures.

The next prominent page of the patent contains the abstract, the background and the start of the detailed description:

SYSTEM AND METHOD FOR FILLING CONTAINERS WITH FLUIDS

CROSS-REFERENCE TO RELATED APPLICATIONS

This application claims the benefit of priority under 35 U.S.C. §119(e) to U.S. Provisional Application Ser. No. 61/937,083 entitled "SYSTEM AND METHOD FOR FILLING INFLATABLE CONTAINERS WITH LIQUID" filed Feb. 7, 2014 and to U.S. Provisional Application Ser. No. 61/942,193 entitled "SYSTEM AND METHOD FOR FILLING INFLATABLE CONTAINERS WITH FLUIDS" filed Feb. 20, 2014, which are hereby incorporated by reference in their entireties.

TECHNICAL FIELD

The present disclosure relates generally to fluid inflatable systems and more particularly, to a system and method for filling containers with fluids.

BACKGROUND

Inflatable containers such as balloons can be filled with a variety of fluids, such as air, helium, water, medicines, etc. In some cases, a lot of inflatable containers may need to be filled with fluids. For example, balloons used as props in conventions, large parties, etc. may number in the hundreds and may require substantial human effort to fill them all in a timely manner. In another example, water balloons used as kids' toys may need to be filled in large numbers to aid in various games. Various methods may be employed to fill such inflatable containers. For example, an individual may blow up and tie each balloon by hand or use a tank of compressed air or helium to inflate the balloon, which then has to be tied. In another example, an individual may fill water balloons with water by hand one at a time, and then tie the balloons, which can all be quite time-consuming. Moreover, the inflatable containers may be damaged or filled to different volumes.

BRIEF DESCRIPTION OF THE DRAWINGS

To provide a more complete understanding of the present disclosure and features and advantages thereof, reference is made to the following description, taken in conjunction with the accompanying figures, wherein like reference numerals represent like parts, in which:

FIG. 1 is a simplified perspective view illustrating an example configuration of an embodiment of a system for filling containers with fluids;

FIG. 2 is a simplified diagram illustrating a cross-sectional view of example details of an embodiment of the system;

FIG. 3 is a simplified diagram illustrating other example details of an embodiment of the system;

FIG. 4 is a simplified diagram illustrating yet other example details of an embodiment of the system;

FIG. 5 is a simplified diagram illustrating yet other example details of an embodiment of the system;

FIG. 6 is a simplified diagram illustrating yet other example details of an embodiment of the system;

FIG. 7 is a simplified diagram illustrating other example details of an embodiment of the system; and

FIG. 8 is a simplified flow diagram illustrating example operations that may be associated with an embodiment of the system.

DETAILED DESCRIPTION OF EXAMPLE EMBODIMENTS

Overview

An example embodiment of an apparatus includes a housing (e.g., casing, covering, etc. with a cavity inside) with an opening at a first end and a plurality of holes at a second end, a plurality of hollow tubes attached to the plurality of holes, a plurality of containers (e.g., receptacles, vessels, ampules, test-tubes, balloons, etc.) removably attached to the hollow tubes, and a plurality of elastic fasteners, each elastic fastener clamping each container to a corresponding hollow tube, such that when the containers are filled with fluid and detached from the corresponding hollow tubes, each elastic fastener seals each container with the fluid inside.

Example EMBODIMENTS

It is to be understood that the following disclosure describes several example embodiments for implementing different features, structures, or functions of the system. Example embodiments of components, arrangements, and configurations are described herein to simplify the present disclosure. However, these example embodiments are provided merely as examples and are not intended to limit the scope of the invention.

The present disclosure may repeat reference numerals and/or letters in the various exemplary embodiments and across the Figures provided herein. This repetitious is for the purpose of simplicity and clarity and does not in itself indicate a relationship between the various exemplary embodiments and/or configurations discussed in the various Figures.

FIG. 1 is a simplified diagram illustrating an example embodiment of a system 10 for filling containers with fluids. System 10 includes a housing 12 removably attached to a hose 14 (e.g., tube, pipe, etc.) on a first end A and to a plurality of hollow tubes 16 on a second end B. As used herein, the term "housing" encompasses a hollow space enclosed by a rigid or semi-rigid casing (e.g., covering, skin, sleeve, sheath, etc.). In some embodiments, end A may include a threaded opening configured to mate with corresponding threads on hose 14. In some embodiments, end A may be smaller in circumference or area than end B. Hose 14 may be connected to a fluid source, such as a water tank, gas tank, water supply line, etc. on end A. End B may include a plurality of holes (e.g., configured in an array), configured to fit tubes 16. In some embodiments, tubes 16 may be permanently attached (e.g., welded, brazed, stuck with adhesives, press-fitted, etc.) to housing 12. In other embodiments, tubes 16 may be removably attached (e.g., with threads, pressure, etc.) to housing 12.

A plurality of containers 18 may be clamped (e.g., attached, fastened, held, clinched, secured, etc.) to plurality of tubes 16 using elastic valves 20. As used herein, the term "container" refers to an object that can hold something, such as fluids. The term "valve" refers to an object that regulates, directs, or controls the flow of fluids, by opening, closing, or partially obstructing passageways of fluid flow. In an example embodiment, elastic valves 20 comprise elastic fasteners, such as O-rings. In another example embodiments, elastic valves 20 comprise corrugations, smocking, elastic fibers, etc. fabricated into the necks of containers 18 such that force is required to pull open the necks of containers 18, and removal of the force causes the necks to constrict and close. In yet another example embodiment, elastic valves comprise internal or external plugs affixed to the necks of containers 18, through which tubes 16 may be pushed through to clamp containers 18 thereto.

US Pat. Nos. 9,051,066 and 4,082,285, Next Pages of the Specifications

Each section presents a different level of detail for the invention, with the *figures* providing visual guidance. They all have a singular purpose though: to support the definition of the invention for which the USPTO grants rights or the deed to the patent monopoly—the *patent claims*.[39] They are found at the end of the patent with little fanfare.

CLAIM YOUR PATENT RIGHTS

Here are representative first claims from each of the patents:

> What is claimed is:
> 1. An apparatus comprising:
> a housing comprising an opening at a first end, and a plurality of holes extending through a common face of the housing at a second end;
> a plurality of flexible hollow tubes, each hollow tube attached to the housing at a respective one of the holes at the second end of the housing;
> a plurality of containers, each container removably attached to a respective one of the hollow tubes; and
> a plurality of elastic fasteners, each elastic fastener clamping a respective one of the plurality of containers to a corresponding hollow tube, and each elastic fastener configured to provide a connecting force that is not less than a weight of one of the containers when substantially filled with water, and to automatically seal its respective one of the plurality of containers upon detaching the container from its corresponding hollow tube, such that shaking the hollow tubes in a state in which the containers are substantially filled with water overcomes the connecting force and causes the containers to detach from the hollow tubes thereby causing the elastic fasteners to automatically seal the containers,
> wherein the apparatus is configured to fill the containers substantially simultaneously with a fluid.

> The embodiments of the invention in which an exclusive property or privilege is claimed are defined as follows:
> **1.** An electronic board game comprising:
> a first playing board surface made up of a number of depressible playing squares;
> a first display means for displaying at each of said squares an image of any one of those playing pieces required for the game; and
> logic circuitry to permit each player of the game to selectively cause said image to be automatically transferred from a first square to a second square upon sequentially pressing the first and second squares wherein said logic circuitry includes replacement means for replacing the predetermined first display image with the second image after the transfer of said first displayed image to one of a predetermined number of playing squares defining a back row of the playing surface, said replacement means including image decoder means for sensing when said first display image is transferred to one of said predetermined number of squares and wherein said logic circuitry includes indicator means responsive to said image decoder means for indicating when a player is allowed to transfer images from one square to another and when the player is allowed to replace the first predetermined display image with the second image.

US Pat. Nos. 9,051,066 and 4,082,285, First Claims

The format of a claim is a numbered paragraph made up of a single sentence, including an introduction, or *preamble*, followed by individual features or *elements* of the claim. The elements limit the claim and are therefore called claim *limitations*, thereby providing the invention's scope.

Each claim includes a *point of novelty* or meaning of the claim, which is not delineated as such in the claim, but is part of the posturing that occurs during the application process at the Office and in later litigation. Claims generally involve either systems or methods, or combinations of these types.

Josh Malone's patent claim 1 has four elements for physical components of a product, including in element 1, a subcomponent with features to connect to other subcomponents; in element 2, more subcomponents for the same purpose; in element 3, the balloons themselves (called *containers* for broader application) attach to other subcomponents and, optionally, become unattached. Element 4 explains that when the swelling balloon's weight and movement exceeds a connecting force, the balloon drops and automatically seals. This is one example of a *point of novelty* or the key to this claim (based on one interpretation; there are others). The next paragraph tells the result—water balloons are ready to explode.[40]

In the electronic chess patent, element 1 is about the board with depressible squares. Element 2 focuses on chess piece images on the element 1 squares. Element 3 is about the electronic circuitry or logic for detecting, validating and indicating movement of the chess piece images around the board. This is an excellent example of the use of computer-implemented technology applied to improve a classic game, which at the time, was granted a US patent.[41]

Twenty Claims for Twenty Separate Patents. A common patent strategy is that patents have twenty claims, with some having more (and even hundreds in some cases, though claims beyond twenty increase the filing cost). Each claim represents a different and distinct invention (also called an *embodiment*) and is technically a separate patent. Importantly, each claim has its own point of novelty and is adjudicated separately in patent litigation, standing on its own for purposes of infringement and validity.

Hopefully you have made friends with patents and now have a better sense of what you are dealing with. Before we move on, though, let's review how claims support the dynamics of the patent system—to advance knowledge and create value for inventions.

SHARPEN YOUR KNOWLEDGE OF CLAIMS

A classic illustration for educating about claims is to envision a property description in a deed that defines the boundaries of real property. Claims each have a varying scope, with broader claims having fewer elements (called *independent claims*) and more narrow claims adding elements (called *dependent claims*, which refer to earlier claims and include the elements of those earlier claims). Independent claims present the least number of elements necessary to define the invention, or the most important features, and are the broadest claims.

Let's use pencils for another illustration. For a foundational patent to a pencil (referred to as P1), an independent first claim 1 includes three elements: (1) a wooden shaft (2) with an aperture and (3) graphite. A narrower, second claim 2 can add a tactile surface to the shaft to enable more precise handling. A third claim 3 can change the composition of clay present in the graphite for more precise lines. Claims 2 and 3 each provide different permutations as separate inventions which could be contained in separate patents.

If we add a later-dated second patent (referred to as P2) to an improvement of the foundational pencil patent P1, we can begin to experience the dynamics of the US patent system. Let's propose that the improvement patent P2 includes a first claim 1 to the same P1 elements of (1) a wooden shaft, (2) with an aperture and (3) graphite, but adds a P2 element (4), an attached eraser. This invention was patented in 1858 by Mr. H. L. Linman, and with honor, I use an illustrated figure from Mr. Linman's patent to explore P2 claim 1:[42]

H. L. Linman.
Pencil & Eraser.
N° 19,783.   Patented Mar. 30, 1858.

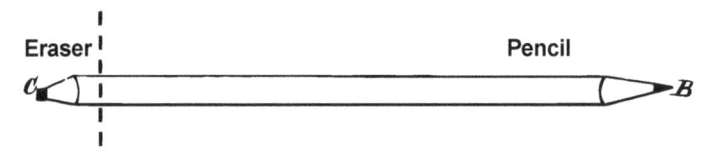

Historic Patent: US Pat. No. 19,783 (with "Eraser," "Pencil" and Broken Diving Line Added for Illustration)

Let's assume both patents are issued and both owners seek to commercialize. The improvement patent P2 owner wants to sell the pencil with the attached eraser. However, even if the eraser is added, the improved pencil P2 still includes the three elements from the pencil patent P1 claim 1, namely the (1) wooden shaft, (2) aperture and (3) graphite. Therefore, even though P2 adds more—or improves upon the first pencil patent P1—P2 is a copy of the elements of the pencil patent P1 and therefore infringes P1 claim 1.

However, at a commercial level, the market for pencils increases when they have attached erasers. As a result, the patent P1 owner cannot attach an eraser without infringing the improvement patent P2 claim 1. In an ideal ending, both owners execute a cross-licensing agreement, while further improvements of the patents P1 and P2 are whittled away by these inventors or others, given the success of pencils.

Use the claims and the pencil illustration to set your own expectations for the US Patent and Trademark Office and patent professionals and to guide your understanding of these assets, despite their dense, anachronistic character.

ANALYSIS

With these highlights about the opportunities for patents, let's turn to the timing basics for when to pursue patenting and once granted, the length of time (or the *term*) of the legal right, followed by the obligatory Patent Lawyerly Litany.

FOR PATENTS, IT'S ALL IN THE "FIRST-TO-FILE" TIMING

To the First Inventor at the USPTO Door, the Patent Spoils Go! Recalling *Edison v. Tesla*, multiple inventors often race to solve a problem. This dynamic is increasing with the internet and advanced technologies' ever-expanding reach in publicizing technology, problems, and potential solutions.

Historically, US laws determined the winner based on the date of the invention. The invention date amounted to a contest for the "first to invent," with the Office examining the facts about when each inventor had her spark of an idea (called *conception*), followed by her diligence in advancing it (called *reduction to practice*, with either an actual physical working version of the invention or filing a patent application).[43] In theory, the system favored small inventors by recognizing their date of creation. In practice, battles about facts and dollars to adjudicate them dominated the topic.

The 2011 America Invents Act (AIA) changed the standard governing dates to the "first inventor to file" a patent application at the USPTO.[44] This filing date is easier to identify than poring through evidence of conception and reduction to practice, although retaining that evidence where needed in litigation is important.[45] For the race to patent—the spoils to the PTO-timing victor go! However, earlier filers are not the only impediment to winning the race to patent.

The Achilles' Heel of Patents—Prior Art. The Office's decision about granting a patent is whether public knowledge, or *prior art*, predates the patent application. The Office will not grant patents for inventions already publicly known (noting the exception of one year under the *US grace period* for the inventor's own disclosures). Prior art is the Achilles' heel of patents; it is a rich and historic area of the law on its own.

Other patents are just one form of public knowledge. Solutions to problems are not always patented. Sometimes they are instead presented publicly before or without the inventor ever seeking a patent. Examples of public activities are publications, presentations or any descriptions publicly available in written, audio or video (or other tangible) form, or commercial information such as business, investor, research, sales or marketing materials—all of which are prior art. Commercialization activities, deemed to make the invention available to the public, also are prior art. This includes selling or offering to sell products or services and even using an invention. Formally, prior art means any previous patent or publicly available writing, presentation or knowledge, including information based on a sale, offer for sale or use of an invention. The PTO researches the prior art to determine, whether alone or in combination, the story of technology presented in the patent has already been told before the filing date.[46]

Prior art is critical evidence for the USPTO or courts to determine whether a patent application should be granted, or once a patent, whether it is valid or invalid. When the prior art date is earlier than the patent application filing date, it's said to be a *statutory bar* to validity.

Don't Bar Your Patents with Your Own Activities. Anyone can be a source of prior art—including you as an inventor. This makes the first and key consideration for prior art the inventor's own creation of it. Inventor-created prior art is within the inventor's control. Therefore, it is the inventor's opportunity and responsibility to seek patents and avoid losing patent rights, respectively, before activities that bar those rights. This timing requirement therefore must trigger consideration of patenting. Be forewarned! When a groundbreaking invention is not timely filed, it cannot become a patent, and its inventor and owner cannot receive the benefits of the patent system.

Prevention before Error. An invention made public before filing for patents (in most jurisdictions, with one example of an exception in the one-year US grace period) loses the opportunity to seek patenting.[47] This does not of course prohibit you from commercializing your invention without a patent, but patent protection requires a filing process and grant by the PTO. A rational business owner, therefore, knows that she needs to plan for this timing requirement.

Top-10 Takeaway 1

#ip2ip-1: Apply for patent rights before an invention is made available to anyone outside of the company.

This topic is the number one takeaway in this book. If only this rule stays with you, it bodes well for your success.

If you research how-to books on patents, you'll find meaningful portions devoted to myriad fact patterns of inventor activity and whether they generate public knowledge. For example, patent rights may rise and fall depending on whether an innovator put an invention on sale or offered it for sale, and whether at the time of such activity the invention was *ready for patenting*.[48]

Some technology owners may believe that a nondisclosure or confidentiality agreement insulates them from this issue of public disclosure. While these agreements support the idea that information is confidential—and therefore not public—they do not cover an offer for sale or a sale. In addition, the information covered by the NDA can prompt evidentiary issues where the NDA is later challenged.

While NDAs have value, any disagreements which later arise will rely on evidence. The strongest evidence of invention is documenting your invention in a patent filing as close to its creation date as possible, ideally before providing it even under an NDA. Therefore, do not place your full reliance on confidentiality and NDAs with third parties as a haven—in addition to the use of NDAs, timely file for patents.[49]

A FALL FROM ONE-YEAR US PATENT GRACE

To those who think the above Top-10 Takeaway 1 is flawed because it glosses over the statutory *one-year US grace period*, let's address that now.

Grace is a form of requesting forgiveness. US patent law allows for one year to pursue a patent application after a public activity. However, in most foreign jurisdictions, the day that you make an invention public anywhere worldwide, you create an absolute *statutory bar* to applying for patent rights, referred to as *absolute novelty*.[50] My recommendation is that inventors with an interest in protecting their innovations globally should file for patent rights before the date upon which public activities occur.

Whether you plan today to pursue global protection, set yourself up in your planning to build to global coverage as your business and IP strategy advances to warrant it. My advice: *do not rely on* the US one-year grace period,[51] and instead follow the overall absolute novelty bar, as presented in Top-10 Takeaway 1.

There are situations where the one-year US grace period offers solace. First, if your invention has been public for less than a year, then there's still time for a US application—pursue it immediately! If you are past the one-year mark, then the one-year grace period is as it says: one year. Period. Take a moment, accept that you just learned the hard way and move on. Patents generally are improvements on earlier innovations, and successful businesses continually innovate. Shift to assessing improvements to your innovations and making timely applications before public activities.

To Rely or Not to Rely Upon the US One-Year Grace Period. For your game plan moving ahead, I propose advanced planning to minimize distraction from the substantive issues of validity and infringement in a litigation. Apply for patents before any public activities—ideally, months before to prepare high-quality filings. IP considerations can be part of advanced planning for a product launch, discussions with third parties, an offer for sale, sale, use in an offering or other public activities, as well as for R & D so that patenting can be pursued as close to the creation date of inventions as possible. Having applications on file helps avoid losing patent rights, and early filings optimize quality.

THIRD-PARTY PRIOR ART YOU CANNOT CONTROL—OR CAN YOU?

Avoid the Rush to Lateness. The topic above relates to the *latest* timing to avoid a negative outcome. You also are competing with other inventors to secure patent rights in our first-to-file regime. Recall that even if you have invented and not yet engaged in public activity, your *priority* as the first to file can be spoiled if another files a patent application before you, thereby creating prior art relative to you.

You can choose to file for a patent as close to the creation date of your invention as possible. This reduces the body of third-party prior art relative to your application date and optimizes your chances of succeeding in the race to patent.

The bottom line: the inventor who maximizes her chances to win the patent race is the person who files first. From this perspective, the inventor has more control over prior art from third parties than gleaned at first blush, and this insight elevates it to Top-10 Takeaway 2.

Top-10 Takeaway 2

#ip2ip-2: Apply for patent rights as early as possible upon the creation of an invention.

A Time for IP Assets. Patent timing can trigger the consideration of other intellectual property assets too. An easy way to ensure that you leverage filing benefits across the IP spectrum is to take the opportunity when prompted to evaluate them holistically. The relationship between IP assets, particularly for computer-related technologies, is an outstanding leverage point to maximize IP protection.

PATENT TERM

The time a utility patent is in force (or term) generally is twenty years from the patent application filing date, with design patents being fifteen years from the grant date. The filing date of the application granted as a patent generally starts the term. Sometimes, multiple applications are filed sequentially in a parent–child format to support a patent grant, with the term for each claim based on the filing date of the earliest application supporting it.

THE PATENT LAWYERLY LITANY

The US Patent Economic Engine. The US Constitutional patent mandate is enacted in Title 35 of the US Code, starting with Section 101, "Inventions Patentable":[52]

> Whoever invents or discovers any new and useful process, machine, manufacture, or composition of matter, or any new and useful improvement thereof may obtain a patent...

101 involves whether an invention is eligible for patenting. It became the focus of patenting in the 1990s and is still doing a command performance, though many view it as the cause of today's broken patent system. Section 101 is further developed in Sections 102, "Novelty"; 103, "Nonobvious"; and 112, "Enablement."[53] Section 102 requires that the invention be *new* (or "Novel") and timely filed, and 103 adds that the subject matter must be "Nonobvious." Sections 102 and 103 are all about prior art, with 102 applied for a single prior art reference, and 103 evaluated for multiple references from the perspective of a skilled reviewer with an identified level of knowledge in the technology (called a *person having ordinary skill in the art*, or *POSIA*). Section 112 involves whether the invention is described sufficiently or *enabled* for a POSIA to make and use it. The meaning of *useful* in the context of 101 means functional, with utility patents focused on functions. Analysis of these sections benefits from the investigatory lens of patent professionals.

PATENT LITIGATION

Once a patent is *issued* by the US Patent and Trademark Office, litigation to enforce it can be brought when a third party copies the patented invention within the patent's twenty-year term. Patents are litigated in federal courts and the International Trade Commission (ITC). Court decisions are appealable first to the penultimate court for patents, the US Court of Appeals for the Federal Circuit (or Federal Circuit, established in 1982 to unify IP law) and finally to the United States Supreme Court.

Infringement. The statute, Title 35 Section 271 for "Infringement of patent," provides: "[W]hoever without authority makes, uses, offers to sell, or sells any patented invention, within the [US] or imports into the [US] any patented invention during the term of the patent therefor, infringes the patent." Recall two key patent litigation issues—*infringement* and *validity*. Infringement tests whether the accused infringer engages in excluded actions for an offering covered by the *claims* of the asserted patent. The primary defenses for the accused infringer are twofold: invalidity and noninfringement.

Patents Are Presumed but Not Guaranteed. Validity, in essence, tests whether the USPTO got it right in agreeing to grant the patent in the first place. Patent owners do not need to assert patent validity, since the PTO's patent grant creates a presumption of validity. The burden in litigation is therefore on the accused infringer to prove invalidity.[54]

To make matters more complicated, not only can courts take a "second look" at patent validity, but the PTO provides *post-grant proceedings*, such as *inter partes review* (*IPR*s, discussed in Chapter 3: Patents: Risks), which invalidate between 60 and

80 percent of patents.[55] IPRs are intensely debated, with patent owners rightfully asking why their assets can later be withdrawn by the government body which issued them in the first place. Accused infringers respond that the invalidity risk is based on the patent owner's decision to bring suit.

The Ultimate Risk for Patent Owners Is Invalidity. An invalidity decision by either a court or the USPTO extinguishes a patent for all purposes. Bringing patent litigation can also result in a finding of no infringement. However, even where a complaint for patent infringement fails, the patent can still be asserted against other parties. A finding of invalidity curtails any further use of the patent in litigation or otherwise because it is no longer in force.

Counterclaims in Competitor Litigation. Litigation between competitors often involves both competitors holding patents. The accused infringer commonly counterclaims that the patent owner plaintiff has infringed the defendant's patents. The parties then engage in role reversal and crossfire. Arrows flying from both directions should in theory incentivize the parties to resolve or settle their conflict more efficiently.

No Counterclaims in NPE Litigation. Note, however, that in litigation in which the plaintiff is a nonpracticing entity (or NPE), there is no basis for the defendant to assert counterclaims, because the NPE does not commercialize by making, using, or selling products or services. Eliminating the settlement dynamics of counterclaims makes NPE litigation more difficult and riskier for defendants than competitor litigation.

PATENT INFRINGEMENT RELIEF

Patent enforcement litigation seeks damages and injunctions. Damages include profits lost from the infringement or, at minimum, a reasonable royalty. If the accused infringer is found to have known about the subject patent and the conduct of copying is found to be egregious, called *willful infringement*, the patent owner can recover up to treble damages and attorney's fees (as explored more in Chapter 3: Patents: Risks).[56] Courts also can award attorney's fees to successful parties to curb overly aggressive or meritless litigation. This contrasts with the general approach, called the American rule, that parties pay their attorneys' fees.[57] The plaintiff's selection of jurisdiction, based on the alleged infringer's state of incorporation or activities that demonstrate a regular place of business, also comes into play. Some jurisdictions are known to be patent friendly and/or fast paced.

Patent Case Law Precedent Weakens Injunctions. Litigation equitable relief can also include injunctions to discontinue infringing activities.[58] Historically, injunctions have been a powerful tool to incentivize settlement. A SCOTUS case, however, has weakened the standard for injunctions by shifting the focus from four factors to two, which are now these: whether the injection would be "too costly" to the defendant and society, and whether the rights holder can be compensated with money.[59] Corporate-accused infringers with deep pockets are disincentivized to settle, given that a full trial may bring monetary incentives anyway. Instead, they are emboldened to lengthen the litigation and its attendant costs to patent owners.

Government Waivers of Patent Rights. Another critical topic is the 2021 US Biden administration's efforts to waive US patent rights for COVID-19-related inventions for certain countries. Fortunately, European countries declined the proposal.[60] Otherwise, as former Director of the US Patent and Trademark Office Andrei Iancu explained, the billions invested by companies to develop vaccines in record time and protections for high-quality vaccines would have been lost.[61] Legislation is the appropriate venue for drug pricing resolution, rather than a substitution of the patent system.

THE PATENT HOW-TOS

With the statutory underpinning of the US patent system behind us, this section addresses the more pragmatic how-tos for getting a US patent and a primer on international protection.

The Patent Applicant and Ownership. An invention is generally created by an individual as an employee or consultant. First, ensure that the ownership of inventions is properly secured by their intended owner. For corporate technology owners, that generally means the corporation. Patents are unique in the spectrum of IP assets in that they require filing a patent application that lists the individual inventor(s).[62]

While the corporation is the owner of the application, confirmation of ownership must be formalized in an assignment filing with the PTO. Therefore, it is strongly advised to contract for ownership—that is, an assignment of all IP rights, including patent rights and the status of work made for hire—in employment and consulting agreements.

UTILITY PATENT APPLICATIONS

Patent Filing Process (and Its Formal Terms). Patent rights derive from the USPTO's determination (called *examination*) of whether an invention is *patentable* and therefore warrants granting a patent. After the inventor or applicant prepares and files a utility patent application (called *preparation*), a PTO official (called an *Examiner*) communicates with the applicant about whether the Office will grant a patent (called *prosecution*). Upon grant, the owner pays fees to issue and maintain the patent over its twenty-year life cycle from filing.

PROVISIONAL PATENT APPLICATIONS

The Provisional Starting Point. The USPTO also provides a path to getting started in a preliminary version or *provisional* of a utility patent application, thereby securing a filing date. The applicant must then file the utility application within one year to gain the benefit of the provisional filing. Determining the subject matter that warrants a patent filing and tools to assist, such as an Invention Disclosure Form, are detailed in Chapter 9: Cost.

The provisional provides a placeholder for the story of the technology described as of its filing date. Where the utility application is timely filed within one year, it adopts the provisional filing date as its official *priority filing date*. Where a utility is not timely filed, the provisional is abandoned and no longer available for reliance in later applications.

Provisionals are often prompted by an imminent public disclosure. Filing the public materials as a provisional ahead of time avoids creating prior art. The materials can be gathered and filed as a provisional for a cost of $60, as presented in Chapter 9: Cost. The higher cost of utility applications, which must meet more formal requirements, also prompts filing provisionals.[63]

However, I strongly caution you to approach provisionals with attention to meeting the statutory terms for a follow-on utility filing. As funds and timing allow for provisionals and even more so for utility applications, work with a patent professional. The examination substance and process are highly technical, and arguments during examination with the Office are key evidence about the quality of any granted patents.

THE USPTO EXAMINATION PROCESS

Here's a brief overview of the formal utility *examination* process. The PTO assesses whether the invention described in the patent application warrants a patent, based on the eligibility of statutory Sections 101, 102, and 103, as well as 112, as previously described.

Upon receipt of the filing, the Patent Office undertakes research for prior art dated earlier than the application filing date. The patent applicant is not required to research the prior art, but rather, under a *duty of disclosure*, must provide the art that she is aware of. The Office then compares the prior art to the *claims* in the context of the *specification* to determine whether and how the claims are different from the prior art.

PTO Office Actions and Claim Amendments. During examination, the Office prepares communications, called *Office Actions*, to present its positions. They include objections and rejections of the claims based on the statutory sections. Applicants optionally can request a meeting with the Examiner, called an *interview*, to receive feedback about the Office Action.

The applicant can then file a formal response to the Office Action, including answering the points set out or *amending* the claims to clarify the differences between the claims and the prior art. The goal for the applicant is to maintain the *scope of the claims* as closely as possible to the invention, but in light of the prior art and PTO positions. A narrower claim scope (for example, adding a new element to the claim) may be required considering the prior art.

Patent Success. Ideally, some or all of the PTO's positions are overcome. Where they are not, the Office prepares a *Final Office Action*, which answers the applicant's arguments and advances the discussion. The applicant in turn responds, ideally prompting the Office to grant the patent. With success at any point of the examination comes a granted patent, which happens with 57 percent of applications.[64] Today there have been about 11 million US patents granted within about 150 million patents worldwide.

Patent Rejection Options. On the other hand, if the Office maintains its rejections and decides not to grant the patent, there are several options to continue to seek patent rights: refile the application, file an appeal or abandon the filing.[65]

The Patent File Wrapper. The USPTO makes available the formal communications between the Office and the applicant in a historical record, called a *file wrapper*. These exchanges, therefore, can be reviewed and are a key evidentiary record should the patent be involved in litigation or other transaction where its value is assessed.

PATENTABILITY SEARCHES

Patentability Searches. An optional activity (at additional cost) which some professionals recommend is conducting a patentability search, or researching prior art.

However, undertaking prior art research prompts costs and the risk of acquiring knowledge of a third-party patent which may later be asserted against you in litigation. This knowledge can trigger a litigation allegation that you knew about the third-party patent, and therefore your infringement is willful, as discussed in Chapter 3: Patents: Risks.

Patentability searches aren't required. Be wary of patent services that present patentability searches as a menu item (and cost) before filing for a patent application. These searches require a nuanced decision and should be considered based on a careful risk–benefit analysis with your patent professional.

Go Global. Another question inventors can consider is whether to file their invention internationally. Remember, if foreign rights are not timely filed, that ability is lost. Foreign patents are a separate treatise in themselves, warranting hiring professionals with specific international experience.

SUMMARY

In patent litigation, the gravamen for the patent owner is the strength of the patent (or its validity) and infringement by a third party. Other issues add costs and distraction. For example, adjudicating time bars for public activity is a non-substantive distraction, potentially resulting in a patent found to be invalid and *all rights lost.* Employing the best-in-class planning of this chapter extends beyond opportunities to prevention to avoid outright errors that destroy future value.

A Preview of the #ip2ip Checklist. Optimizing the timing and quality of patents also yields benefits across the IP spectrum because, as you'll see in the additional substantive IP Chapters 2 through 7, this timing also can prompt leveraging additional IP assets. Then, these IP strategies are accumulated in the Chapter 10 checklist, with the encouragement to *Do Business in the Bullseye.*

When viewed in the broader context of competition, you are subject to the obligations of others who will leverage all legal, business, and competitive strategies, regardless of whether you do. Your reading of #ip2ip demonstrates your interest in gaining this competitive advantage for your innovation and its protection.

CHAPTER 3

#IP2IP PATENTS: RISKS

PLANNING FOR PREVENTION

ACTions

3.1 Apply intentional strategies for computer-implemented inventions, given the downward pressure on patents.

3.2 **Generate a litigation playbook for bringing and defending against litigation, including corporate policies which demonstrate good IP citizenship.** *Top-10 Takeaway.*

I hope the majesty of our US patent system inspires you. The file-or-lose-it proposition also offers a risk of declining to participate. That risk, however, is within your control.

There are additional risks which are unfortunately outside your control—the greatest risk being the state of the US patent system. To repeat an unfortunate truism—the US patent system is broken. A high percentage of patents are invalidated based on a 2014 US Supreme Court decision changing the Section 101 standard for whether an invention is eligible for patenting.[66] What resulted was a 914 percent increase in the number of patents found invalid from 2009 to 2019, reflecting the decision's five-year impact. Today, researchers estimate that 60–80 percent of patents judged in court have had claims held invalid.[67]

Add to these dire statistics additional challenges for patent owners: First, success in patent litigation is reversed on appeal about half of the time.[68] Second, litigated patents also can be challenged in "second look" or *post-grant proceedings* by the US Patent and Trademark Office—most commonly, inter partes reviews (IPRs). Patents tested in an IPR have at least some claims invalidated about 92 percent of the time, and some patents are subject to multiple IPRs.[69]

The risks related to asserting a patent in litigation to protect your innovations is only one form of risk in patenting. From an IP owner's perspective, litigation seeks to remedy the infringement of patents. However, competitor litigation often prompts a counter assertion of infringement. Even high-quality IP assets are subject to the IP rights of others.

Finally, your receipt of IP litigation is not a function of your ownership. Risk management therefore must include preparing to defend against patent (or other IP) litigation against you.

Let's next turn to these risks:

1. Section 101 Eligibility: The State of Play Needs Correction

2. USPTO Post-Grant Proceedings: Repeating Assessments of Patent Grants, Repeatedly

3. Litigation Readiness: A Litigation Playbook for Planning and Prevention

SECTION 101 ELIGIBILITY
THE STATE OF PLAY NEEDS CORRECTION

The colloquial use of 101 to suggest the simplicity of a topic does not apply to Section 101 of the US patent laws and its impact on computer-implemented inventions, or 63.2 percent of all patents today.[70] Section 101 is the patent eligibility standard for categories of inventions deemed patentable. It applies to specific technologies, including computer-implemented inventions, such as software, as well as areas outside of computers, such as medical techniques and pharmaceutical technologies.[71]

As we turn to 101, let me first offer a respectful apology to inventors and patent owners for the US patent system. The state of patents goes beyond unfairly invalidating patents to a missed opportunity for case law precedent to fairly guide innovators to achieving strong patents, and in turn, a strong innovation economy. This US void is pronounced and is being filled by our global competitors at the expense of our economy and protection of our American ingenuity. However, self-selected clear-thinking leaders also are committed to its correction. I can tap the informative and elegant reasoning of those striving to return the patent system to its original intention—to inspire innovation. With respect, these judicial leaders are Federal Circuit Judge Pauline Newman and retired and esteemed Judges Kathleen O'Malley and Paul Redmond Michel (who devotes his retirement to this cause).

The Legal Standard. Recall that Section 101 is about what can be patented, including:

> ...any new and useful process, machine, manufacture, or composition of matter, or any new and useful improvement thereof.

A 1981 SCOTUS decision reminded us that "Congress intended statutory subject matter to 'include anything under the sun that is made by man.'"[72] However, the same Court has presented limits or *judicial exceptions* to the Section 101 definition of patents, including that "*laws of nature,*" "*physical phenomena*" and "*abstract ideas*" are *not eligible* for patent protection. Courts deem computer-implemented inventions to be abstract.

101 jurisprudence has been likened to a rabbit hole in Wonderland, derived from the seminal 2014 SCOTUS decision described above, with the parties *Alice v. CLS Bank*.[73] *Alice* involved a review of whether innovations for software or business methods are eligible for patent protection with a two-step test:

> Step one, whether the *patent claims are directed to a patent-ineligible concept*, such as an *abstract idea*; and

> Step two, *if so*, then whether *the additional claim elements, individually or in combination, demonstrate an inventive concept*. The inventive concept also has been expanded to mean that it is *significantly more* than the abstract idea itself.[74]

I'll pause for a moment...as I anticipate your reaction. I still experience it to this day, encountering what should be informative language and instead being confounded by it. *Abstract idea, ineligibility, inventive concept, significantly more* and *transform*. What? Federal Circuit cases have since layered additional words in pursuit of clarity, but instead confirm their inaccessibility.

Many would say *Alice* is impossible to apply. As one district court judge noted, "[a]t this point, it is trite to comment on the confusing abyss of patent eligibility law."[75] Leaders from every government branch have formally plead for guidance by the SCOTUS and Congress and await action, with cases passed over and Congressional bills stalled. Unfortunately, this is the state of affairs for 101.

Insider Lawball

Patent Uncertainty under 101 Dominates in a Descent Down the Alice Rabbit Hole
By Robert Rando

This Insider Lawball follows the 101 twists and turns that are not the way a body of law should develop. Patent news highlights lawsuits filed by some patent owners who assert patents acquired for litigation rather than "practicing" or commercializing them, called *nonpracticing entities* (NPEs). This is not malfeasance, in and of itself. However, some NPEs have blanketed industries with monetary demands at amounts below litigation defense costs. They accumulated micro-settlements into small fortunes and gained newsworthy cries of foul from companies and even charities, giving rise to the label "patent trolls." The patents fueling these controversies are often computer-implemented inventions.

Historically, computer-implemented inventions and software were not recognized as patentable. In 1998, the Federal Circuit declared that business methods and computer-implemented inventions were patentable so long as they yielded "a *useful, concrete and tangible result*," triggering floodgates opening for filing and litigating these patents.[76] The exploding influx of new filings at the US Patent and Trademark Office, itself ill equipped to assess computer-implemented inventions, resulted in some low-quality patents. Add to this the 2008 economic downturn, yielding patents in bankrupt companies for fire-sale purchase by bad-acting patent trolls. Patent litigation of questionable patents started to make headline news.

The judiciary reacted at the highest level, with the SCOTUS transitioning from a historic trend of declining to review patent decisions by the US Court of Appeals for the Federal Circuit (the penultimate appeal court for patent issues) to rendering opinions in patent cases. In the 2010 case of *Bilski v. Kappos*, the Court, in a splintered decision, struck down the *useful, concrete, tangible result* test.[77] Congress passed the 2011 America Invents Act (AIA), including post-grant proceedings IPRs, to reduce abusive litigation based on perceived poor-quality patents.[78] More SCOTUS decisions ensued, culminating in the controlling 2014 *Alice* precedent.

I posit that the transcendence of 101 had more to do with the litigation climate rather than a 220-year-old spark of insight into US patent law. Since this time, here is a review of efforts across the USPTO, Judiciary and Congress to make corrections.

USPTO. The PTO proactively issued a series of official Examination Guidance drawing on court decisions for use by PTO Examiners in evaluating patent applications under *Alice*.[79] A 2019 Guidance publication presented that *abstract concepts* which are "*integrated into a practical application*" of a *judicial exception* support eligibility. The Federal Circuit, however, has held that the Court is not bound by the Office's Guidance.[80] The Honorable Kathi Vidal, as the currently serving PTO director, has been focused on post-grant proceedings more so than Section 101.[81]

Judicial Efforts. While rendering numerous decisions post-*Alice*, courts have not sufficiently clarified 101. Interestingly, in the *Alice* decision, the SCOTUS itself admitted "[a]t some level, 'all inventions…embody…laws of nature, natural phenomenon, or abstract ideas.'"[82] Judge Pauline Newman cautioned in June 2021 that "…inconsistency and unpredictability of [101] adjudication have destabilized technological developments."[83] Retired Judge Paul Michel presented that "recent cases are unclear, inconsistent [and confusing]. I myself cannot reconcile the cases… [With 22 years of experience, I cannot predict outcomes]."[84] Hope was raised in 2022 as the Supreme Court considered reviewing a Federal Circuit split 6-6 on a rehearing. The highly anticipated outcome was a denial of the petition for certiorari in June 2022, maintaining the status quo, followed by further denials of 101 cases in 2023.[85] Given what appears to be the SCOTUS pens in suspended animation, the focus has shifted to Congress for action.

Congressional Efforts. Congressional efforts have been bipartisan, with Senators Chris Coons (D-DE) and Thom Tillis (R-NC) leading patent reform. A June 2023 Senate bill, the PREVAIL Act, is the latest effort striving to expand eligibility for software. It maintains the statutory categories of eligible subject matter by listing areas which cannot be patented, such as algorithms or processes that are substantially economic, financial, business or mental, etc. To address uneven case law interpretation, language is added to convert the exceptions to being designated patentable subject matter where, on a practical basis, they require the use of a computer.[86] The Honorable Michel pronounced that the "boldness of the new bill is stunning."[87] With earlier bills falling short of passage, supporters of inventors' rights hope the sentiment is worthy of the outcome.

Economic and Innovation Impact. The consequences, as elegantly penned by esteemed attorney Robert Rando, are: "clear empirical evidence demonstrate[s] the devastating effect Section 101 uncertainty has had. [Patents routinely denied US issuance...are granted in China and Europe, threatening America's] leadership role and innovation defense and economic superiority on the global stage."[88]

This brief history of US patents for software illustrates the descent down the *Alice* rabbit hole, plus the complexity and uncertainty in achieving value in the US patent system today. The connection between a strong patent system and economic opportunity is unquestioned.

Since IP protection of innovation must evolve, the courts and Congress should work to increase the certainty of the value of patents. Patent risk based on Section 101 implicates US innovation and economics. The risk has gone unanswered now for nearly a decade. With a properly functioning patent system, our public and private sector resources could have been applied to building innovation leadership for economic opportunity in the US. Innovators cannot justify an investment in patents that are subject to uncertain future value and expensive litigation, diverting money that could be invested in R & D.

The present uncertainty is a rallying cry to reinstate this critical institution to its mandate of incentivizing innovation. Therefore, the task is now left for the SCOTUS to clarify 101 through judicial precedent or for Congress to step in for a better patent day.

ACTIONS TO MANAGE 101 FOR COMPUTER-IMPLEMENTED INVENTIONS

Uncertain legal standards prompt a need for expanding technology descriptions in patent applications. They must anticipate legal standards written not for engineers or innovators, but for judges. A framework follows which can be handed to your patent professionals to bolster your chances of being granted a patent. The exercise can yield separate business value too.

Deconstructing the Legal Standard. Let's start with deconstructing the legal patenting standard, starting with a negative (despite my optimistic penchant): a software program that merely runs on a computer is ineligible for patenting. Think back in history to the days before computers, where processes were completed with paper and pen. When these known processes are simply programmed for execution on a computer, they become ineligible.

Why? The two-step *Alice* analysis governs with this:

> Step one, it is an *abstract idea* as an exception to Section 101 and

> Step two, the abstract idea does not have *something more* than what is well understood, routine and conventional. It is simply an instruction to implement the abstract idea on a computer, using the computer merely as a tool.[89]

Cases and the PTO have also identified categories which are commonly deemed abstract, listed in the PTO Guidance in three groupings: (1) *mathematical concepts*, such as mathematical relationships and mathematical formulas; (2) *mental processes* or concepts performed in the human mind (including an observation, evaluation, judgment, opinion); and (3) *certain methods of organizing human activity*, such as fundamental economic principles or practices, commercial or legal interactions, or managing personal behavior or relationships or interactions between people.

Innovations broadly related to these subject areas should heighten the exploration of additional technology descriptions to add to your patent application. The Guidance attempts to accomplish this exploration with the notion that the innovation is "*integrated into a practical application*."[90]

Some Computer-Implemented Inventions Are Patentable. At first blush, this seemingly eliminates any computer program from being patentable. In 2016 however, the Federal Circuit refused a rule "that all improvements in computer-related technology are inherently abstract…"[91] This left a window open for some computer-implemented inventions.

Which ones? The Supreme Court has yet to define precisely what subject matter is 101 eligible by either being outside of the abstract idea category or, while abstract, including additional elements to constitute an inventive concept. Instead, courts mine fact patterns from earlier precedential decisions to explain the reasoning for their 101 conclusions. Therefore, adding descriptions of your innovation which match or are similar to the fact patterns held by courts (or presented by the USPTO in its Guidance) to be patent-eligible is the singular aim.

Fact patterns surviving 101 in court often follow this general reasoning:

Under 101, the computer-related invention is one of the four enumerated categories, such as a *process* or *machine*, or an *improvement on it*, and it is not a *judicial exception* because:

Under *Alice* step one, the invention *improves the underlying functionality of a computer* or specific improvements in computer capabilities;[92] and

Where step one ineligibility applies, under *Alice* step two, the individual claim elements alone or in combination provide *something more* by *improving the underlying functionality of a computer*, do not constitute *well-understood, routine or conventional activity* or are a *practical application* of an idea.[93]

The analysis for each of the steps is close because often, *Alice* step one is a given in case decisions. As a result, the computer-functionality improvement is most often applied in *Alice* step two. However, arguing it in both steps doubles the chance of satisfying 101.

While the Federal Circuit has declined to be bound by the USPTO Guidance, the Patent Office necessarily assesses 101 in deciding whether to grant patents. The patent is then available to enforce in court for a twenty-year term from filing. Consider that a commercially valuable invention meeting the Office's Guidance produces a patent extant for a period where ideally the standards will be corrected to accommodate the PTO's approach.

Business Concepts. With a focus on business value as our guide in patenting, let's also approach 101 from a business mindset. Computer-implemented inventions, including software and even business models, are created because they provide commercial value to your business. We are in a digital age where business offerings are increasingly implemented in technology, and necessarily involve technological solutions to technological problems. It is at this level of describing your invention that you optimize your chance of patenting under 101.

The business concept then is as follows: focus on technological solutions to technological problems, their technological results and how the invention achieves the intended solutions or results.

Just the Facts. Patents are found eligible when they can be analogized to earlier successful case law fact patterns. Your story of technology in your patent application should do the same, by analogizing to individual descriptions or combining multiple descriptions in the fact patterns below. Approach the exercise as a matching game of features of your invention with the fact patterns. Detailed and expanded individual and combinations of facts may support patentability (or validity) over their twenty-year term and maximize your chances of exceeding present or future 101 standards.

Simply apply your best efforts. The descriptions can be presented as alternatives which conflict with each other, so do not focus too much on internal consistency across descriptions. Recall that each individual claim based on one of alternative technology descriptions is a stand-alone invention. Above all, do not focus on getting the "right" answer. Judges and courts are pleading for help because there is no right answer.

Here goes—fact patterns found to support patent eligibility:

- *Fact Pattern 1. Improving the Underlying Functionality or Operation of a Computer Itself:* Software with specific rules or hardware features that improve the operation, performance or components of a computer system itself, in contrast to processes that are simply run on a computer. A 2021 Federal Circuit case found eligibility based on fewer computer resources, less human interaction and simpler devices as an advance over prior systems.[94]

- *Fact Pattern 2. How the Invention Improves Computer Functionality:* Technology descriptions in the specification support patent claims which present *how* or the specific way the invention solves the problem rather than merely presenting results or functions, such as what the invention does.[95]

- *Fact Pattern 3. Steps Using Unconventional, Specific Rules:* Software or hardware that is part of a special purpose computer, or "steps using unconventional specific rules," solutions or improved technological results.[96]

- *Fact Pattern 4. Distributed Architecture:* Hardware or software is distributed across computers/hardware over networks with components being remote from each other and with the processing of data performed close to the source.[97]

- *Fact Pattern 5. Machine or Transformation Test:* The subject matter "effects a transformation or reduction of a particular article to a different state or thing." However, the SCOTUS noted that while this test may provide a "useful and important clue" for eligibility, it is not the sole test.[98]

- *Fact Pattern 6. A Practice Application Beyond an Abstract Idea Itself:* Within the 2019 PTO Guidance, technology descriptions *integrated into a practical application* of an abstract idea and not simply an abstract idea itself are eligible. This applies for inventions within the enumerated abstract idea categories of (1) *mathematical concepts*, (2) *mental processes* and (3) *certain methods of organizing human activity*. Presenting how they satisfy the Guidance is particularly important.[99]

It is also worthwhile to note a trend in software development under environmental sustainability to reduce power usage even within software code and its interactions with hardware and systems under sustainability goals, such as green software to increase energy and hardware efficiency. We can apply these principles to support 101 as well. When considering sustainability for computer systems, add your technological solutions to your patent application.

I close with this advice: Assume that your inventions are patent eligible under Section 101—especially if the invention does something new and is commercially valuable. Present your patent professional with multiple technology descriptions which relate to individual, multiple or a combination of features of your invention—with confidence! The rest is outside of your control.

Finding Business Value in the 101 Exercise. Let me also offer to lift us from the patent doldrums in two ways. First, the exercise of preparing materials to describe your invention necessarily prompts you to think of your invention in new ways, similar to a SWOT analysis using patenting standards (called *forward* *inventing*). In addition to the fact pattern matching above, consider these questions: Which innovations will competitors most want to copy? Which innovations will be hardest for competitors to compete against without copying? Where do you see innovations in the market in one, three or five years, as patents can include future innovations beyond your current commercial offerings? It may even prompt a new feature for commercialization with patent protection in mind. Second, consider more broadly the IP spectrum and capture additional protective strategies for computer-related inventions. These strategies, including trade secrets and copyrights, can complement or, if needed, replace the efficacy of patent rights today.

WHAT SHOULD BE THE STANDARD FOR PATENTING?

Not Section 101, according to the Honorable Pauline Newman who referred to 101 as a "'coarse eligibility filter,' not the final arbiter of patentability," and generally regarded 101 as a low hurdle, while considering other statutory requirements, such as Sections 102, 103 and 112, as placing more meaningful limits on patentability.[100]

Sections 102 and 103 Are Foundational. 102 and 103 enable an objective use of evidence in prior art, and an application of the law to the facts to reach logical conclusions. This objectivity provides precedent and guidance to innovators. They have always been, and many posit still should be, the steadfast bulwarks to determine and challenge validity.

With the hopes that 102 and 103 will rise again to prominence at the expense of 101, for now, it's back to the trenches...

USPTO POST-GRANT PROCEEDINGS
REPEATING ASSESSMENTS OF PATENT GRANTS, REPEATEDLY

When granted, a patent is deemed valid and has a legal presumption of validity in court. However, the validity of patents can be reviewed again and reversed. This occurs most commonly as a defense to infringement litigation. The alleged infringer argues that the patent is invalid in federal district court, and often in parallel post-grant proceedings at the US Patent and Trademark Office, such as IPRs. Through either path, a patent held invalid is extinguished as if it were never granted in the first place.[101] An invalid patent has no value.

The Frustration and Basis for a Second Look at Patents. How can the USPTO grant a patent and then, when the patent owner goes to enforce it in litigation, take a "second look" and reject its own work? The policy basis presented for this second look is the societal interest in terminating patents that never should have been issued.

Patent challenges at the USPTO started in 1981. Today's IPRs were established under the 2011 AIA as minitrials to be handled by a new panel of specialized Patent Office judges as part of a Patent Trial and Appeal Board (PTAB).

Inter Partes Review. IPRs involve a more limited set of invalidity grounds than can be presented in court, namely Sections 102 and 103, based on prior art in the form of patents and publications. While Sections 101 and 112 technically do not fall under invalidity bases in IPRs, some cases have expanded to indirectly evaluate them when claims are amended during IPRs.[102]

IPRs are Billed as Fast and Cost-Effective, but for What Purpose? The policy for post-grant proceedings is a fast and cost-effective alternative to litigation, albeit with an expensive PTO filing fee. Accused infringers may only bring IPRs within one year of the patent litigation filing.[103] Unsurprisingly, IPR filers generally result from being sued in parallel lawsuits, with litigations often being stayed (and delayed) pending the IPR outcome.[104] Third parties not in a lawsuit with the patent owner can bring post-grant proceedings at any time. IPRs also are statutorily directed to be concluded by the PTAB within one year of accepting a petition to challenge the patent. This rapid determination adds fees to the patent owner's legal actions against the infringer earlier in time than in the historic course of district court litigation.

The Interplay between AIA USPTO Proceedings and Court. AIA proceedings have important differences from federal court, easing challenges to patents. The PTAB's analysis of validity requires proof by a "preponderance of the evidence" (or more likely than not, think 51 percent more likely). This is a lower burden than the "clear and convincing standard" (think more than 51 percent likely) applied to validity challenges in federal courts and the ITC.[105] Also, while patents have a starting presumption of validity in court, that presumption does not apply in post-grant proceedings. The PREVAIL Act, as discussed above, is pending legislation to improve the US patent system; it includes harmonizing PTO IPRs with the court evidentiary standard of clear and convincing evidence and presumption of validity.[106]

IPRs are a Mainstay of Litigation Defense. As a result, when a patent owner sues for patent infringement, the owner should prepare for the likelihood that a challenger or third party will challenge the patent in an IPR.

Validity Is Reviewed in Multiple Proceedings with Different Appellate Tracks. Appeals of AIA determinations are made to the Federal Circuit. Therefore, cases arrive at the Federal Circuit either by route of appeals from district courts or from USPTO decisions. The PTO generates rulings about patents in its decisions, but of note, it is only when Office decisions are challenged in an appeal to the Federal Circuit and that Court renders its appellate decision that its decision is legally binding on federal courts and the USPTO.[107] The Federal Circuit decision is also appealable to the SCOTUS. The patent owner therefore also has to manage separate appellate timing and tracks from the district court and separately from the USPTO to the Federal Circuit.

Misuse of IPRs. In practice, parties in litigation and others in the market use IPRs as a means of leverage to run up the patent owner's costs. Dozens of IPRs can be filed against a single patent asserted in litigation (although filing an IPR is expensive). Parallel tracks in federal court and the PTO, combined with the nonbinding nature of the Office's decisions until an appellate decision, can result in timing differences that produce the opposite of their intended timeliness for most patent owners.

LITIGATION READINESS
A LITIGATION PLAYBOOK FOR PLANNING AND PREVENTION

This focus on patent quality for substance and process bodes well not only for protecting your innovations but also for creating strong evidence in court against third-party copiers. Enforcement addresses the opportunities side of IP assets.

IP strategy also must address risks. While we have explored risks in the value of your patent assets, these strategies must also include defending against the patent and IP assets of third parties being asserted against you in litigation. This is common in business strategy, with threats being part of the strengths, weaknesses, opportunities, and threats (or SWOT) analysis, bringing us back once again to business-aligned IP strategy.

Nowhere are the consequences of IP strategy more apparent than in litigation. Success in litigation is a function of litigation counsel and high-quality IP assets. However, with a mindset of planning for prevention, I offer two areas for your consideration that can be well ahead of hiring litigation counsel to optimize evidence of your high-quality assets and risk mitigation: (1) a Litigation Playbook and (2) Willful Intellectual Property Infringement.

A litigation playbook involves planning for a complaint that you will assert (offense) or receive (defense). Offense is the opportunity in litigation to receive relief for IP asset infringement provable by your companies' evidentiary support. Defense or risk when sued is about defending yourself in the event your company is accused of infringing third party IP assets. However, defense can start long before the receipt of a lawsuit.

Litigation Role-Play. The ideal planning approach is a modeling exercise.

Top-10 Takeaway 3

#ip2ip-3: Generate a litigation playbook for bringing and defending against litigation, including corporate policies which demonstrate good IP citizenship.

Presume that right now on your desk, you have a complaint suing you for IP infringement, such as patent infringement. Think through this scenario with the full logical and emotional reaction of being faced with actual litigation. You'll have your own reactionary topics, but consider these: Who is your first call internally, and how do you manage that person's reaction and set her expectations? Now consider contacting her and asking her to role-play along with you. Do you have a litigator in mind or a path to retaining one? What budget line items are available for funding? Do you have insurance coverage (noting that often these policies require notice and advocacy for coverage)? Are you a member of any industry organizations which provide defense services; is this a good time to consider them?

Above all, imagine the potential of this happening now, as you are reading this. You cannot control the timing of third-party legal actions against you. However, you can control your planning to react to them, including strategies to implement today to address issues likely to arise in future litigation. Work with your in-house and outside litigation professionals to embark on preparing a privileged litigation playbook for reacting to and undertaking a defense. This exercise alone will ensure that in the event you are sued, your first reaction is an improvement over what many experience as panic and uncertainty about where to begin, but with absolute certainty of the high cost of litigation.

Upon the heels of this exercise, you can shift to a playbook for the reverse situation of bringing IP litigation. Think of this book as a litigation playbook for offense, with high-quality IP assets at the ready to enforce if need be.

Document Retention. A complimentary area to develop in the playbook is document retention. The discovery phase of litigation is costly and elongated due to identifying, designating, and producing evidence, whether as plaintiff or defendant. Naturally, the more materials in your corporate repository, the more expansive the exercise. Document retention sounds mundane, but it can build a corporate culture that views the information at your office as potentially positive or negative trial evidence. Policies about these materials should be grounded in quality and integrity, but also tactically in a protective manner to reduce litigation risk and discovery cost.

WILLFUL INTELLECTUAL PROPERTY INFRINGEMENT

IP litigation often carries with it an accusation that infringement is willful. The term "willful" on its face speaks of bad conduct, the consequences of which are similarly bad. Where infringement is found to be willful, the decision can support enhanced damages and payment of the patent owner's attorneys' fees.[108] Much of #ip2ip is focused on setting up IP rights which give the potential of attorneys' fees. If you are on the receiving end of patent litigation, the obverse is at work, with the potential of a loss expanding to multiples for financial damages and attorneys' fees. Advanced planning in this area is therefore warranted.

The Good and the Bad for Litigating Parties. An underlying theme of litigation is an aggrieved party as the plaintiff in conflict with a defending party, with the scales of justice in the outcome elevating one at the expense of the other. This is facilitated by each party portraying themselves as a good actor (or good IP citizen) in contrast to their bad actor opponent. A willfulness accusation is a powerful label in the arsenal of patent owners seeking to show their alleged infringer's bad virtue.

Planning for Prevention. For IP owners, a willfulness claim is part of litigation planning, following the applicable marking statute and strategically giving notice to bring litigation. Defenses to an accusation of willful infringement are more complicated because they arise from the action and timing of others. Third-party litigation against you is outside of your control and based on unique facts with a yet unknown third party.

Changes in the Law: A Halo for the Good Party. Changes in the law also are difficult to plan. Willfulness is a good example of such a change.

Courts historically treated willfulness based on objective standards determined in the first instance by a judge.[109] An exemplary fact pattern meeting the objective standard was a legal opinion prepared as part of the litigation (or post-litigation). In addition, the factual presentation of willfulness and its attendant good and bad actor theme generally was not heard by the jury. In 2016, the US Supreme Court changed the law on willfulness in a case brought by plaintiff *Halo Electronics*

("*Halo*").[110] The Court shifted the standard for willfulness from an objective to a subjective one and the decision on willfulness to the trier of fact, which is a jury in a jury trial. The evidentiary standard was also lowered, making it easier for the new trier of fact to find willfulness. Where willfulness is found, a judge can then determine whether to enhance damages separately.[111] A 2021 Federal Circuit decision, including Cisco as a sophisticated party, clarified that willfulness requires "a jury to find no more than a deliberate or intentional infringement."[112] The SRI case is instructive to review for guidance on conduct which supports willfulness and enhanced damages.

Evidence of Willfulness before Juries. Juries historically determine infringement, where the good and bad actor themes are impactful. Adding willfulness gives a new arena to litigators to influence jurors' decision-making. And it has, with an increase in the incidence of finding willfulness. In addition, where willfulness evidence and posturing are presented to a jury, jurors are more apt to find infringement.

Key Evidence: Legal Opinions and Knowledge. Two key evidentiary areas in post-*Halo* decisions are knowledge and legal opinions, and their presence or absence relative to the timing of the litigation filing. It gets complicated and costly fast.[113] Build IP strategy around demonstrating that your company is a good IP citizen through corporate policies, practice, and culture for risk management, guided and directed by legal professionals.

Summary

A Call to Action for Correction of the Patent System. Patents and IP can drive the new story of how America enables the next generation of Edisons. Those with a common interest in thinking and innovating see a fork in the road in America's prosperity. With an increasingly information-driven global economy supported by computer software, patent reform must occur to keep the economic engine healthy. Each branch of government must embrace a shift to reignite the power of a single idea and the American dream of patents.

Risk Is in the Details Best Managed by Litigators. Details govern, and those details are best evaluated and planned for with your litigation counsel in the context of your company, market, and competitors. Formalizing your approach in corporate policies sets up an intentional assessment and decision for your litigation playbook. Risk mitigation strategies too can build your corporate culture to make intentional decisions as good IP citizens to avoid infringing the intellectual property rights of others.

CHAPTER 4

#IP2IP PATENTS: YOUR FUTURE SUCCESS

INNOVATING THE PATENT SYSTEM
GUEST AUTHORS: JULIE MAR-SPINOLA, ERICH SPANGENBERG WITH JONAS BLOCK, AND RUUD PETERS

ACTion

4.1 Be a guest author. Write your ACTions for *Your Future Success* along with your guest authors. Visit cherylmilone.com.

FUTURE LEGAL FRAMEWORKS WITHIN THE PACE OF ARTIFICIAL INTELLIGENCE AND OTHER EMERGING TECHNOLOGIES

Today, we find ourselves in a technology explosion. We are experiencing an accelerating pace of emerging technologies that advance more quickly than the law. Witness artificial intelligence (AI), machine learning and blockchain. These technologies perform computer tasks outside the interaction of individual human inventors or creators.

The offerings created from these technology advancements, such as ChatGPT™ (OpenAI®) and Bard™, built on large language models, are today's headliner news.[114] The technology arms race and the media focus on the highs and lows of opportunities and societal risks, overshadows rational security, economic, legal and ethical AI safeguards.

Generative Artificial Intelligence. Generative AI dominates IP news as it does business. Topics include AI innovations and IP asset opportunities and risks, and involve both owners and users of AI systems, as well as inventors and creators of data used to train the systems. For AI innovations, IP laws have been applied to clarify that while AI is credited with extraordinary capabilities, a computer using artificial intelligence cannot be a patent inventor—that honor is reserved for humans! The conclusion draws on the legal standard requiring conception, or formation in an inventor's mind, of an invention. However, like other tools which augment human innovation, AI technology descriptions have been identified in early 1960 US patents building on an acceleration of AI in the 1950s, with AI-related patenting soaring since 2013. For example, from 2013 to 2016, fields showing at least 28 percent growth in AI-related patenting include banking and finance, transportation and computing in government. In 2023, the advancement of generative AI, and inventors asking patent offices and courts to declare AI as an inventor, prompted formal inquiries into whether inventions made by humans with the assistance of AI, or with AI as a component, may be patentable. The US Patent and Trademark

Office has requested public views on the topic. For additional IP assets, such as copyright, the US Copyright Office has presented that some degree of human involvement is required in how AI is used to create a final work and that AI-generated features which are more than de minimis must be excluded from copyright as nonhuman authorship.[115]

Risks arise because AI systems train using data potentially owned by third parties. Input into public AI systems also risks the loss of confidential data. IP laws cover these activities. However, boasts by AI systems owners of vast training on colossal amounts of data scraped from the internet have prompted concerns that IP laws generally have been ignored. While IP infringement lawsuits are accumulating, US courts are far behind advancements.[116] We'll start to see decisions on preliminary relief, with precedent-setting decisions years and appeals later.

In mid-2023, the United States Supreme Court issued opinions about copyrights and trademarks supportive of innovator rights.[117] While not AI cases, they present directional guidance for the treatment of IP assets in AI-related infringement lawsuits.

For US AI regulation, an October 2023 executive order advanced voluntary requirements set out earlier by the White House to improve "AI safety and security." Two key areas are labeling AI-generated content, such as using watermarks, and sharing safety test results for new AI models with the US government where the tests show a risk to national security (drawing upon a federal law generally applicable in national emergencies). The order falls short of providing for enforcement, and executive orders are subject to being overturned by future administrations. Major tech companies generally have welcomed the step, emphasizing testing of new models rather than limitations on building models, as well as their voluntary efforts to address risks. For example, the Coalition for Content Provenance and Authenticity (including Microsoft, Intel and Adobe) and its affiliated open-source community have been developing watermarking techniques. Other experts argue that the order does not go far enough in providing testing standards through the National Institute of Standards meant to break models in order to expose vulnerabilities, but without a requirement that companies apply the standards. What is clear is the lengthy path to enforceable regulation, with US AI regulation unlikely prior to the 2024 presidential election. US Congress has hosted debates, and lawmakers have introduced nascent bills and proposals. Individual state efforts in many cases are leading those at the federal level. As of July 2023, US state legislators have enacted four bills aimed at privacy frameworks, including collection, use and disclosure, with opt-out rights for AI use in specified automated decisions.[118]

The EU leads in AI regulation, with advanced planning resulting in the AI Act 2021, focused on privacy rights for personal data, and a follow-on June 2023 proposal requiring AI providers to publicly disclose "sufficiently detailed" documentation of copyright works in training. The Act's application and how companies can comply with it remains to be seen. OpenAI has suggested, for example, that as a result of the required documentation, it may not be able to operate in the EU. The AI Act's effective date likely is 2025 at the earliest.[119]

Blockchain and Web3. The advent of Web3 and decentralized applications based on blockchain-enabled technologies seek to drive transactions directly between individuals. Blockchain is a database containing immutable and secure records of transactions, secured by the majority consensus of all network participants. Familiar blockchain networks are cryptocurrencies Bitcoin and Dogecoin. These currencies are not backed by governments nor regulated by central authorities. Cryptocurrencies being used alongside fiat currencies (government-issued legal tender) demonstrate the power and reach of blockchain technology. Within the noise of Bitcoin pronouncements and denouncements, one leading global financial institution still deemed Bitcoin to be the best performing asset at the start of 2023.[120]

Non-Fungible Tokens. The immutable and transparent recordation of assets has vast societal implications beyond money. Assets tokenized as non-fungible tokens (NFTs) can enable standardized transactions and unlock characteristics to build new assets. Using intellectual property assets tokenized as NFTs, for example, inventors and creators can receive ongoing royalties automatically triggered by subsequent transactions of the NFTs, giving creators access to increases in the asset value. Artwork is the most notable use case to date, with artists realizing the increase in value of their art, regardless of the variability and fraud accompanying these opportunities.[121]

NFT transactions are governed by smart contracts, with their simplicity and transparency driving efficiencies and productivity by reducing dense legal negotiations. It is fascinating for inventors and creators because technology is driving a focus on the value of the assets while automating historically inefficient processes to determine that value. It is for this reason that blockchain is said to herald a creator economy.

Open Source. Another feature of the technology explosion is the use of software distributed under open-source licenses. Examples of open-source software include Linux®, Chrome™ and Android™. Open source generally arises within the copyright context, as licenses provide royalty-free access, use, sharing and even modification by anyone.[122] Open source seeks to increase standardization, adoption and efficiency, and to reduce costs through community development, debugging and maintenance.

However, part of the legacy of open source is to require its licensees similarly to apply open-source requirements to their software where the software incorporates licensed open-source code. This presents a need for due diligence by those who use open-source software in assessing their use and distribution of software inheriting these restrictions. There also are issues of combining open source and other IP rights for features of offerings, as well as potential antitrust implications among large-market open-source users. Open source and AI also overlap as an additional arena for litigation; recently, a class action lawsuit was filed by developers who contributed code to the open-source platform and service GitHub. The suit accuses OpenAI of training its systems with code from GitHub repositories and illegally reproducing GitHub code without complying with open-source license terms. These are areas for awareness of both opportunities and risks.[123]

Metaverse. Also on the horizon is the execution of these technologies in the virtual world, described as the *metaverse*. For example, NFTs can be used to exchange goods and services in the metaverse. Virtual worlds built in the metaverse are the new frontier in creating parallels to our physical world. Intellectual property and open source will provide anchors for how to govern the interaction of parties and entities as part of the legal foundation in the metaverse and their application from the physical to the virtual worlds.

These futuristic areas can best be leveraged upon a solid foundation of intellectual property basics, upon which are built strategies anticipating that technology is far ahead and accelerating relative to the law and providing novel questions testing boundaries across IP assets. The future of IP and open source perhaps will be created with colleagues using virtual reality devices as avatars in the metaverse, along with AI colleagues.

INTELLECTUAL PROPERTY TO INCREASE PROFITS FROM SMES TO GLOBAL ENTERPRISES

As IP protection is accomplished for your first innovation or set of crown jewel IP assets, you can pursue next-level IP strategies focusing on your market share and how to plant the seeds of monetization.

I am fortunate to have several of the world's most formidable IP strategists to provide a glimpse into these next-level strategies. Julie Mar-Spinola espouses building quality IP assets as the foundation of her industry-leadership monetization through patent licensing best practices and litigation successes. Erich Spangenberg and Jonas Block focus on driving hockey stick growth of SMEs, and Ruud Peters transformed a global, historic, leading brand to leverage and grow its historic patent portfolio, converting its IP program into a leading global profit center. They share their visions for supporting your journey to *Your Future Success*.

STRIVE FOR QUALITY PATENTS AND ADDITIONAL IP
BY JULIE MAR-SPINOLA

My parents, 1950s Chinese immigrants, intuited the nature of each of their four eldest of five children and aligned our personalities with compatible career paths. Number One Son was a good writer and enjoyed history, so he became a journalist, black belt and beloved grade school teacher. Number Two Son loved to take things apart, so he became an engineer. Middle Child Daughter (me) was quiet, observant and precise, so a pharmacist I could be. Number Three Son, the charismatic, natural athlete who couldn't sit still, would do well as an entrepreneur and tennis pro. Last but never least, the baby sister—too young to have her destiny tagged—was free to do as she would and has become fearless, generous and independent.

I pursued a clinical pharmacy career, specializing in compounding and administering intravenous solutions, particularly nutritional and cancer medications, for more than ten years until product literature warned against exposure to these meds if of "child-bearing age." This warning compelled me to seek a new career path where my pharmacy-related knowledge and skills are helpful. The idea of becoming a patent attorney came to me in a dream. Distinctly, an image of a lone man (female patent attorneys weren't yet featured, even in my dream!) sitting at a drafter's desk in an attic under a bare incandescent light bulb drafting a patent (LEDs weren't yet commercially viable, though it would have been life changing if I had dreamt about the LED then). At the time, a requirement to take the patent bar exam was a hard science degree, so I promptly changed my major to chemistry.

With a background in pharmacy and chemistry, my patent

practice would have naturally been in the pharmaceutical, life sciences or medical device industry. Still, I found myself in the heart of Silicon Valley, building a healthy practice in computers, electronics, software and cybersecurity. My former clients included, among many others, Texas Instruments (computer hardware), Tencor (semiconductor wafer scanners), Telex (communications), Atmel (semiconductor), Alta Devices (high-efficiency photovoltaic cells) and Finjan (cybersecurity and software).

With each client, I worked with and learned from some of the world's most prolific inventors and technology pioneers, such as the inventor of nonvolatile memory and a nominee for the 2010 Nobel Prize in Physics. Indeed, I learned about technology within the confines of patent law and big business by working with the abovementioned companies and their founders, investors and other brain trusts. This valuable experience made me think about IP, particularly patents, in the business context beyond defending them in infringement disputes. The problem I wanted to solve as early as 2005 was transforming a cost center into a profit center through intellectual property. The solution manifested some ten years later.

One of the first steps to monetizing IP is to fortify them against invalidity challenges. A strong patent asset is a valuable business asset to both the patentee and would-be licensees. There are two main ways in which to profit from your IP, namely through licensing or litigation. Enforcement via arms-length licensing negotiations is much more economical and can achieve quicker results than in the context of litigation. My non-litigation negotiations averaged between twelve to twenty-four months, versus litigation resolutions which averaged about three to five years, plus several millions of dollars in fees and expenses. I negotiated an estimated $80 million in non-litigation licensing deals and another $200 million in litigation by following a set of "Licensing Best Practices" we developed at Finjan.[124] By following these best practices, you or your organization can create a reputation as a credible patent owner/licensor. Your "battle-tested" patents will gain durability and accrue more royalties with each license you enter. If litigation is inevitable, litigation tends to fare better if the asserted patent(s) are licensed to third parties because, in patent law, one of the factors to prove the validity of a patent is that the asserted patent was recognized as worthy by others. Because a notice of infringement is required to start the "damages clock," provide adequate information about the perceived infringement as early as possible, either in writing or by marking your patented products.

In sum, align IP strategies with business strategies and find the pulse of competition in your space. Indeed, once you have a good sense of your business strategy and the competitive landscape, build your IP portfolio wisely. Find patent attorneys with deep experience drafting patents, engaging with patent officials at the PTO (such as Examiners during prosecution or PTAB judges) and working with patent litigators, preferably with their own patents being successful in litigation. Whether the business model is an individual, a startup, a spin-off, an SME or a VC, success can only come with quality IP assets (i.e., patents, trademarks, applicable copyrights and trade secrets). It doesn't require a vast IP portfolio, but a portfolio that reaches the four corners of a business is ideal.

MONETIZATION FOR SMES TO ENTERPRISES
BY ERICH SPANGENBERG, WITH JONAS BLOCK

IS IP REALLY IMPORTANT TO AN SME?

Investing in obtaining IP rights is a significant undertaking for most SMEs. The money and time you spend on IP are resources you are not spending on other business needs.

In fact, significant research presents a connection between the most successful SMEs which account for generating the most jobs and attracting the most capital—referred to as high-growth firms—and their ownership of multiple patents (and trademarks and copyrights).[125] Patents also generally are acknowledged as a qualitative signal to attract VCs and other funders.[126] Obviously the nature of your business may dictate that IP is a greater or lower priority, but this is a decision that should be contemplated with the risk of losing the option to patent. If you do not file within certain time periods (often a year from when you conceived of the invention) or certain events (the first time you make a disclosure of your invention not under NDA), you probably cannot patent that invention.

Now What? Once a patent issues, the most common reaction of SMEs is, "Great, now that I have a patent, what do I do with it?" Then comes the second most common question: "What is it worth?" Assuming you maximized the quality and relevance of your patent and didn't just get a patent issued, there are answers to these questions that can be obtained without significant additional investment.

Valuation. Depending on your needs, there are two types of valuations available that range from under $100 to over $100,000.

Due diligence for a bank for a line of credit can prompt the expensive version. Information simply for intelligent business decision-making gives access to the less-expensive option. At IPwe (www.ipwe.com), we provide a "valuation" on a patent-by-patent basis and on a portfolio basis at the low end of this price scale. It provides a reference range of valuations and lets you compare your patent to other similar patents. Focus on the relative value as a better indicator of value than the precise range.

Alternatives. What follows are additional objectives with IP ownership. This is not meant to be an exhaustive list—and there are variations to each alternative. Our goal is to prompt options as starting points to further explore for your intelligent business decisions.

Acquisition and In-Bound Licensing. One of the quickest ways to improve your IP position is to acquire relevant IP. You can identify the IP yourself and contact the owner or hire a lawyer or IP broker to help you. You need to get over the "not invented here" syndrome and recognize that maybe there are some other relevant IP assets out there that you did not invent, but that are still highly relevant to your business or strategy. If you can't afford to buy, consider licensing. Many intermediaries can handle this for you.

Sale and Out-Bound Licensing. Some companies could simply sell some of their IP, particularly where the IP is no longer relevant to their product road map. Many companies prefer licensing their IP (while retaining ownership). To help you evaluate this alternative, there is no shortage of service providers. IPwe offers the "IPwe Marketplace," and it is designed to keep costs low and success rates high by ranking the offerings on a scale that takes into account the valuation of the IP and the price being asked by the seller.

Smart Pools. Smart Pools are a creation of IPwe, as a place where patent owners (what we call "Founders") make their patents available for license to many other companies (what we call "Members"). The model involves a high volume of Members attracted because of low-cost entry points and freedom to innovate, while Founders receive consistent revenues (unlike uncertain and appealable litigation outcomes) and adoption. The Smart Pools are organized around emerging technologies like blockchain, metaverse, digital link and drone—with new areas announced every quarter. Representative technical areas are relatively early in their adoption phase but recognized as likely to be widely adopted. How do Smart Pools benefit SMEs? An SME as a Founder can generate a return at a very low cost. There are no fees for an SME to be a Founder and make its patents available for license under a Smart Pool. The SME Founder collects a known share of the Smart Pool gross revenues every quarter and can withdraw from the Smart Pool at any time with no long-term commitments.

An SME Member can get access to many patents for a nominal cost—if your revenues are less than $50 million, the cost is typically $1,000 per year; if your revenues are less than $10 million, the cost is $500 per year; and if your revenues are less than $1 million, the cost is $100 per year, typically with the first year free. As a Founder, you make money and pay nothing. As a Member, you pay little and get access to great technology that gives you freedom to innovate and allows you to tell your customers that you are licensed to critical technology.

Financing. A quick-growing area of financing is IP-based

financing. Historically, the only way an SME could finance its IP was through IP litigation financing—not exactly optimal when building a business as litigation is expensive, uncertain and time-consuming. Today, companies like IPwe can offer credit terms that are often far more attractive than raising equity.

How Do I Figure out What to Do? As an SME IP owner, it is critical that you seek good advice and information. Do your research, pull together a list of leaders with proven track records and talk to them. Ask them about your alternatives of interest, the number of transactions executed for each and references. Be careful of long-term commitments not tied to performance.

Bottom Line. For many SMEs, obtaining IP is the right decision. The IP should work hard for you; you should not have to put it in a drawer and wait for an external impetus to prompt a benefit. Like other corporate assets, we advise that you affirmatively seek a return on your IP investments. Fortunately for you, the industry provides a range of cost-efficient and potentially revenue-producing models. IPwe is one of them.

VALUE-DRIVEN IP PORTFOLIO MANAGEMENT
BY RUUD PETERS

The main activity of patent professionals in IP departments of most companies is portfolio management, including building and maintaining their company's global patent portfolio. Highly educated and skilled patent professionals are needed for this complex and laborious activity. Companies would not undertake these huge efforts and spend the substantial cost on their patent portfolios if that would not serve a purpose.

IP departments know that the IP strategy needs to be fully aligned with the business strategy. Although a majority of companies present this alignment, when one scratches the surface, this alignment is weaker than expected. For example, most business strategy documents do not contain IP strategy information and many IP departments do not have access to business strategy documents.

This low involvement of IP departments in the business strategy and vice versa means patent portfolio management in many companies is based on the number of historic filings for R & D groups and their portfolio budgets. With these quantity objectives in hand, mostly out of an uncontrolled inflow, those invention disclosures are selected for filing that best protects the company's own technologies and products under development. The portfolios built in this way generally are only activated when a competitor copies features of an offering protected by patents without authorization or when the company is accused of infringing a competitor's patents. Building and using a patent portfolio in this way can result in suboptimally supporting a business in realizing its business strategy.

The goal of patent portfolio management is to create control positions in the market, which can be leveraged to generate sustainable advantages for businesses. This requires a proactive, forward-looking approach to building a portfolio that has the biggest impact on potential competitors in spaces where you want to operate your business. Those spaces need to be defined in a structured process involving relevant people from the businesses, R & D, design and IP departments in a company with a good view on where the markets, industry and technologies will be going in the future—in short, a company with a clear business strategy. For each of those businesses, an IP strategy must be defined that not only supports the business strategy but also enables operation in the company's desired position in the market.

The IP strategy defines the IP value model, or dominant model for how IP is or will be creating value for a business, impacting the way the patent portfolio for that business is built and managed. There are four primary IP models: exclusivity, commercial, defensive and liberty.

Exclusivity. When a business aims to create exclusivity for its products, services or elements of those, the IP value model is focused on creating the broadest exclusivity to generate profitability and durability and to increase market share. This requires a focused and dedicated effort in which IP filings must be made, prosecuted, monitored and when needed, enforced. Exclusivity requires an approach of looking at your IP portfolio from the perspective of your (potential) competitors seeking to enter the market in a space you want to operate exclusively. The optimal impact is that you have built an IP portfolio that discourages your (potential) competitors from entering your space or circumventing your IP. Of course, you can only create an exclusive IP position if the IP landscape allows for that. Therefore, the IP function must be part of your strategy right from the beginning.

In spaces where offerings are covered by patents from different companies, the interdependencies make companies cross-license their relevant patents to commercialize their offerings. Strong technology companies may build up larger, more impactful patent portfolios, which they may use to gain commercial benefits (mostly by collecting royalties) from other market participants with weaker portfolios in relation to their relative market positions.

Commercial. Companies operating in this so-called commercial IP model tend to patent heavily for their core strength technologies. This IP commercial model is practiced, for example, by companies that are large contributors to technical standards. They file as many patents as possible on their technical contributions to that standard. These patents may become essential and necessarily infringed when these contributions are accepted into the standard. Given the high-volume markets for many standards, companies can generate substantial revenues by licensing their standard essential patents to other market participants with a relatively weaker patent position.

Defensive. Companies may operate in product or service markets as a technology follower or in catch-up mode. They may be faced with some leading technology companies having strong IP portfolios that are using their patents to collect royalties from their competitors. They are mostly forced to operate in the mitigation model, in which they build up a portfolio, organically and/or inorganically, to offset or mitigate at least part of the royalty payments those third-party IP holders demand. In building their "defensive" portfolio they usually focus their own patent filings on product features or cost-saving product implementations that may be attractive to the leading technology companies, and on possible improvements of the products and technologies of those leading technology companies in areas where the impact of patent infringement would be largest. For the latter, product road map forecast analysis based on IP filings could be used. Building a portfolio that reduces IP risk takes time, and if that time is not available, companies can also seek to acquire patents. Superfluous to mention here is that the mitigation model does not likely provide any relief in case of nonpracticing entities.

Liberty. In situations where a company wants to participate in a market that is dominated by another company with a strong IP portfolio that it enforces to keep new competitors out of their space, a different IP strategy is needed to secure market access. This is the so-called IP liberty model for quickly building an IP portfolio focused on the products of the dominating player prior to entering that market. For the latter, product road map forecast analysis based on IP filings may be used. After having entered the market with its own products and faced with enforcement actions, the company can use this portfolio as a lever against the enforcing company to secure market access.

An IP strategy aligned with a business strategy requires a more proactive and granular approach to IP portfolio management. Depending on the IP value model selected in support of the desired business model, you should build an IP portfolio each time that is optimized for that value model. In a first step, companies can apply this approach for their patent portfolio management, and once deployed and working, can integrate the other forms of IP into a single IP portfolio management approach.

Summary

#ip2ip endeavors to place its reader in the rarefied company of those who have achieved best-in-class success in monetizing patents and IP, and who apply their strategies to innovate the patent system. Witness historic best-in-class patent monetizers Julie Mar-Spinola, Erich Spangenberg, Jonas Block and Ruud Peters.

These best-in-class owners align IP strategy closely with business to drive a profit component of their IP operations. This makes (common) sense, too, since IP assets have the same purpose as any corporate asset—to increase shareholder value. My appreciation to these global leaders and dear colleagues for spending their valuable time with us—we are honored.

CHAPTER 5

#IP2IP COPYRIGHTS

IT'S ALL IN THE WRITING
CO-AUTHOR, J. CHRISTOPHER LYNCH

ACTions

5.1 **Register copyrights to receive statutory benefits as or before a work is published.** *Top-10 Takeaway.*

5.2 Use a copyright wrap technique to protect key trade secrets, particularly for computer-software businesses.

The power of copyrights in intellectual property laws is their simplicity in securing and formalizing this right. Copyrights have a long duration and protect original works from a broad range of copying. While few are granted a US patent, every American is granted a copyright by virtue of their works. Every email, communication and audio, physical or video work of art, as examples, is protected by copyright. While patents capture headlines, there is strength in the quiet and direct nature of copyrights.

COPYRIGHT WORKS AS ARTISTIC ENDEAVORS ARE HONORED

Copyrights are showcased alongside patents in the US Constitution *Limited Times* clause and referenced in two phrases: "science and the useful arts" and "authors and inventors." Acknowledging the US Constitution itself as a work of authorship, subject to copyright protection (had it not predated the Congress it created)—copyrights are referenced a third time. Three times is the charm.

Express Yourself with Copyrights. Copyright protects the expression of ideas in original works you have authored. It gives you ownership of your personal expression communicated to others. Your expression contrasts with general ideas, which are free for everyone to use with their own expression.

Copyrightable subject matter is broad—all *original works of authorship, fixed in a tangible medium* are protected immediately. Examples are literary works, musical works, performing arts, visual arts, digital content (including computer software code, databases, data models and additional digital works), motion pictures, photographs, sound recordings and architectural works. The rights of copyright owners are protection from copying and commercialization such as distribution, reproduction, display, performance and licensing others to do the same.[127]

The public is used to seeing the copyright notice—©, year of publication, owner name—which I advise to continue using even though technically (since 1989), it is no longer required.[128] Notice reminds the public that rights are claimed. Your adding notice should be a prompt to formalize registration through a filing process at the United States Copyright Office (USCO), as I advise and will re-advise you to avail yourself of.

Copyright versus Patents. So why do patents historically dominate intellectual property discussions? Inventions are the stuff of the American dream. They are bold. Patents cover inventions, drawing a boundary around ideas. Copyright does not cover inventions, ideas, or facts. Instead, it embraces the *expression* of ideas. The ideas remain free for the expression of others, but your expression, if *fixed* or captured, is yours.[129]

Copyright protection comes into existence automatically, or immediately from that moment of fixation. This is another fundamental difference between patents and copyrights. Patents must be granted based on a government determination.

With copyright, what you see is what you get. The original work is known. For copyright infringement, either an infringer had access to the work or not. Either the work was copied or it wasn't. The copier must be aware of the expression. Infringement requires deliberate abuse of the owner's right—access and copying, whereas the patent infringer can be held accountable regardless of his knowledge of the patent or intent to infringe it. Comparatively then, because copyrights only protect deliberate copying of your expression, copyright scope of protection is more narrow or quiet than patents.[130]

Copyright for Software. Computer inventions, whether non-confidential or trade secret, are entitled to copyright protection. The uncertainty for patenting computer inventions makes copyright more important as an alternative or addition to patent protection for software.

An amendment to the 1976 Copyright Act and subsequent federal court cases confirmed that computer programs can be protected by copyright. Protection extends to lines of software code called *object* and *source code*, as well as *literal elements* and *nonliteral elements* not reduced to code, including "structure, sequence, organization, user interface, screen displays and menu structures." Analogizing to a book, words are literal elements, and their organization—such as in chapters, the table of contents, characters and plot—are nonliteral elements.[131]

Copyright Fair Use. Copyright law also permits some copying under the societal consideration of *fair use* as a complete defense. Fair use narrows what can be enforced, but it requires some societal benefit. Copying for the sake of commercialization is infringement.

However, as discussed in this chapter's risk section, recent cases regarding copyrightability and fair use present limitations on the historic precedent for copyrighting software. It is notable that in each case, at least a portion of the code was in the public domain or open source.[132] While copyright continues to present a more straightforward path to IP protection of software than patents, software owners are encouraged to consistently register for copyrights and, when presenting a litigation position, to cogently articulate bases for protectable expression.

Fair use is also the subject of a high-profile case involving famous artists Andy Warhol and Lynn Goldsmith, with implications for artificial intelligence (AI), NFTs and the metaverse, as discussed further below.[133]

Copyright Rapid Relief. For a literal copy of a registered work, such as in counterfeit or knock-off situations, copyright litigation, including injunctions and impoundment of counterfeit goods, can be swift and impactful.

Copyright and Patent Cost Alignment. These comparisons also align with costs and respective rights. Patent filing and maintenance fees dwarf that for copyrights. For the scope of IP rights, a patent may present twenty separate inventions in individual claims describing invention boundaries. Litigating competing views of the boundaries per claim makes patent litigation the (expensive) sport of kings.

OPPORTUNITIES

Copyright embodies the fundamental human activity of expressing ourselves. It reflects the balance of intellectual property generally between protecting the work of an author versus ideas available to the public.

THE COPYRIGHT REGISTRATION SHOWSTOPPER

Statutory Benefits from Timely Copyright Registration Are a Showstopper. Copyright law provides authors with the opportunity to gain a strong advantage in copyright litigation by perfecting their copyrights through registration at the USCO, including a deposit of the work cataloged for access by the public through the Library of Congress.[134] Timely registered copyrights afford the option for statutory damages, plus the potential for attorneys' fees in copyright litigation. These statutory benefits are a showstopper for the value of copyrights within the IP spectrum.

What Is Timely Registration? The optimal timing for the copyright owner to register is at the same time or before publication. Outside of this event, which is under the control of the owner, there is a ninety-day grace period after publication to retain full benefits under the law.

Top-10 Takeaway 4

#ip2ip-4: Register copyrights to receive statutory benefits as or before a work is published.

Let's further explore the statutory benefits to solidify your pursuit of them. Quite simply, copyrights follow patents in my presentation of IP because, while some rights are automatic, registration brings additional statutory benefits. They include statutory damages and the potential for attorneys' fees.

Statutory Damages. Statutory damages are part of the law for registered copyright owners. These monetary awards can be selected by the copyright owner without proving actual damages from infringement. The judge sets the amount as a deterrent to infringement of works. The award ranges from $750 to $150,000 for willful infringement for each work infringed. Damages provided by statute are important because it can be difficult to prove actual damages in an infringement litigation. Instead, once infringement is proven, the copyright holder has the option to present no further evidence regarding monetary damages. Predetermined amounts and less evidence mean less ammunition for litigation gamesmanship.[135]

Attorneys' Fees. Prompt copyright registration sets up the potential for reimbursement of litigation attorneys' fees in a successful copyright infringement litigation. If litigation must be pursued, timely filed copyright registration increases your chances of getting your attorneys' fees back. For litigation deterrence and settlement, the heightened chance of attorneys' fees cannot be overemphasized.[136]

Cost. Cost further demonstrates that registered copyrights are such valuable assets. The benefits presented above for copyrights are attainable at a de minimis cost where you file a DIY registration (using the ample free resources provided by the USCO) or, as detailed in Chapter 9: Cost, with professional help, at an estimated cost of between $750 and $1,500. Copyrights do not have any maintenance fees or renewal obligations. With the copyright term of the life of the author plus seventy years, the investment over its lifetime makes copyright the optimal IP asset.

Reap the Statutory Benefits as Rewards. Probably the best reason to rush to the USCO, though, is not what you get but what you miss by failing to leverage this asset. So I suggest we cease the chatter and instead go right to defining works subject to copyrights and how to register them.

COPYRIGHTS IMPACT CULTURE

Copyright embodies the fundamental human activity of expression and connection with one other. Among the very first inventions at the beginning of civilization was writing, as celebrated in the ancient Sumerian culture in 3000 BC. The ability to distribute writings based on the invention of the Johannes Gutenberg Press in 1440 AD was a watershed. Our Bill of Rights codified the First Amendment, freedom of speech. The US Constitution and the First Amendment have in common the goal of dissemination of expression. These policies have a simplicity, and quiet strength, in making available to authors the protection of their expressions.[137]

ANALYSIS

Copyright is a part of every business, just as trade secrets and trademarks are. Not every business needs patents. This book has a computer-software focus because software touches all four of those IP areas. Many other businesses have important copyright cores such as content creation, design, fashion or entertainment businesses. All those enterprises have expression at their heart, just as copyrightable source code is the heart of a software enterprise.

Copyright also is quiet in its manner of creation. The preceding sentence is protected by copyright for example.[138] As long as the work is (1) original (e.g., not copied, even if not unique) and (2) fixed in a tangible medium of expression, then copyright attaches from the moment of fixation, and the author can control the commercial exploitation of that work for the long copyright term.[139] Businesses should consider all of the works that contribute to the business as candidates for express copyright recognition and protection.

Examples of copyrightable works for technology companies are published materials associated with offerings, such as advertisements, websites, mobile apps, literature, users' manuals and any written or visual work. In the modern day, computer code is also subject to copyright protection, even when the code is a trade secret.

Insider Lawball

For Trade Secrets, It's a Copyright Wrap
While the visual of copyrights often involves a yellowed, curled-edge historic relic—which is a joy—the cutting edge of not only copyrights but trade secrets are computer software code, along with inventions and commercial information. Software is commonly protected by either patents or trade secrets, with a decision to publish the code in a patent or retain it as a secret. What is less well known is that trade secret software can be copyrighted and receive statutory benefits.

Copyright Deposit of Secrets. Recall that copyright registration "deposit copies" are cataloged for public access. A public deposit can be retained as secret because redactions are permitted in deposits, including pre-defined formats for blocking out and identifying portions of, as well as properly designating, trade secret software code.[140]

As a result, trade secrets can be "wrapped" within a copyright registration, retain their secrecy and receive copyright statutory benefits. If later needed in litigation, the un-redacted deposit can serve as clear evidence not only of its substance but of optimal IP strategy.

Finally, while foreign copyright is generally beyond the scope of this book, here is an introduction. Copyright is essentially a global set of common rights, enforceable globally under the international Berne Convention.[141] Your US copyright can be enforced (even without registration), for example, in France against a French infringer. Your counsel can help you navigate international waters, but the law is designed to help the author.

May the opportunity for copyrights inspire you to understand their value. It may justify the attention we now have to spend on the more mundane but necessary timing and process areas.

COPYRIGHT TIMING: STATUTORY BENEFITS ARE THE COPYRIGHT OWNERS TO LOSE

One well-known adage is that anything written is copyrighted. Words themselves or short phrases are not copyrightable subject matter (they can be trademarks), but a simple work of original authorship is copyrightable. For example, this haiku can be registered for copyright—short phrases aren't protected/ but your haiku is/copyright is powerful.

Copyright comes into existence at the moment of creation—the moment the work is created and fixed in a tangible form. The establishment of copyrights is true whether or not the author avails herself of the copyright registration procedure. The terminology of a "copyrighted" work means that US copyright law protects the work, not necessarily that a copyright registration on the work has been received from the USCO.[142]

Statutory Benefits Require Registration. To trigger the key benefits of statutory damages and potential attorneys' fees, the Copyright Act requires a formal filing with the USCO within a timing schedule. The formal registration puts the public on notice based on a public record of key facts about (1) the author, (2) the owner, (3) whether the work is published or unpublished, (4) if it may contain elements of a trade secret and (5) the year of creation.[143] A copyright must be registered to bring litigation for copyright infringement. For a special government fee, registration can be expedited to less than two weeks.

Registration and Publication. Two words to unpack in copyright law are "registration" and "publication." Registration is the formal process of a copyright filing at the USCO. Publication means that the work is made available for access by the public through a publicly available version or an electronic program or process running based on a computer program.[144]

Convert "Encouraged" to "Required." The USCO uses the word "encourage" for submitting an application before a copyrightable work is published. However, the opportunities for statutory benefits triggered by registration should immediately convert the term "encourage" to "require."[145] Let's shift our thinking about copyright applications: they must be filed before publication. Where this isn't feasible, then backup procedures are the default, but they too require timeliness of three months from the date of publication. If the three-month backup date is missed, the copyright owners lose the benefits should infringement commence.

In addition, even where statutory rights are lost based on the timing of publication, an issued copyright registration is required to bring litigation for copyright infringement.[146] The owner must execute this filing anyway to enforce her rights. This identical process, though, yields reduced benefits.

Infringers Control the Timing of Infringement. Infringement is conducted by a third party outside of the control of the copyright owner. It is therefore illogical for a copyright owner to connect her filing to an activity by a third party over which she has no control. Rather, the analysis should shift to timely registration at or before publication to allow its effective date to predate infringement, opening all potential remedies and benefits.

Copyright Owners Control Their Timing, and Their Success or Failure. The timing of copyright registration is entirely within the control and responsibility of the owner. We, therefore, under our #ip2ip "Do Business in the Bullseye" philosophy, endorse treating the timing requirements for copyrights as aggressively as for patents. Filing for patents and copyrights should be the same. That is, the earliest that the subject matter is available for copyright or patent protection, it should be filed. Copyrights are easier than patents in this sense because copyright registration is a fraction of the cost and consternation of patents. Do not allow a breakdown in simple planning of timing registration versus publication to undermine this outstanding IP asset.

COPYRIGHT TIMING: TERM

A copyright term for a work authored by a corporation is a minimum term of ninety-five years from the date of publication. If a person is named as the author of the application, the term extends for the life of the author in the application plus seventy years. Like patents, the term of copyrights is limited by the Constitution, but "life plus seventy years" is an outstanding economic time frame.

THE COPYRIGHT LAWYERLY LITANY

Copyright law is exclusively federal in the United States Code, Title 17, with the Copyright Act of 1976 providing the basic framework for today's copyright law.[147] Section 102 defines copyright and sets its boundaries, all in a single section:

(a) Copyright protection subsists...in original works of authorship fixed in any tangible medium of expression, now known or later developed, from which they can be perceived, reproduced, or otherwise communicated, either directly or with the aid of a machine or device.

THE COPYRIGHT HOW-TOS
KEY TERMS FOR OPTIMIZING COPYRIGHT REGISTRATION

Key Term: The Author's the Thing. Authorship is a key term to explore. As copyright represents the beauty of expression, particularly in words and phrases, let me with respect invoke Shakespeare to assist us in scripting the optimal process for authorship. With due respect to Shakespeare, folly is afoot about who or which collection of writers authored Shakespeare's masterworks. Imagine, if you will, projecting these valuable assets into today's legal gladiator contests. The debate over copyright ownership would distract from the playwright's brilliance to who owns the copyright in them. In this fanciful hypothesis, a royal treasure would be in jeopardy.

Generally, where a person creates a work, the person is considered to be the author of the work. Shifting to corporate owners often adds multiple contributors to works of authorship (for example, a software product or a marketing project). Authorship is so important that copyright law created a statutory exception to the general rule of the writer being the author, called the *work made for hire* (WMFH) exception. Under WMFH, the employer is the *author* and the *owner* of the work.[148] When the copyright application is submitted, the employee names are not required.

Ensure Work for Hire Provisions Work for You... However, copyright law unwittingly sets up a false sense of confidence about automatic corporate authorship. A "[w]ork made for hire may be found where the work is created by an employee as part of the employee's regular duties."[149] The uncertainty of "may" and "regular" prompt a consideration of whether you would want to invest your corporate resources in litigating them. Instead, create certainty in your own tangible work of authorship in buttoned-up employment agreements presenting clear WMFH and assignment provisions.

...Even When You Hire Independent Contractors. You may wonder, particularly with the common use of consultants for software, *I use a consultant for some of this—does that matter?* It does since *only* the works of your employees are initially owned by you.

In addition, the Copyright Act WMFH exception pertains solely to employees of a corporation. This authorship exception does not pertain to independent contractor work, leading to a common dispute between commissioning parties and their contractors over who owns what, even after the contractor has been fully compensated. Most commissioned works from nonemployees, including almost all software prepared by independent contractors, are not WMFH under copyright law. The commissioning party can only be the "owner" of a copyright by express assignment in a signed writing. Independent contractor engagements, therefore, require a clear consideration if the copyright is being assigned. Anyone with a hand in contributing to your valuable assets should do so under an agreement that protects your interests, authorship and ownership.[150]

Insider Lawball

Clarifying Rights in Existing Agreements

Where contracts are not buttoned up for clear ownership of IP rights vis-à-vis employees, consultants and third parties, the stage is set for confusion. Asking a contractor to confirm an assignment after the fact may invite a reaction to question the confirmation, particularly where it is confirming a loss of rights or benefits. For example, the contractor may not have fully considered its capacity to offer an assignment or license for any commissioned work.

Consider instead introducing the topic at a natural point in the relationship, such as during the next renewal of the contract for which you are seeking to confirm WMFH or at the next opportunity to benefit the recipient. Memorializing a benefit also meets the contract law requirement of a quid pro quo when confirming the rights and liabilities.

The Author's the Thing, If Only the Bard Had Written. Let's close the curtain on these forebodings—do better than the Bard by not leaving authorship to chance in clear agreements and processes. Check agreements for terms to ensure your clear ownership of these corporate assets. Treat your works at the same level as a Shakespearean treasure and feel smug in the notion that you are outsmarting the Bard by validating your authorship and ownership of copyright (and all IP for that matter) in agreements.

Key Term: Date of Registration. When the USCO registers a work, it grants an effective date of registration associated with the certificate of registration. The effective date marks the date of receipt of required filing elements in acceptable form, including the application, deposit and nonrefundable filing fee. If the elements are not in proper form, the applicant must supplement the application with acceptable and complete materials, deposit and/or sufficient fees.

Key Term: Publication. Publication is defined by copyright law under Title 17, Section 101 as "the distribution of copies...of a work to the public by sale or other transfer of ownership by rental, lease, or lending." Interestingly, Section 101 also provides "[a] public performance or display of a work does not of itself constitute publication." Under the standard presented thus far, distribution to the public is key, whether direct distribution to the public or indirect distribution to a group for the purpose of further distribution.

The copyright application requires identification of whether the work has been published. The publication date can determine the copyright term. Statutory damages and attorneys' fees may not be available for infringement of an unpublished work. The deposit requirements and exceptions to the exclusive rights of the copyright owner also differ for an unpublished versus a published work.[151] The USCO similarly will not affirmatively investigate the owner's presentation unless there are clear and contrary facts within the application. The Office instead generally relies on the affirmative statements of the applicant that either the work is unpublished (that is, the applicant does not present a date of first publication in the application) or is published.

While the Copyright Office Believes You, Opposing Litigators Won't. The autonomy granted to an author affords an opportunity to register the author's copyright based on the clearest facts then known. Any ambiguity will later be tested if the copyright is litigated with a six-figure legal bill. The best way to fix a problem is to avert it in the first place.

RISKS

Limitations to Copyrightability of Software. A 2023 Federal Circuit case potentially limits the historic precedent for copyrighting software. The case involved nonliteral code elements and found that the owner failed to identify and filter out unprotectable constituent parts of the nonliteral elements. The nonliteral elements included unprotectable open-source elements; unoriginal elements; mathematical and statistical elements; well-known and conventional display elements, such as tables, graphs, plots, fonts, colors and lines; and third-party elements. An expert report presented by the owner also was rejected.

A dissenting opinion cited to historic precedent that the selection and arrangement of individually unprotectable elements with a minimal degree of creativity supports copyrightability. The takeaway from this case is for software owners to pay greater attention to consistently registering for copyright, considering the impact of open-source code and preparing litigation positions and evidence of copyrightability of nonliteral elements. In addition, owners should avoid simplistic positions that nonliteral elements are creative or there are alternative design and architecture options.[152]

Fair Use. Fair use is a statutory exception to infringement. It requires that the defendant engage in criticism, comment, research or teaching. Four factors are considered: (1) the purpose and character of the accused use, (2) the nature of the copyrighted work, (3) the amount and importance of the portion of the original work used and (4) the effect on the original author's market.[153] A common test for the first factor is whether the use *transforms* the original work by adding new expression, meaning or message. Fair use narrows what can be enforced, but it requires some societal benefit. Copying for the sake of commercialization is infringement.

A 2021 US Supreme Court case found that portions of an API software interface are fair use even when copied for precisely and the same reason as their creation in the original work, based on the use of new implementing code designed to operate within a new environment. The Court emphasized the subject of the computer code copyright as a functional work, with potentially less application to creative works.[154]

Derivative Works. Copyright owners have the right to control making *derivative works* where a second work is made using the first as a basis. In software, most "versions" are derivative works of others. This is one strategy where the commissioning party can have leverage over the contractor: do not engage the contractor to create a new solution, have the contractor create a derivative work of your old solution.[155]

In 2023, the SCOTUS decided a high-profile case between two famous artists. While not based on artificial intelligence systems, the decision favors innovator rights, presenting insights into how IP assets may be treated in AI-related copyright infringement lawsuits.

Andy Warhol incorporated a photograph by Lynn Goldsmith

into a new work under the guise of appropriation as an artistic innovation. Goldsmith discovered the use of her photograph as part of a Warhol magazine cover honoring Prince and sued for copyright infringement. Warhol defended that the artwork had transformed the photograph and was fair use.

The case tested whether adding new meaning or message to the original work is sufficient to transform it into creating a derivative work under fair use, or whether fair use should only be allowed for works when the use is necessary to convey the copying artist's message. The Court found Warhol did not alter the first work with new expression, meaning or message, and therefore failed to transform it to support fair use. The majority also looked at the similar purpose and commercial uses of the artworks, for magazine stories about Prince, outweighing any transformative nature of Warhol's work.

Critics express that the decision negatively impacts disciplines such as appropriation art, which present thematically what can be expected when AI generates images. The case also has implications for transformative and derivative uses regarding non-fungible tokens (NFTs).[156]

Characters. Literary and artistic characters are protectable. J. K. Rowling has copyright in her seven *Harry Potter®* books and in the myriad of characters, meaning other authors cannot use them. Character licensing often pushes the boundaries of idea/expression.

Infringement Litigation Requires a Registered Copyright. Where the author or copyright owner does not avail herself of registration, doing so in reaction to infringement has disadvantages beyond a loss of statutory benefits. The average time from filing for registration to receipt of a certification of registration is 2.7 months, delaying the timing of seeking relief for infringement.[157]

Determining Publication. A primary example of a key non-substantive issue is whether a work has been published. It is highly impactful to meeting the timing requirements for statutory benefits of copyright. Again, if the work has not been registered before publication or within three months of publication, then the statutory benefits may not apply. One aspect of determining publication is whether the owner's distribution or offer of distribution is *authorized*.[158] This is another area of copyright where there is legal posturing, similar to the topic of publication.

The Five-Year Rule. Copyright registrations made within five years of first publication also are afforded presumptions that streamline any copyright trial, such as the copyrightability of the code and its authorship/ownership lineage.[159] However, after five years, the presumptions need to be proven by the copyright owner, even with a post-five-year registration.

The Thirty-Five Year Rule. Copyright assignments and even licenses can be terminated under US law in a five-year window period starting at the thirty-fifth year from publication. Assignors of copyrights have value through longevity to renegotiate for a better deal three decades later. This termination right does not apply to WMFH (since there is no assignment of authorship, and the employer is the author) and it only applies to assignments and licenses.[160]

Performance and Display. Copyright allows the owner to prohibit copying, and also to prohibit commercial performance or display of the copyrighted works (except in fair use).[161] Many entrepreneurs are unaware of this; for example, any commercial use of music or art is prohibited, even though you may have otherwise "paid for" the music or art by buying a copy.

Defendant Attorneys' Fees. Accused copyright defendants can win attorneys' fees in court without having to prove vexatious litigation or other customary obstacles to fees in US courts for defendants who prevail at trial. Given copyright's roots in the Constitution, exonerated defendants were engaged in non-infringing behavior—just as society wants—so they can receive fees for being accused and then prevailing.

Copyright Trolls. BitTorrent and other peer-to-peer technologies allowing rapid copying of large files can lead to piracy, some of it commercial in nature. Users of those technologies are vulnerable to IP address harvesting used to support copyright lawsuits. Similarly, many commercial photographers use metadata and other techniques to locate infringing uses to support copyright lawsuits.

Joint Authorship. Joint authors each make a copyrightable contribution to a unitary whole work. Setting specifications for software, for example, does not create a joint authorship relationship with the programmer, because each party must make a copyrightable contribution. Because the contributions of joint authors may differ wildly (author and illustrator), a contract is the only commercially sensible solution.[162]

The Merger Doctrine. Copyright protects expression and not ideas, but sometimes in software the expression and the idea *merge* because there is only one way to code the function. Copyright owners need to recognize that some code will not be enforceable under copyright law, but the merger doctrine code does not defeat the copyright in the original and nonfunctional aspects of the work.[163]

Fleeing Employees. Repeating a common theme of this book, honor your valuable employees but remain realistic about today's competitive landscape—especially in software. Strong employee agreements can buttress the act of locking in your rights through patents, trademarks, copyrights and trade secrets. Set expectations at the commencement of employment and then confirm alignment of those expectations.

Summary

Copyright rights are quiet, but powerful. Copyright policy respects its foundation in the US Constitution—arts and sciences are advanced by the provision of the limited monopoly. Society enjoys access to the works as they are protected, and then society enjoys the works without cost once the monopoly is extinguished. Indeed, on January 1, 2024, the copyright on Walt Disney's masterpiece, *Steamboat Willie*, and with it the beloved character Mickey Mouse® will enter the public domain—free for public use (as long as it is not confusing, but that is an area for trademarks).

CHAPTER 6

#IP2IP TRADE SECRETS

THE TRADE SECRET PROGRAM YOU DIDN'T KNOW YOU HAD

ACTions

6.1 **Formalize a list of trade secrets as part of your patent and copyright strategies.** *Top-10 Takeaway.*
6.2 Document trade secrets as they are created.
6.3 Leverage a trade secret program as a tool against espionage and everyday employee movement.

TRADE SECRETS AS TREASURED IP ASSETS

Trade secrets are often inventions that a company chooses to keep as an internal secret instead of publishing them through patenting. The dichotomy is instructive—trade secrets are secret, and patents are public.

However, trade secrets also go beyond protecting inventions and can include all valuable information. In fact, some trade secrets have nothing to do with inventions at all. Non-inventive trade secrets have the same opportunity as inventive ones to be equally protected by trade secret laws.

A simple definition of trade secrets is information, created and maintained as a secret, that gives its owner economic value. Owners protect trade secrets from competitor discovery by making reasonable efforts to maintain their secrecy, as one would a treasure. The broad coverage of trade secrets is achieved without any formal government registration. It is based instead on the actions of their owners and the evidence produced based on those actions. Trade secrets similarly have no formal duration. Rather, they are extant for so long as a trade secret remains valuable and secret. However, no matter how carefully protected, trade secrets are subject to independent and lawful development of the same trade secret information by others.

The government can become involved if there is theft of trade secrets. Sometimes their involvement extends beyond civil remedies to criminal penalties and jail time, with the US Department of Justice increasing their intervention, particularly relative to foreign country misappropriators. This backdrop of criminal law gives trade secret law an elevated strength and opportunity for strategic use and enforcement.

The richness of trade secrets is separate and apart from other IP assets. It is therefore a privilege to focus on trade secrets in their own right, as well as part of the corporate treasure chest of IP assets.

OPPORTUNITIES

Trade Secrets Are Newly Defended. Perhaps the most significant affirmation of the IP stature of trade secrets came in 2016 with the passage of a new federal law called the Defend Trade Secrets Act (DTSA).[164] The DTSA is the "most significant expansion" of federal IP law in decades because it created a federal claim for trade secret theft, contrasting previous adjudication through state laws only.[165] The Act also added new causes of action and forms of injunctive relief, with its sustained value as a body of precedent based on greater consistency across federal courts.

Identifying the Definition of Trade Secrets. Formally, trade secrets involve secret inventive or non-inventive information. The information provides its owner with independent economic value and is not knowable or readily ascertainable by others based on reasonable measures taken by its owner.

Trade secrets must be identified formally for the first time when they are enforced in litigation. As a result, judges must manage the public nature of the proceeding while protecting the confidentiality of the alleged trade secrets. A common approach is to disclose information about the secrets in multiple phases. Early on, they are presented in broad categories, then as the litigation progresses, with increasing detail. The expanding breadth protects the owner from disclosing the secrets in initial court filings while, over time, providing sufficient clarity so that the accused party receives notice of the allegedly wrongfully taken property. The identification starts with "categories." Categories of trade secret information in the DTSA include "financial, business, scientific, technical, economic or engineering information, compilations…formulas…programs, or codes to name a few."[166]

Commercial Information. Trade secrets also involve a large swath of financial or business information, commercially valuable but not necessarily inventions (called *commercial information*). Examples include pricing and financial models that provide value for production, cost of goods, labor, supply sources and inventory. Customer lists, industry research and marketing strategies potentially are included because they provide commercial value.

Customer Lists. Customer lists are highlighted as a common form of trade secrets. Elements of these lists that are not "readily ascertainable" (and preferably result from documented expense and effort) provide strong evidence, particularly when identified long before litigation. The greater the detail of a customer list (who buys what, when, for how much and why), the more likely it is protectable as a trade secret. Examples of trade secrets as part of these lists are nonpublic sales terms, contact details, custom information about the products purchased, shipping, payment history and even preferences.[167]

A Formula for Trade Secret Success. One of the best-known trade secrets is the formula for the famous Coca-Cola® soda. The Coca-Cola Company has kept the formula for its flagship beverage secret since 1891.[168] The Coca-Cola formula exemplifies the key to trade secrets under the control of its owner—maintaining a secret throughout the lifetime of the secret.

"Lifetime" is measured by the period of secrecy and therefore is theoretically unlimited. For Coca-Cola, that timeframe clocks in at over 130 years now. Another feature of this trade secret formula is its ability to provide commercial value to its owner. The story of Coke, the brand, is so well known because of the formula as its flagship product's commercial success.

Trade secret rights are extant for so long as the trade secret remains valuable and secret. Examples of activities that are common themes for litigation are when companies fall short of protecting their trade secrets or unscrupulous employees engage in theft.

Driving Modern-Day Trade Secret Litigation. A high-profile example of a litigation theme takes us into the modern day, in the Waymo (Google's, now Alphabet's, self-driving car company) versus Uber trade secret litigation.[169] It is compelling because of its storytelling qualities, with a center stage technology (lidar or laser technology for self-driving cars to avoid obstacles), smoking gun emails and a fall from grace by Uber employee Anthony Levandowski (including criminality and bankruptcy). The punch line is Uber and Levandowski lost, with Uber disavowing its prodigy Levandowski. The case settled on the eve of the technology trial in part because the parties worried that their trade secrets might be revealed in presenting their evidence in open court. After extensive arguments, the court allowed merely the repositioning of a screen to show visual evidence solely to the jury, but with the audio and arguments accessible in open court. Levandowski later pleaded guilty under criminal statutes and declared bankruptcy. The saga didn't end there as Mr. Levandowski's criminal case was later pardoned by former President Trump in 2021.[170]

Trial circuses aside, the Waymo case also had someone en route to jail, highlighting that trade secret theft is a crime. When a bad actor is discovered to steal, or *misappropriate*, a trade secret, the person or company that benefited from such unlawful actions can face consequences beyond civil litigation relief to criminal penalties.

In September 2023, a group of leading litigators, judges, academics and scholars prepared a *Trade Secret Case Management Judicial Guide* to support the emergence of trade secret litigation for federal judges, with the judicial bench having a range of experience in trade secret litigation. It is a masterwork of statutory and case law analysis, which I hope further informs the strategies presented below. I look forward to using it as a resource as well, with my focus on avoiding creating fact patterns for future additions.[171]

TRADE SECRETS CAN CONTRIBUTE TO AND STRENGTHEN THE CORPORATE CULTURE

Trade Secrets Can Contribute to the Corporate Culture... Innovation is a point of pride in a company culture. Trade secrets' commercial information, such as customer lists and marketing and sales data, can provide a culture boost because they expand recognition of corporate assets beyond technology innovations traditionally produced by engineers.

Commercial trade secrets derive from employees in business operations. They therefore are understood by a broader community within your corporate culture. With understanding comes buy-in about their value and potentially their successful use to protect your company.

...and Protect the Company and Strengthen a Protective Corporate Culture. Planning and executing a trade secret program demonstrates a protective inclination, which employees can reinforce based on their penchant toward personal protection. Based on their own experience with privacy and hacking, employees can understand the damage to business operations which can result from trade secret theft. Leaders and employees alike, as a result, can be vigilant not just in handling trade secrets, but also in policing threats from inside of the company and out. Trade secrets can become a rallying cry as part of the corporate culture to view corporate trade secrets figuratively as gems in a corporate physical or digital safe and as under continuous threat. As corporate performance protects their livelihoods, employees must also protect corporate assets that drive that performance.

EMERGENCY ACTION FOR STOLEN TRADE SECRETS

The secrecy of assets also sparks an urgency to retrieve them when stolen because their knowledge outside of the company causes harm. Trade secrets lend themselves to emergency relief, which is a critical outcome, coloring the court's approach to the disagreement and likely reflecting the ultimate outcome. The most common form of emergency relief is a preliminary injunction (ideally preceded by a temporary restraining order), or a court order enjoining the accused party from using the trade secrets during the litigation.[172] This relief requires proof of two conditions based on strong evidence: first, the owner has a high likelihood of success; and second, the theft has caused irreparable harm. If both conditions are met, then the court considers additional factors of whether the relief is remediable by money damages, will result in even greater harm to the nonmoving party or other interested parties and is counter to the public interest. At the litigation's conclusion, the court then decides whether to make the preliminary injunction final or lift it. The success of this preliminary proceeding, and its likely impact on the overall outcome, is a function of sufficient evidence. Often strong proof relies on evidence generated long before a theft.

ANALYSIS

Now that we have highlighted the opportunities of trade secrets, let's ramp up the basics of timing for their protection and pendency.

TRADE SECRET TIMING

Trade secrets begin with creating commercially valuable information that meets the criteria for protection. A logical touch point for formalizing protection is at the time of creation.

We have already evaluated the timing to consider patents and copyrights, but that same timing can also prompt us to consider trade secrets. If these rights are part of bringing IP into business, then the same business strategy meetings can drive timing.

Trade Secret Procurement Timing. Another consideration relies not on subject matter but rather the person creating it. This timing consideration also precedes the date of creation. Rather, the timing is the start of the working relationship and the legal terms governing that relationship, regardless of the type of working relationship.

Upon onboarding, employment or other agreement terms are gating items for establishing accountability for employees for corporate trade secrets (and confirming the employee will not use trade secrets from a former employer). Then, formal phases of employment, such as reviews and exit procedures, afford additional touch points. They are systematic opportunities to acknowledge the company's sole ownership of trade secrets and to reinforce each employee's responsibility to protect them.

Trade Secret Pendency Timing. The term of a trade secret is the period that the subject matter is retained as a valuable secret, or theoretically unlimited. Coca-Cola again is the exemplar, whose formula has a long pendency for corporate secrecy, independent economic value and a failure of third parties to discover the trade secret.

THE TRADE SECRET LAWYERLY LITANY

The 2016 landmark DTSA, as introduced above, made it easier to bring litigation in federal court based on its new federal cause of action for misappropriating trade secrets, while using the same definition-driven enforcement mechanism as historic state court legal standards.[173] A recent law was enacted in January 2023 to build upon a concern about national security and trade secret theft by foreign actors. It requires the president to follow a process of sanctioning foreign entities and related perpetrators and their supporters (such as the entities' CEO and directors) involved in significant theft of US-owned trade secrets, where activities are likely to result in threats to national security, foreign policy or economic health. The law fails to define what constitutes "significant," and "theft" for that matter, creating uncertainty as its foundation.[174] The impact of the law remains to be seen, particularly since a July 2023 reporting deadline to take action under the law has come and gone without any presidential or agency action.

Let's return to the DTSA language for the definition of "trade secrets":

> (A) All forms and types of financial, business, scientific, technical, economic, or engineering information...

(B) the owner thereof has taken reasonable measures to keep such information secret; and

(C) the information derives independent economic value, actual or potential, from not being generally known to, and not being readily ascertainable through proper means by, another person who can obtain economic value from the disclosure or use of the information[.][175]

This definition, along with the examples presented earlier, demonstrates the expansive breadth and scope of information potentially subject to trade secret protection. Any type of information may constitute a trade secret. The information must derive "independent economic value" that is not "generally known" or "readily ascertainable" by others, and its secrecy must be protected using *reasonable steps*.

Independent economic value requires a nexus between the information and economic impact on the business, either actual or potential, or a showing that a competitor would have to expend time and money to develop the information. The phrases "generally known" or "readily ascertainable" refer to whether the actor who may obtain economic benefit is already aware of it, such as based on it being public or subject to discovery. An owner may also combine individual trade secrets into unique combinations that meet the standard. Reasonable steps are particular to each owner, with smaller companies having a reduced burden relative to larger companies. Courts have defined reasonable efforts to include advising employees of the existence of trade secrets, limiting access to the information on a need-to-know basis, requiring employees to sign confidentiality agreements and keeping secrets under lock and key.[176]

The DTSA also created two important tools for trade secret enforcement. First, in a nod to the importance of exigent relief, it started a right and process for trade secret owners to seek an ex parte (or one party) seizure of misappropriated trade secret property. Second, whistleblowers received an exemption from trade secret liability by alerting authorities about misconduct.[177]

Eight-plus years later, in 2023, have the DTSA goals been realized? With our focus on rights holders, there's mixed news.

Ex Parte Seizure Orders and Other Exigent Relief Post the DTSA. Creating civil seizure orders was significant—and, therefore, good—for rights owners. But it requires a high level of proof of "only in extraordinary circumstances" and where the party "would evade, avoid, or otherwise not comply" with other equitable relief. Due to this high level of proof, stakeholders have had a low expectation of getting ex parte seizure orders.

Additionally, traditional injunction standards have been applied to balance the harm to the asset owner and the legitimate interests of the person or third party who may be harmed by the seizure.[178] Even without seizures, defendants can be required to surrender the property to the court or opposing counsel that likely contains trade secrets, or to not access or modify them.

The Actual versus Threatened Trade Secret Proof Problem. However, for the bad news, in gaining consistency across states, the DTSA reconciled inconsistencies across jurisdictions in misappropriation theories, namely *actual* or *threatened* misappropriation.

Actual Misappropriation Is the Most Actionable. A common pattern of *actual* misappropriation in the 2020s features a computer tucked under a foreign citizen's arm as the person is en route through an international departure terminal to her home country. The computer contains electronic data purloined from the US company. Let's throw in a stuffed briefcase with hard-copy materials as well. For effect, you can picture the perpetrator dressed in a disguise. Let's posit that the insider has physical and digital company files marked confidential stored not only on her devices, but later input onto a competitor's network for misuse.

Thankfully, courts do not have difficulty identifying this fact pattern as actual trade secret misappropriation, and then taking action to protect the asset owner. If you are dealing with trade secret threats, this is the one to uncover. It provides the strongest proof, and with high-performing litigation counsel, the swiftest remedies.

Threatened Misappropriation Is a Threat to Trade Secret Protection. Moving away from the brass ring of actual is *threatened* misappropriation. With threatened misappropriation, there is no perpetrator at the airport nor flashlight shining on the keyhole of the corporate treasure chest. Instead, threatened misappropriation requires either evidence of actions or circumstances that have a high likelihood of leading to actual misappropriation. What are the actions? Conduct or words? How do the circumstances play into it—is some misappropriation *inevitable* regardless of the accused's intentions? If this sounds like a proof problem, it is. And it depends on where you live. The evidentiary and geographic variables are the definitive bad news for employers.

A walk around threatened misappropriation travels through historic state and common laws, as well as the DTSA. We'll take the walk, but let's jump to the finish line first and list the common winning and losing threads. Threatened misappropriation requires evidence of bad behavior by the former or departing employee, and whether that behavior shows the employee "can't be trusted to honor the integrity" of the former employer's trade secrets.[179] The bad behavior must connect to an imminent and provable threat of actual misappropriation.

Common threads for successful fact patterns include unusual retention or previous improper use of company data, improper post-employment conduct or misinformation and rapid creation of a new competitive business.[180] Activities often falling short of misappropriation are retaining trade secret property with an explanation for the retention and an affirmation that the property wasn't accessed or used or was destroyed. Threatened misappropriation is harder to support as a basis for the all-important emergency relief.

The Inevitable Disclosure Doctrine, as Interpreted by Judicial Activism. One historic doctrine for threatened misappropriation was based on the knowledge of the former or departing employee, called the *inevitable disclosure doctrine* (IDD).[181] It was judicially created to address a former employee with trade secret knowledge working for a competitor. Courts reasoned that a person with trade secret knowledge from a former employer inevitably would use trade secrets at a new company that is competitive with the former employer. The doctrine did not necessarily require bad conduct on the part of the employee. Instead, an employee could be found to have misappropriated trade secrets under this doctrine unintentionally—by doing the job at the competitor.

Fast forward past the introduction of the IDD in 1965, through a fascinating case in 1995 where the IDD was found to prevent a former employee of Pepsi® from going to a different beverage manufacturer, to post-DTSA precedent.[182] Many commentators view the DTSA as codifying the demise of the IDD based on requiring "evidence of threatened misappropriation and not merely on the information the person knows"—but IDD is still good law in the states that have adopted it.[183] As cases continue to apply the DTSA, there is an emerging split on applying the doctrine, with some courts finding that the DTSA does not allow the theory.[184]

As a result of the rejection of the IDD in certain jurisdictions and uncertainty in others, enforcement strategy and timing should focus on proofs of actual misappropriation, leaving IDD for assertion only when warranted in particular jurisdictions and as necessary in the absence of better evidence.

Where a trade secret program is straightforward and managed, and high-performing litigation counsel is at the ready to seek emergency relief (ideally based on actual misappropriation), the technology owner maximizes her chances of success.

THE TRADE SECRET HOW-TOS

For the more pragmatic how-tos of satisfying legal standards, the fact that a company has trade secrets and a program to support them should be well known to employees.

While initiating a trade secret program from scratch may seem daunting, fortunately trade secrets can be identified and managed as a jump start, and their costs absorbed, within existing corporate functions. Trade secret protection also can be pursued as part of patent and copyright strategies.

On the other hand, some companies may want to approach this IP asset affirmatively and independently from the outset, or a program expansion can take place over time. An affirmative program is also covered in this section. So while trade secrets as secrets are absolute, their procurement and management offer flexibility.

Reasonable Standards for Reasonable Efforts to Maintain Secrecy. That flexibility extends to how to show reasonable efforts to maintain secrecy. Case law generally sets out a wide range of efforts to meet the reasonableness standard, and the Federal Trade Commission has provided a guide to support business owners.[185]

Human Resource Functions Welcome and Advocate for Trade Secrets. HR functions provide a critical connection between employees' creation of trade secrets and the company's sole ownership and control of them. HR administers employment and related agreements and associated policies and procedures. Like other IP, trade secret protection starts and succeeds with clear agreements for employees, setting out corporate ownership and employee responsibilities.

HR policies also must cover safeguarding secrets during employment phases, including onboarding, annual reviews and exit. You can use the onboarding process to level-set your ownership of trade secrets for your new employee, including respecting the rights of prior employers. You should ensure that a new employee affirmatively rejects unauthorized access or use of the third party–owned IP upon and during her tenure at your company. Not only do you demonstrate that you honor her prior employer's IP rights, but you also set an expectation that the same respect applies to your corporate assets too.

The Author Is Still the Thing for Trade Secret Protection in Employment and Related Agreements. Three general IP terms found in employment and related agreements are key to trade secrets. They are confidentiality, work for hire and noncompete terms.[186] IP terms generally convey employer ownership of information and sole direction and control of employee interaction with the information.

Confidentiality Terms and Trade Secrets. One key provision applicable to trade secrets is an agreement to maintain their confidentiality. It may be in stand-alone agreements, such as widely used confidentiality agreements or nondisclosure agreements (NDAs) or mutual nondisclosure agreements (MNDAs), or included in others, such as employment, purchase, customer, supplier, joint-venture, partnership or licensing agreements, etc.

Confidentiality terms involve the company's ownership and management of confidential information, including trade secrets. They present that employees must maintain the confidentiality of all such information designated as confidential and have an obligation not to disclose that information and not to access or use it except as authorized. Employees in turn acknowledge employer ownership of that information and their obligation to maintain it as such, perpetually.[187]

Trade secrets are not just confidential information; they are the most crucial form of confidential information. Therefore, make their safeguarding a key component of your company's reasonable efforts, including access to them solely on a need-to-know basis. In addition, your risk and security leadership should guide the designation procedures for information under the agreements.[188] For example, one common designation approach is placing a notice on trade secrets of confidentiality. Failure or unevenness in this notice is a common litigation issue. While notice shortcomings alone do not cause a failure of reasonable efforts, it is advised to set straightforward designation approaches for disclosing and receiving confidential information.[189] Confidentiality agreements covering third parties, such as NDAs or MNDAs with customers, suppliers or partners, should also have need-to-know and handling restrictions.

There is also an opportunity to specify a perpetual duration term for trade secrets so that this protection survives the termination of the subject agreement. This term can allow trade secrets that become public, and therefore lose their trade secret status, to remain covered as confidential under the agreement. Similarly, confidential information also covers proprietary information that might not rise to the level of a trade secret. If the trade secret is later found to be publicly known, a breach of contract claim may still be available.

In a Competition between Trade Secrets, Noncompetes and Judicial Activism, the Self-Proclaimed Winners Are Judges and Governments. Noncompete terms are a limitation on an employee (or contractor) competing with their employer after leaving the company, and are only enforceable under state law, if state law allows them. They generally involve a duration or geographic area within which a departing employee agrees to refrain from competing with their employer.[190] Noncompete terms would seem to meet the classic definition of a contract: an agreement between parties with a promise to take legal action in return for a benefit (employment). However, enforceability is uncertain.

In early 2023, the Federal Trade Commission issued a Notice of Proposed Rulemaking that would bar noncompetes, with proposed language which is so broad as to decline limitations on noncompetes that are reasonable in scope (such as the duration or geographic area limitations). Nondisclosure terms generally are not covered by the proposal, unless they are so broad as to function as noncompetes.[191]

State laws reflect a range of views. Some states, like California, have statutory prohibitions against noncompete agreements while others have statutory qualifiers, such as Washington, where these agreements are void for any employee below an income cap. When enforceable, the duration of a noncompete sometimes causes the term itself to be voided, and if the duration is determined to be lengthy, the entire employment agreement is sometimes struck down.[192]

In some cases, the duration of a noncompete now may be assessed based on the pendency of trade secret protection, representing a view that trade secrets don't last beyond one or two years anyway. When the former employee works at a competitor, the question then becomes whether the other IP terms under a private employment contract survive beyond the length of the contract's noncompete. Trade secrets potentially have an indefinite pendency due to the secret remaining so. Therefore, one reasonable situation between a trade secret owner and her departing employee is that the noncompete aside, the departing employee can work at a competitor but refrain from accessing or using trade secrets owned by the former employer. Try telling Coca-Cola that.

With this context, what can employers do? Decisions are state law and judge dependent, but here are recommendations: ensure you meet your jurisdictional standards on duration and consider with your employment lawyer additional terms which have the potential to protect against anticompetitive conduct and reduce judicial objections (such as customer or employee non-solicitation and garden-variety leave terms). Have a strong trade secret program, so if misappropriation happens, your evidence maximizes the likelihood of proving actual theft. In addition, set HR standards to select, manage and compensate employees for their success in using and accessing trade secrets for the company's performance as a source of their livelihood.[193]

IDENTIFY HOW BEST TO IDENTIFY TRADE SECRETS

With employees' awareness of ownership, rights and responsibilities from their employment contracts, the next step is to identify the trade secrets themselves.

Formalize the Identification of Trade Secrets. Ideally, you have confirmed your company's rock-solid employment and related agreements to govern trade secret protection. With the protections so delineated, next arises the question, what is being protected? A gap between protecting trade secrets in theory and in fact creates strong evidence to assist misappropriators, who argue that they don't know what is considered trade secret or confidential. The owner's ability to seek exigent relief is bolstered by employees confirming the existence of trade secrets and their responsibility to protect them during their interaction with these assets.

Bring the Approach Home. Let's drive this point home by shifting our perspective from your office door to your household door. Locked in your private safe at home is a gold and diamond heirloom as a family treasure. In this fact pattern, though, nostalgia is upended by a robbery. You immediately call the police to catch the thief during her getaway to return your property. Unfortunately, things go further awry because you don't have at-the-ready documentation or even a photo. Finding identifying evidence will require time. The chance of recovery is inversely proportional to that period. Further imagine the heirloom as a locket holding the passwords to your cryptocurrency wallets worth millions. Failure to recover the property exposes your family to further harm.

Plan for Emergency Relief in the Event of Theft. Alleged misappropriators commonly assert that they don't even know what trade secret they are accused of stealing. In addition, unprotected disclosure becomes more damaging over time. An unscrupulous third party in possession of trade secrets will seek both to benefit from the property and obfuscate his theft of it. On the other hand, emergency court relief, where successful, returns your property to the corporate vault, heightening risk for the alleged misappropriator. It alerts all actors that further illegal conduct will have severe civil and criminal consequences. Fast and aggressive actions introduce uncertainty and deterrence for the perpetrators about continuing their risky conduct.

Imagine a summary level list of trade secrets, ready for immediate presentation in proceedings. Think photos, internal business materials or software code captured at the time of the trade secret creation, called *contemporaneous evidence*. Add to it an annual acknowledgment by employees of the list and its purpose.[194] This may be accomplished by maintaining an internal list of trade secrets for use in HR policies and procedures. It also sets expectations of employees' obligations and documents their agreement to do so, reducing their ability to later claim a lack of knowledge.[195] The investment to prepare this list is far more productive and beneficial than undertaking the exercise post-theft in litigation.[196] You may also consider trade secret insurance, with such lists being compulsory in working with your insurer.

Top-10 Takeaway 5

#ip2ip-5: Formalize a list of trade secrets as part of your patent and copyright strategies.

For Documenting IP, If Not a Patent, Then an Inventive Trade Secret. Information considered for patenting can help identify trade secrets as a default when an inventor or owner decides to decline patenting. One tool traditionally used to evaluate inventions is an Invention Disclosure Form (IDF) to document and then determine whether to file for patents. IDFs traditionally include the inventors, title, summary description, dates and documentation of the invention (with versions readily available online) and are completed by inventors and sometimes decision-makers.[197] They also can include an assessment for business alignment, as explored in Chapter 9: Cost, specify considering trade secret protection and document the inventor's acknowledgment of the innovation as a potential trade secret.

Trade Secrets Are a Copyright Wrap. The approach of copyrighting valuable assets can also encompass identifying and filing for copyright protection of trade secrets, recalling the copyright wrap technique from Chapter 5: Copyrights. The US Copyright Office adjusts the filing requirements to include a redacted deposit of trade secret information. The result is a list of trade secrets on file with a government office, creating strong evidence for a trade secret enforcement case.

A similar strategy is recommended for public contracting. Recognize that the public has access to government records, and therefore a need to protect trade secrets in submissions that accompany, for example, a bid to provide custom software. Like the copyright registration system, most governmental entities have processes to protect trade secrets within the public nature of government recordkeeping.

A SEPARATE AFFIRMATIVE TRADE SECRET PROGRAM

Identify Trade Secrets, Affirmatively. This chapter title, *The Trade Secret Program You Didn't Know You Had*, is a jump start or default trade secret program within existing IP strategy touch points, reducing the burden of launching a program from scratch and creating strong evidence of reasonable efforts. In this way, an affirmative and independent program may be considered while executing the fundamentals provided by the IP strategies above.

A separate trade secret program is warranted because these key assets, in their own right, are worth addressing and managing affirmatively. This is particularly true where trade secrets are a primary corporate asset, such as in internet or software companies.

To set up a separate program, begin with each line of business and identify the types of information that maximize your competitive advantage. Initially, the DTSA list of categories may surface potential subject matter. With a recognition that trade secrets relate to information that has value to its owner, the assessment can also expand to information about your offerings and their commercial value and competitive advantage (or conversely, what your competitors would benefit from knowing).

After surfacing potential subject matter, next consider whether the information is readily ascertainable by competitors. You may treat this step as competitive intelligence by researching public sources, such as educational or academic industry resources, or reverse engineering companies, industry standards companies, or suppliers or customers in your industry. Where the information is hard to find by others using lawful means, prioritize it on a list. Where there is concern that researching public sources using a description of an actual trade secret may provide a path for a third party to uncover it, one option is to research a broader subject. For example, where a trade secret solves a problem, then research the problem to investigate whether your solution is shown, and potentially provide additional competitive intelligence such as its commercial value. Where publicly known solutions embody your trade secret, then relinquishing that particular trade secret will allow you to prioritize more valuable ones.

The Trade Secrets List. Whether the identification of trade secrets derives from patent or copyright filing strategies or an affirmative program, these efforts will generate an official internal list of trade secrets.

An advantage of the DTSA is that an ex parte seizure does not require disclosure of the trade secret. However, this benefit for owners is inconsistent under various state laws. Therefore, having the list of trade secrets ready for exigent filings should be treated as required.

Be forewarned, however, that the list itself can be the subject of litigation posturing in failing to identify the company's trade secrets with reasonable particularity. This defense is raised in motion practice and discovery with constant pressure for additional disclosure. Courts have added guidance that the list must be of "actual trade secrets" rather than "a list of categories of business information" that are in no way unique to the plaintiff and not merely "generalized trade secrets." In other words, the simple DTSA definition category names are inadequate because they are not specific to the plaintiff. I hope that this glimpse into the evidentiary posturing (as the tip of the iceberg)[198] reinforces why you should generate a trade secret list. Imagine a program including, long before litigation, an official list of trade secrets, at varying levels of description available on a selective basis and acknowledged by employees with access to the assets.

Maintaining an internal list offers broader benefits than evidence for litigation and meeting the reasonable efforts standard. The benefits expand to celebrating employees as they honor their employment agreements by acknowledging trade secrets as valuable corporate assets. Internal awareness of the list at varying descriptive levels buttresses a corporate culture that protects corporate assets.

Insider Lawball

Identification of Trade Secrets

Let's review an exemplary approach for generating a trade secret list. Each trade secret can have its own numbered or otherwise categorized general reference title, prepared for employee review and with an eye toward being published in litigation. Grant only those employees with a need-to-know access to the trade secret list beyond the general reference titles (and log and retain employee access).

Add supplemental evidence for individual trade secrets as a function of the particular secret, such as a summary, a detailed description or contemporaneous business records aligned with an escalation of disclosure required over the course of litigation.

Individual secrets may also be grouped, or evidence can be used for multiple secrets. Combinations of trade secrets increase the number of assets, and therefore opportunities, to assert in the event of enforcement.

The list order can also be prioritized when new trade secrets are added or at a natural assessment point within business strategies. Prioritizing trade secret assets once again can leverage the approach used in prioritizing patents (see Chapter 9: Cost). However, one important advantage for trade secrets compared to other IP is they do not require a government filing. Even when filing for them under copyright, the estimated cost of between $750 and $1,500, plus additional costs for redacting the trade secret material, is cost efficient.

After Identifying the Basics, Leave the Program to Professionals. Initiating a program of matching commercially valuable corporate secrets to the comprehensive DTSA list of categories, adding general reference titles and initiating reasonable efforts to secure the secrets listed will put you a long way on the road to generating valuable evidence. Beyond this, trade secret identification is highly fact and business dependent. It is also a hot spot for litigation disagreements. This sensitive exercise warrants the input of IP specialists in trade secrets, including litigators knowledgeable about your company and the standard applicable to its location.

RISKS

Trade Secret Management through Risk and Security Functions. Employment and related agreements executed upon onboarding provide the foundation of accountability for employees regarding trade secrets. Compliance with these agreements is managed by HR, along with legal functions. HR also oversees employee manuals, policies and procedures which provide additional touch points.

Topics relevant to trade secrets also overlap with two additional vital corporate areas: risk management and technology security. Here is a list of topics for consideration under risk and security management to further support reasonable efforts to safeguard trade secrets:

- **Human resources management:** Reconfirm employment or related agreements annually, such as in employee reviews, along with the appropriate detail level of the company's trade secrets list. The review can be in writing and connected to compensation to satisfy contract consideration. Audit employee compliance with confidential and trade secret rights and responsibilities. Establish employee exit phase agreements (even between different areas within the company when access to specific trade secrets changes) and procedures, including reconfirming confidentiality terms and continuing duration and duties, plus a confirmation of a return of all property.

- **Human resources, key employee management:** If access or use of confidential information is customary, or information is secret, then confirming policies and responsibilities can be more frequent and used as a basis to build relationships with key employees as partners in protecting trade secrets.

- **Human resources, enforcement policies:** Plan specifically for monitoring to detect violations of trade secret policies. Where problems are detected, provide notice, consequences and remediation. HR should implement responsive actions consistently and immediately.

- **Risk management:** Establish rules around access to and use of trade secrets, keep interactions on a need-to-know basis and employ compliance monitoring and consequences. Establish these as affirmative actions to take at each interaction with trade secrets. For example, some companies require that employees use corporate technology and devices for business rather than personal devices.

- **Risk management and document retention:** As part of your litigation readiness, consider retention strategies to address specific trade secret safeguarding, including retention of trade secret evidence and key employees' interactions with them.

- **Security:** Provide notices of confidentiality or watermarking, passwords and encryption tools for confidential or trade secret information. Set formal rules for physical access to and protection of physical locations with trade secrets. Monitor and document transfers of information and the parties involved. Enact and execute specific visitor procedures, including confidentiality and nondisclosure agreements and where applicable, escorts and limited or controlled access.

Even a high-performance trade secret program does not obviate risks for trade secrets. Make addressing these risks part of the foundation of a trade secret program. In some cases where trade secret theft occurs, litigation may be unsuccessful or unavailable.

Trade Secret Owner's Preparation and Execution Are Key Factors in Early Intervention and Success in Trade Secret Litigation. Have success stories of Coke and Google's Alphabet, or the espionage headliner cases, inspired you to embrace trade secret protection? If so, then maintain that enthusiasm. While they are the best stories, they are not the greatest opportunities nor risks. The most common fact pattern today lies between these dramatic extremes.

One path for trade secrecy loss has nothing to do with anyone's bad conduct. In the end, you have no control over the legitimate discovery of your hard-earned secret sauce by third parties. Your secrets can be discovered through the lawful actions of third-party individuals and companies in discovering for themselves the information providing you with a competitive advantage. Alternatively, some secrets lose their commercial value over time, subsequently losing their need for protection. In other words, there is an element of luck in the information not being deconstructed over time and retaining commercial value.

LOSS OF TRADE SECRETS THROUGH LAWFUL ACTIVITIES

Lawful actions of third parties can impact the theoretical unlimited lifetime of secrets through no fault of the corporate owner or its employees. Competitors are actively and legally seeking to discover competitive information too. A healthy form of competition is to engage in lawful activities to reduce the advantages of competitors. Examples of lawful activities are research, investigation, deconstruction or independent invention.

Herein lies the risk, because the trade secret owner cannot control the actions of others. Where the secret is valuable, competitors naturally seek to uncover or approximate it. If or when others outside the company legally uncover the trade secret, the treasure chest is opened, and the value of the former secret is extinguished. Once the secret is out, the discovering third party can use it to gain their own value or remove their heretofore competitive disadvantage. Every litigation defendant insists the trade secrets were lawfully uncovered.

Coca-Cola Continues to Teach. Let's continue to use the Coca-Cola story to explore these *lawful* actions of third parties. Since 1886, other companies like Pepsi have tried to replicate the famous Coca-Cola formula. Have they succeeded? Well, as a fact finder, which do you like better, Coke or Pepsi? Coke presents folks prefer their beverage because of its superior secret formula. I say "presents" because who knows? Perhaps Pepsi's formula is nearly the same, but we don't know because neither company (nor the public) has access to either company's formula. Another possibility is the Pepsi taste is better. On an even more subjective basis, are we so conditioned to experience Coke's formula as unique that we "taste it"?[199] We have no way of knowing, short of accessing the formulas not just of Coke, but of Pepsi and other competitors. Even in litigation, this information would be filed under seal. Trade secret strategy therefore has an element of the unknown, with this illustrative analysis serving to highlight, once again, to control your controllables and optimize protection of your treasured corporate assets.

Changing Times Change the Environment for Trade Secrets. The second most significant risk to achieving trade secret longevity and success derives from changing technology and work environments. As of the 2020 COVID-19 pandemic, this shift of work from physical offices to online and virtual became a chasm with the trend toward virtual work accelerated to become a debate. This shift will forever change how we work, and information transmitted electronically and globally will be at greater risk from unauthorized access and security threats.

In addition, data and technology today is unprecedented and will continue to expand in the future. Witness artificial intelligence, machine learning, blockchain technologies and 3D printing. This pace of data and technology advancement can only shorten the longevity of secret information by increasing the possibility of lawful analysis.

Another development for this IP asset is employee mobility. For example, the average tenure of employment at a given company has decreased dramatically in recent decades, with news reports calling 2021–22 the great resignation. Some employees today with exposure to your company's trade secrets will leave your company to join your competitors. Employment law trends increasingly protect the rights of employees to work freely.

While Coke's historic success is sweet, it continues to have a bit of good fortune in the business, industry and societal conditions supporting the result. Coke's storyboard drives home the richness of this topic, which perhaps is best enjoyed as a break from this dense learning with a beverage.

Summary

Managing Risks of Lawful Activities. It is unsettling to know a secret that you have worked so hard to keep confidential can be found and lawfully acquired by others. How do you manage the risks of lawful actions by third parties? First, you can acknowledge that lawful actions extend to the opportunity for your own lawful actions. In this respect, legal actions are an even playing field for competitive behavior. Second, you gain opportunities to address risks, whether based on lawful or unlawful activities, by paying attention to trade secrets and receiving their benefits.

It has been uplifting to end a section on risk with the realization that risk also derives from lawful conduct as part of the cost of doing business, making risk less foreboding. Trade secrets therefore offer riches in the law, business strategy and honoring the contributions of employees that are at the level of a treasure. Through a focus on valuing people, we end this chapter on a high ground from which trade secrets can be leveraged for business success.

CHAPTER 7

#IP2IP TRADEMARKS AND DESIGN PATENTS

MAKE YOUR MARK AND SUCCEED BY DESIGN
CO-AUTHOR, J. CHRISTOPHER LYNCH

ACTions

7.1 Create marks—names and logos—as crown jewel assets to showcase your company and its offerings.
7.2 **Prioritize a strong mark which minimizes your investment over its lifetime.** *Top-10 Takeaway.*
7.3 File for US federal trademark protection upon selecting your mark, with an option to register before you use your mark.
7.4 **Consider design patents for the visual look and feel of key commercial design features when you assess utility patents.** *Top-10 Takeaway.*

TRADEMARKS AND DESIGN PATENTS AS FINISHING TOUCHES FOR CORPORATE BRANDS

Trademarks and patentable designs are borne in creative minds, often as the finishing brand touches for a company and its products or services. As the face and energy of the company to the marketplace, they spark the user experience and build brand loyalty. Some are unique or notable from the start. Others gain strength and become iconic over time. For a few companies, these IP assets are a path to global recognition and generational wealth.

Think visual and not just iconic company names and logos. Trademarks can protect product names and logos, as well as product designs, colors and packaging. They serve to tell consumers which company makes a product (or service), as distinguished from similar offerings made by others.[200]

Design patents protect the way something looks. Formally, they involve the look or appearance of visual qualities on articles, called *ornamental features*, such as industrial, package or fashion designs, and features of computer graphical user interfaces (GUIs).[201] Design patents prohibit similar designs on articles that would be confused side by side by a person making an ordinary observation, called an *ordinary observer*.

Recall that design patents are different than utility patents, which protect functions or structures. Often both are at play by breakaway success companies talked up by their adoring customers. Take Apple®, for example. Steve Jobs was the iconic creator of the sleek modern design of the iPhone® and is famously known for his central role in Apple's marketing and brand efforts. He not only transformed industrial design but was equally prescient in investing in design patents to protect his transformations, resulting in a litigation win with design patent damages outshining those for utility patents.

Visual Identity. While trademarks and design patents have differences, their overlap in protecting the visual elements of products makes them beneficial to consider together. Copyright too can be part of a layering approach. Marketing and brand leaders consider these three IP assets as part of a company's "visual identity," or all that the consumer can see about the company and its offerings.[202]

Brand elements are creative stuff, playing a starring role in elevating ordinary products and services. Their selection is a critical business strategy to protect your customers and your corporate brand. So make your mark and succeed by design!

OPPORTUNITIES
THE MARK OF TRADEMARKS

Trademarks are the connection in the marketplace beyond a product to its company, with the best examples being a company's name and logo. Creativity also applies beyond the selection of trademarks to what can be a mark, such as a word, phrase, design, or even a color, sound or smell.

Marks must be used in the marketplace (or *in trade*) to indicate their *origin* so that they distinguish between other offerings (formally, *goods or services*) from other sources. In this way, they avoid confusion in the marketplace. They also must be monitored and infringement addressed to maintain their strength and, therefore, your brand value.

Goodwill. Trademarks also represent its owner's *goodwill* by identifying the company as the origin of the marked product to the consumer.[203] The consumer can then apply her perception of the source to the product's characteristics, enabling her trust in the brand. Goodwill has real, tangible value—as reflected in corporate valuations and legal agreements.

Select Trademarks in Their Market Context. Strong marks also avoid the same or similar marks already in use in commerce; thus, trademark searching is advised. When searching, two factors applied to determine a likelihood of confusion dominate: first, the similarity in the trademarks and second, the relatedness of the offerings. Marks do not have to be identical. Similarity is tipped when they are close enough so that a likelihood of confusion would exist between them, such as by visual, oral, commercial impression or semantic views. The relatedness of products depends on their commercial relationship in the marketplace, such as channels of trade.

Thus, selecting a trademark includes examining preexisting trademarks, their goods and services and marketing channels, and evaluating the strength of them in the minds of the consumer. Upon completion of this type of clearance, the nascent trademark is a candidate for adoption and registration.

TRADEMARK AND DESIGN PATENT INFRINGEMENT

Trademark Infringement. A strong trademark avoids confusion in the marketplace, facilitating fair trade. Where marks from different companies are similar in meaning, appearance or other characteristics, consumers could mistakenly believe they come from the same company. This is deemed a *likelihood of confusion* and is the test for trademark infringement. Factors to weigh are the strength of the owner's mark, the degree of similarity between the marks, evidence of actual confusion and their marketing channels.[204]

Design Patent Infringement. As described below, design patents employ a variation of the test based on the ability of an *ordinary observer* merely looking at designs side by side to tell the difference between them.[205]

The only limit on creativity for trademarks is the creative decisions represented by existing marks for the same or related offerings, as tempered by legal rules of thumb. For example, trademark rights are not available for generic terms or designs dictated by function, not form.

TRADEMARKS THAT HIT THEIR MARK

Trademarks with Artistic Aspects Must Still Respect Owner Rights. A recent trademark infringement challenge heard at the US Supreme Court involved trademarks for a classic liquor company—Jack Daniels®. In addition to a number of potentially confusing marks, the alleged infringer added off-color parodies of the Jack Daniels bottle, work and logo marks to a dog toy. Jack Daniels won on the basic question of trademark infringement; subtext issues and facts remain to be sorted out on remand to the lower courts.

The mimicker argued that the First Amendment and free speech protected the toy, and therefore shifted the infringement standard from a likelihood of confusion to a focus on free speech. The First Amendment allows the use of another's mark as an expressive work, unless devoid of artistic relevance or explicitly misleading as to the source.

The majority focused on the basic question of trademarks—whether the public is likely to be confused as to the designation of source for the product. Infringement was found because the toy was intended to be source identifying, so a First Amendment defense did not apply. This doesn't preclude freedom of expression completely from trademark law. But it does provide a clear standard for mimickers of source based on parody.[206]

While artificial intelligence was not involved, the decision favoring owner's rights provides directional guidance for imminent AI-related trademark cases involving AI-generated content.

Iconic Trademarks: Apple® and Tiffany Blue®. Common words placed on unrelated offerings can be protected by trademark. Witness "apple." Which description comes to mind first, the fruit or the technology company? The use of the word "apple" for a product unrelated to the word's common meaning, such as a type of fruit, is a strong trademark. We'll explain why below in exploring the key to trademarks—trademark categories.

Brand elements covered by trademarks also include colors. Consider Tiffany Blue®. For those with a taste for old-world timeless jewelry, Tiffany® fits the bill and the paradigm of trademark success.[207]

TRADEMARK DYNAMICS

Trademarks through Time. Trademark rights can last as long as the trademark continues to be used in commerce. This period contrasts with those of other IP rights, such as fifteen years for design patents. So, while perhaps of interest to know the dates that Apple and Tiffany secured trademark protection, it doesn't dictate how long trademark rights exist. Hence, the potential for them to drive generational wealth.

Trademarks Protect Consumers... These iconic trademarks sound exciting, right? Trademarks represent the accurate source of offerings to consumers, as distinguished from competitive or counterfeit versions. That recognition is quantifiable goodwill engendered by the mark.

...and Companies. Suppose you work hard to earn an excellent reputation for your "A+" product. In that case, competitors with potentially inferior products B, C and D, and counterfeiters with a defective product E, should not tap into your hard-earned loyalty and market share based on confusion. Where competitors infringe your rights, there are two immediate problems.

First, trademarks help set consumer expectations because they represent the goodwill, authenticity and reputation of the source. When consumers see a familiar brand, their assumptions are prompted about the quality they have learned to expect. Your A+ product is favorably known to consumers based on their knowledge and confidence about your product's quality and consistency.

Second, trademark infringement is disruptive. Trademark success enables your company to focus on business performance and consumer loyalty. On the other hand, where the marketplace includes third-party products B, C, D or E presented in a confusing manner, the competitive dynamic is unfair. Consumers are needlessly confused, and your business is harmed. The third-party products B, C, D or E do not have your company's goodwill and may be inferior or even counterfeit.

Judicial remedies can include an infringer discontinuing use of the trademark on their product or removing the product from the marketplace. However, even where remedied, consumer goodwill has been disrupted and requires rehabilitation.

The dynamics of trademark infringement warrant planning to identify and act upon infringement as quickly as possible. Monitoring and enforcement of trademark rights is vital to the maintenance of brand value.

THE TRADEMARK LAWYERLY LITANY

Brand elements are critical to consumer decision-making, resulting in consensus about the value of building a trademark portfolio. While there are some rights triggered by actual use in commerce, formally registering the mark on a federal level and providing notice increases its value and therefore is strongly advised.

Federal Registration under the Lanham Act. Registering for federal trademark protection is based on a federal law called the Lanham Act. This registration is the only way a trademark owner may lawfully display the ® insignia and the powerful notice and deterrent it provides.

The US Patent and Trademark Office administers the Lanham Act by maintaining registrations under two listings, the principal and supplemental registers. A principal register listing establishes a presumption of a valid mark entitled to nationwide use for the designated offerings, the owner as the mark's senior user and litigation enforcement rights. Federal registration also enables potential attorneys' fees and triple damages where an infringer's conduct is found willful. It also allows recordation with US Customs and Border Patrol to help prohibit importation of infringing goods or services. If having a mark on the principal register sounds intimidating for competitors, it is.

A listing on the supplemental register does not confer immediate enforcement rights. Still, it serves as a stepping stone to the principal register if additional evidence of consumer perception can be developed over time. One example of proof is the exclusive use of a mark over five years to establish acquired distinctiveness (or *secondary meaning*).

Use in commerce is required to establish trademark rights and establish the date for identifying the mark's senior user. However, the Lanham Act also offers an intent-to-use (ITU) application if a mark has been selected but is not yet formally used for an offering in commerce. ITUs benefit the mark owner because once the use commences and the registration issues, the trademark has as its filing date the earlier date on which the ITU was filed.

Both the principal and supplemental registers also enable adding the ® symbol to the listed mark—a significant deterrent. Additionally, ™ or ℠ (trademark and service mark) symbols can be added upon use before registration, whether or not there is a formal trademark application. They at least provide notice of ownership rights. Federal registration therefore has both offensive and defensive advantages over the mere use of a mark without securing federal rights.

If You Have Been Using a Trademark, Still Assess and File for Federal Registration Where Available. For those readers with trademarks already in use but without federal registration, you'll find guidance to rely on alternative state and common law rights based on simple use. Reliance on this is akin to a DIY trademark, and with the DIY costs and ample resources, the time to learn alternatives can be better spent on the Trademark Office resources to file for DIY federal registration. Some unwittingly believe that filing for a domain name, a corporate entity, or a d/b/a "tradename" provides trademark rights. Again, I discourage it. Although common law usage rights may work against knowing, willful infringers, the best protection is federal trademark registration.

Opportunity Favors the Prepared. Without federal protection, the mark in use is vulnerable to others for related offerings who earlier sought federal registration or used the same or a similar mark in commerce for related offerings. These risks are minimized by a federal trademark registration as early as possible after selecting your trademark. The USPTO's system defers to the "first-filed" application as the default *senior user* for competing marks, even though the first user in commerce will ultimately prevail under the law if it can meet its burden to overcome the senior user.

THE TRADEMARK HOW-TOS

Another reason to get excited about trademarks is that, like copyright, they are cost-efficient and accessible for DIY filings given the ample resources at the PTO at less than $500 for a single-class federal trademark application, or with professional support as detailed in Chapter 9: Cost, **the estimated cost is less than $3,000 over 11.2 months where registration is successful.**

ESTABLISH A LIFETIME INVESTMENT THEME

Every company and offering, by definition, has a name. Failure to seek federal trademark rights not only represents a missed opportunity but an unnecessary risk in favor of a potentially better-prepared senior user as the first to file. Delays prompt additional costs to then address the missed opportunity. Let's continue with the most cost-efficient approach for trademarks: keeping your attention on simply registering for federal protection.

Trademark Selection Determines the Investment over the Lifetime of the Mark. OK, trademarks are a must. The next step is to determine what to protect. If you already have a trademark in use without an earlier filing, it is not necessarily fatal, as such inaction might be under patent law. You may still apply as the senior user, depending upon whether another has already filed or is using your mark.

Trademark selection is a creative choice as to what can be imagined. It can move beyond the descriptive boundaries of the offering or even known terms or phrases by creating a new lexicon, or it can embody words or phrases from unrelated goods and services. The creativity of trademarks is limited only by the earlier creative decisions of others with the same or related offering. The more creative the selection of a trademark, the harder it is for others to defend using the same or similar mark as anything other than an attempt to confuse consumers. In short, the more creative a mark, the stronger it is. This characteristic of trademarks is called *distinctiveness*.

KEEP A LIFETIME INVESTMENT THEME IN FIRST PLACE

Top-10 Takeaway 6

#ip2ip-6: Prioritize a strong mark which minimizes your investment over its lifetime.

Trademark selection and registration impact not just your success in procuring a trademark but also your investment over its lifetime. A strong trademark makes it harder for others to infringe and therefore reduces enforcement instances. As we examine distinctiveness in more detail, please keep cost in mind. Trademark procurement and enforcement trigger escalating costs the further away the mark is from being distinctive and, therefore, are a potential cause for confusion with marks of competitors.

The Distinctiveness of Trademarks. The theory of distinctiveness is that a trademark "distinguishes" the source of the offering from others. Consumers and companies both benefit from avoiding confusion, thereby enabling competition based on fair commerce.

TRADEMARK CATEGORIES FOR DISTINCTIVENESS

Trademarks are placed in categories 1 to 5 based on increasing distinctiveness: 1. *Generic*, 2. *Descriptive*, 3. *Suggestive*, 4. *Arbitrary* and 5. *Fanciful*. Generally, the categories represent two types of marks, those that *are not* inherently distinctive and those that *are* inherently distinctive.[208] Trademark distinctiveness is best learned by example, such as a category 1. *Generic* mark "Apple," when it is applied as a species of fruit. For a category 2. *Descriptive* mark, "Big Rock" is exemplary for a boulder delivery company because the mark describes the goods or services.

Marks fall into the *Generic* and *Descriptive* categories because either the trademark itself is the product's name or it is descriptive of the product's characteristics—more so than the trademark acts as an indication of source. *Generic* and *Descriptive* marks are not inherently distinctive because they do not distinguish between sources.

On the other hand, where a mark readily can be understood to distinguish products from one company versus another, they are assigned to categories 3, 4 and 5, and deemed *inherently distinctive*. Here are examples of categories 3, 4 and 5 marks. Category 3. *Suggestive*, At-A-Glance® (for calendars); category 4. *Arbitrary*, Banana® (for tires) or Apple® (for computers and without reference to an offering of fruit); and category 5. *Fanciful*, Kodak® (for the film) or Verizon® (for telecommunications service). With increasing distinctiveness comes the potential for more robust trademark protection.

When the Trademark Office assigns a mark to one of the categories 3, 4 or 5, it is eligible to be placed on the principal registry. Marks allocated to categories 1 or 2 fall short of being inherently distinctive. Category 1. *Generic* marks are ineligible for federal trademark protection. By contrast, however, category 2. *Descriptive* marks can be placed on the supplemental register with the potential for elevation to the principal register once distinctiveness is acquired by consumer recognition. Indeed, some *Descriptive* marks can become valuable assets by building acquired distinctiveness. McDonald's Quarter Pounder® and Microsoft's Word® are examples of strong marks based on acquired distinctiveness. Let's now explore each category for trademark distinctiveness.

1. Generic

We were fortunate in 2020 to have a United States Supreme Court trademark decision that provides an assessment of whether a mark is generic and also represents a historic shift in the court's jurisprudence. *Generic* marks generally are the easiest to identify and rule as ineligible for trademark rights, reducing litigation about them.

The 2020 United States Supreme Court Booking.com® Case. Why did the SCOTUS review an appeal about genericness? This case involved the term "booking" for a company that makes travel reservations. Your reaction likely is the same as mine—it's generic. However, it was not an easy rejection because the trademark sought to be registered added the e-commerce syntax ".com" or dot-com. During the application phase, the USPTO found "Booking.com" to be generic and therefore ineligible for trademark protection because it ignored the syntax. Booking.com appealed at the PTO, and then to the courts.

It finally achieved success before the Supreme Court as Booking.com®.[209] However, don't get too excited and start conjuring up a corporate name with well-known words plus ".com" just yet. Instead, consider the cost of this success. Was the investment in Booking.com by the company worth it? For a celebratory moment, let's give Booking.com its due (kudos to its trademark attorneys) and revel for a few paragraphs in its success.

Booking.com won because the SCOTUS overruled the Office's decision that combining a generic term with a dot-com syntax yields a "generic composite."[210] Instead, the SCOTUS relied on how consumers perceive the mark with .com with the potential for distinctiveness. At base, the SCOTUS found that Booking.com is not generic to consumers because consumers recognize it as a trademark from a single source.

In *Booking.com*, the Supreme Court focused on two principles for trademarks: class and consumer perception. The Court's analysis extends beyond category 1. *Generic* to further build our understanding of categories 2–5 distinctiveness. If the mark is the name of a class of offerings, it is category 1. *Generic*, and therefore cannot be assigned to categories 2, 3, 4 or 5. Consider again Apple. While Apple is a generic name for a fruit company selling apples, Apple is not generic when used as a mark for selling computers because computers are a different class of goods and services. Consumer perception, as the next principle, leads us right into the follow-on category of distinctiveness, category 2. *Descriptive*.

Insider Lawball

A Check on the Lifetime Investment Theme

What is your guess regarding the quantity and quality of evidence Booking.com likely needed to prove its case? The decision did not provide this data, but the PTO provided in its decision "the oft-repeated principle that 'no matter how much money and effort the user of a generic term has poured into promoting the sale of its merchandise…, it cannot deprive competing manufacturers of the product of the right to call an article by its name.'"[211] My suggested answer is a figure too high for SMEs to contemplate.

2. Descriptive

This type of mark describes the attributes of products, such as a feature, quality or characteristic, such as "Big Rock" for a boulder delivery company or "Creamy" for yogurt. Because they include terms which literally describe offerings or a prominent feature of them, protection is more challenging, and the marks are weaker.

Descriptive marks are not eligible for the principal register unless the owner can show "significance 'in the minds of the public' as identifying the applicant's goods or services—a quality called *acquired distinctiveness* or *secondary meaning*."[212] Secondary meaning is a recognition by consumers that even though the term may have a first meaning as descriptive, it has a secondary meaning as a trademark. Proving secondary meaning sounds evidence intensive because it is.

Interesting-use cases for descriptive marks include a combination of generic or geographic references and descriptive terms, or surnames. For example, a mark can include a phrase containing a generic term—recall "Big Rock" for boulders or a geography such as "Little Italy NYC Pasta" for pasta from that locale. One commonly misunderstood area for descriptive trademarks is whether an individual can trademark their surname. The answer is "not likely" because it falls under category 2. *Descriptive*, with the law prohibiting "merely a surname."[213] One's full given name is more likely to be protected because it includes multiple words, establishing it as unique to its owner.

In the Booking.com case, the SCOTUS continued to regale us about trademarks by exploring category 2. *Descriptive* marks. After deciding what Booking.com is *not*—generic—it then decided what Booking.com *is*—descriptive. Not only was it descriptive, but all parties including the mark's owner conceded that it was descriptive at the lower court before the SCOTUS appeal. Booking.com further acknowledged that descriptive marks are "'weak' thus making it 'harder...to show a likelihood of confusion.'"[214] Booking.com now has an admittedly weak trademark, but a clear victory at the SCOTUS.

A Second Check on the Lifetime Investment Theme

I return to the investment theme and the mindset of a consumer of legal services. Let's add a factor to the investment question: filing and then litigating a mark the owner acknowledges is "weak." However, paradoxically, some weak trademarks can also be valuable in the end based on additional investments.

3. Suggestive, 4. Arbitrary or 5. Fanciful

On to the more straightforward categories 3, 4 and 5 for stronger trademarks. Legal precedent presents these categories as inherently distinctive because the public can readily understand that the marks identify products from a single source as distinguished from those of other sources. As a result, they foster the mark's owner to maintain its goodwill with consumers. The titles of the categories themselves indicate how they achieve distinctiveness and an immediate listing on the principal register: 3. *Suggestive*, 4. *Arbitrary* and 5. *Fanciful*.

3. Suggestive

These marks present a characteristic or description of an offering but necessitate some "mental gymnastics" to suggest the offerings type. Examples of suggestive marks are Odor-Eaters® for shoe insoles with deodorant protection, and Habitat® for home furnishings. Debate, either when filing at the PTO or in litigation, is most often between whether a mark qualifies as category 2. *Descriptive* or 3. *Suggestive*, and the distinction is the dividing line between entry on the principal register or rejection.

4. Arbitrary

These marks are commonly known words used outside of their ordinary context. As a result, they do not describe the product, nor are they associated with it in common parlance. In addition to the example of Steve Jobs's Apple® are Tide® for laundry detergent and Bananas® for tires.

5. Fanciful

The strongest or most distinctive type of trademarks out of the gate are made up of newly coined words with no dictionary or other known definition, like Kodak® or Exxon®.

Examples of category 5. *Fanciful* marks are often found in pharmaceutical names. If you are like me and recoil at drug commercials, anticipating the unseemly list of side effects, you may also relate to another frustration I have with them. They often present a newly coined word as their name, limiting one's ability to remember them where valuable. Consider, though, the cost of drug commercials. High. The investment in R & D for drugs. Very high. Most importantly, confusion about drugs can mean life or death. One study showed that "mistaking one drug for another with a similar name account[s] for approximately 10 percent of all reported medication errors."[215] Drug companies' marks therefore involve a higher level of due diligence and often a selection of newly coined words as trademarks to minimize confusion. The costly commercials, marketing and branding are invested in the strongest types of trademarks for both investment returns and risk reduction. [216]

A TRADEMARK SELECTION MINDSET

Let's take another pause to consider your takeaways so far. Two are likely. Decide to file for trademarks and consider distinctiveness in selecting your mark.

My personal approach: Why would anyone select a trademark for any category other than a 5. *Fanciful* mark? Your answer depends upon your mindset, the business you have chosen and your approach to sales and marketing. You can also choose to bring your natural perspective or adjust it in consultation with your team, investors and trademark professionals. In some cases, those decisions—say to name a computer hardware company Apple®—may have iconic implications.

The Trademark Selections of Yours Truly. Let's add a punch line (and lightheartedness) to options and peer into my historic choice with my startup name. My mindset? Conservative. My branding story? Simple: I readily picked a three-word phrase, Article One Partners®. My company was about patents, as honored by a specific inclusion in Article 1 of the US Constitution. I wanted the name to be worthy of this legacy, and I considered our customers and crowdsourcing research community to be my partners. "Article One Partners" was evident to me.

The reaction of trademark professionals, a simple recommendation to file, no rigorous searching nor PTO rejection. The name breezed through. There similarly was no confusion as I moved to launch and build the business, all due to my rock-solid, conserva... (or boring?) name. So while we're at it, please judge: Was my name selection—Article One Partners—conservative, boring or something else?

Your Trademark Mindset. Similarly, your personality will influence your corporate name selection and additional brand elements. You may also work with brand experts. Let's see what they have to say. In an article titled "What's in a Brand? How to Define Your Visual Identity," brand expert Ben Matthews provided this guidance:

> Your brand's visual identity is its style... If brands are people, then visual identity is the walk, the talk, the clothes, and the hair...

Does your brand strut down the street...rocking a peacock feather jacket, or does it somberly stroll in a well-tailored suit? ... That's a first impression working its magic...[217]

It is interesting to note that the USPTO provides a warning that branding companies generally advise clients to use descriptive marks based on the ease of conveying what the company does and setting consumer expectations.[218] Descriptive marks are harder to register and usually require the assistance of trademark attorneys, prompting additional cost, uncertainty and a more complex application process. Work with trademark attorneys early in the process to drive a productive selection of a protectable (and robust) mark.

A "Three Times Is the Charm" Check on the Lifetime Investment Theme

Brand decisions carry risk, and risk impacts cost. You can reduce risk by trademark registration. Once registered, further reduce risk by policing the competitive market to address infringement by a third party who would seek to compete with you unfairly, or even unintentionally, by using the same or similar trademark for related offerings. Policing includes monitoring and, if warranted, engaging with attorneys to give notice to third parties, negotiate or litigate.

While a counterfeiter or thief may undertake such theft of a mark within any of these categories, selecting marks in categories 3, 4 or 5 makes it harder for others to infringe your mark and thereby deters at least rational actors. It also would be hard for an infringer to present evidence that a newly coined word is used unintentionally. Under an investment theme, selecting a fanciful trademark reduces lifetime costs and risks.

In the end, Booking.com® may very well be the next Apple®, but placing and continuing that bet from selection to potential enforcement depends upon your mindset and investment theme.

Bring in Trademark Attorneys Early. Consider whether to do a trademark availability search, called a *clearance search*, to assess whether another company is already using the same or similar mark you are considering for your goods or services. These are all areas to explore fully with trademark attorneys at the table.

While the marks of iconic brands readily come to mind, companies have a long list of business investments to make on their road to global domination, as well as when they arrive. Be forewarned: where you achieve success, policing and enforcement is de rigueur, and fast action against wrongdoers may be necessary. Failure to do so can even cause you to lose your trademarks (as detailed in the following Risks section).

You as a Consumer and Your Customer Delight. Finally, let's finish this area of trademark selection by emphasizing the role of creativity. Trademarks can offer surprises, and sometimes pleasant ones. Trademarks, after all, involve marketing and branding, and a current focus of marketing is "customer delight."

Why should your customers have all the fun? While these legal areas require rigorous analysis, they also allow for equally robust creativity in visual brand elements intended to make your vision accessible to the market (and ideally clearer to you). In selecting your trademark, you will not only explore your style and level of creativity, but you may even randomly spark a pleasant surprise. While undertaking the selection exercise, let's also expect and accept some delight as trademarks owners.

Returning with a smile to my startup, I had this experience. My unexpected delight in choosing my corporate name was the fact that it started with an "A." I know; it doesn't sound like much. The kismet moment did not even involve trademark law. Rather, the name gave me market presence. "A" as the first letter of "Article" was the epiphany! Why? "A" placed my startup at the top of alphabetical lists. Fast forward to one of the highlights for my startup life in winning the 2009 Business Insider® Startup of the Year competition (with the then-startup Expensify® losing to me as the second-place recipient). The event was based on a Shark Tank® format where I appeared for my pitch at the top of the order. As a result, a name starting with an "A" became one of my favorite recommendations for clients. It also applies to this #ip2ip book reference with the "#" mark being listed ahead of the alphabet in many hierarchies.

The Investment Theme Has the Last Word. We have reached a point where we have procured trademark rights and we may even find delight in our selection and its effects. While I want to leave you with a sense of wonder about creativity in trademarks, remember first and foremost the underlying lifetime investment theme. Invest wisely.

THE TRADEMARK WORD GAME

Trademarks, and their legal and statutory standards, also cover service marks and trade dress.

A *service mark* is a name, logo, symbol, word, phrase or design placed on a service that identifies the service provider. "Service mark" has the same legal meaning as "trademark" except that trademarks cover products while service marks cover services.[219]

Trade dress is the way a product, its packaging, advertising or interior design looks, which is distinctive and design based, rather than functional.[220] Two leading trade dress concepts are distinctiveness and functionality. Trade dress must be distinctive to be protectable—in that same source-identifying manner as a strong trademark—and trade dress must be a designer's choice and cannot be dictated by function.

Trade dress in packaging can be inherently distinctive based on a similar assessment as other trademarks in categories 3, 4 and 5. Product designs, by contrast, are not afforded the opportunity for inherent distinctiveness. Instead, the owner must prove "acquired distinctiveness" through secondary meaning established over time—akin to a category 2. *Descriptive* trademark.

Recall that consumer perception drives secondary meaning, with evidence grounded in the subjective response of consumers. For example, one easy tip for bolstering trade dress protectability and generating evidence of consumer perception is to tout the design of a product even more than its function. This "look for [the genuine design]" advertising can help reinforce brand awareness in consumers, leading to acquired distinctiveness.[221]

Functionality is a limitation on trade dress rights. If the trade dress is "functional"—driven by cost or ease of manufacturing or use—then the trade dress cannot be protected, even with acquired distinctiveness. Trade dress law imposes the functionality restriction to prevent ownership of features that are necessary for the functionality in manufacturing or use of similar products, and therefore the ability to keep competitors from using them.

Unfair competition and false advertising are causes of action in litigation that generally go hand in hand with trademark protection, prohibiting passing off (or presenting one's goods as those of another) and most forms of false advertising. Trademark cases generally include these causes of action. The common theme is consumer protection, leading to a more vibrant and robust marketplace—all of it strengthening trademark rights.

The federal Lanham Act provides for parallel enforcement rights of unregistered trademarks and false advertising—all under the power of the Lanham Act, but with none of the presumptions that accompany a federal registration. So if a competitor is copying design elements other than your registered trademarks, or a competitor is making untrue statements about its own or your products or services, the Lanham Act provides remedies and relief.

THE DESIGN PATENT LAWYERLY LITANY AND HOW-TOS
THE DESIGN OF DESIGN PATENTS

Design patents are a part of the IP spectrum protecting the "visual identity" of products and services. They generally involve the look and feel or the way an article looks, embracing the shape, ornamentation, texture or color of an article or a portion of the article on which the feature is placed.

Protection by design patents also covers visuals of functional products such as tools and designs used in the digital world, including design features of computer graphic user interface (GUIs) or portions of them. Formally, the exclusive right for this asset prevents others from copying a "new, original, and ornamental design" for an "article of manufacture."[222]

These patents historically have been the lesser-known of higher-profile utility patents. Remember: utility patents protect function or structure, including the way an invention works or how it is used, versus the ornamental features protected by design patents. Design patents fall under the same timing requirements as for utility patents. They apply in the US to designs that have been in public use for under one year.

Design Patents Validity Challenge. In the same way that utility patents are alleged to be invalid in court, challengers to design patents assert invalidity. A recent Federal Circuit case tested a historic standard for applying prior art in an invalidity challenge based on United States Supreme Court precedent. The long-standing approach identifies a primary prior art reference with characteristics which are basically the same as the visual impression of the claimed design as a whole. The proposal instead aggregates features from multiple prior art references (in a manner similar to utility patents). The Federal Circuit declined to avoid cherry picking of prior art references and therefore maintained the long-standing approach, but kept the door open for follow-on challenges.[223]

Apple's Breakthrough Success with Design Patents. Steve Jobs elevated these patents to prominence in the Apple® iPhone® design patent portfolio. The story begins with the 2007 launch of Apple's first-generation iPhone. For some stories, a picture is worth a thousand (or million) words. Figures 11 and 12 show a key Apple design patent that played a starring role.

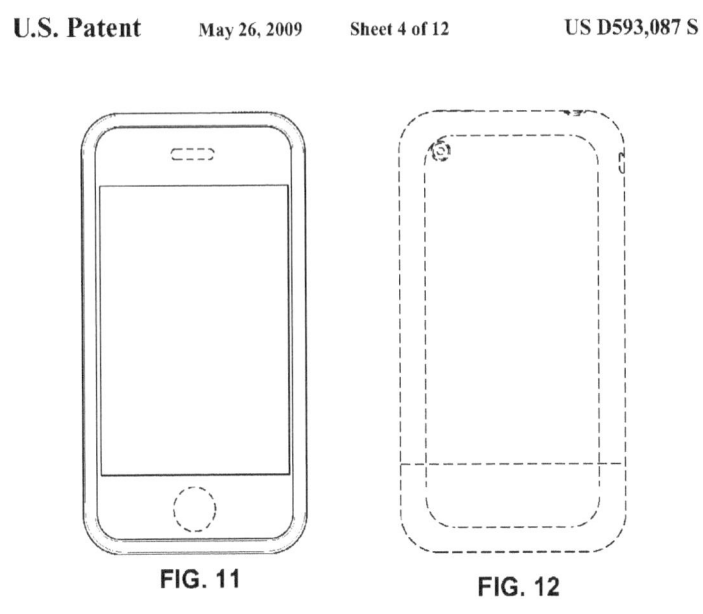

U.S. Patent   May 26, 2009   Sheet 4 of 12   US D593,087 S

FIG. 11

FIG. 12

US Des. Pat, No. D593,087 Asserted by Apple® in a 2011 US litigation, Figures 11 and 12[224]

The illustrations above are from Apple's US Design Pat. No. D593,087 (the D'087 patent) asserted against Samsung® in a 2011 patent litigation. Here's the litigation summary: the suit was part of a global circular firing squad of mobile device litigation known as the "smartphone wars," including multiple utility and design patents. Ultimately, after trips up and down appellate courts, Apple won $539 million for the design patents and $5 million for the utility patents—quite a difference in award quantities! It should be noted that the parties eventually settled the long-running suit."[225] The design patent proved more valuable because the design is presumed to be material to every consumer purchasing decision. In contrast, patentable features are not presumed to be as universally material to a consumer's purchasing decision.

Recall that a utility patent has multiple claims, each presenting a written description of a function with a differing scope (or an embodiment). In contrast, a design patent consists of a single inventive claim based on figures as various embodiments of one ornamental design. The figures set out the design within the context of the article on which it is placed. The visual appearance needs to be unique, not an ordinary adornment, and the design aspects of the article must dominate over its functional aspects. The PTO provides this definition of design:

> A design for surface ornamental is inseparable from the article to which it is applied and cannot exist alone. It must be a definite pattern of surface ornamentation, applied to an article of manufacture.[226]

The figures in design patents include solid and broken (or dotted) lines. The solid lines show the claimed invention, enabling the inventor to control the claimed design. In contrast, the dotted lines show the background or the look of the remaining article. The background is not part of the claim embodiment shown in the figure. Broken lines are used to avoid functionality, prior art and other obstacles to design patenting.

Now that we have set the stage, we can continue the Apple story by returning to Apple's D'087 patent, covering the iPhone's rectangular front face with rounded corners and a raised rim (or bezel). The Figure 12 embodiment excludes as background the screen, based on presenting it in broken lines. The Figure

11 embodiment similarly excludes as background the home button.[227] The D'087 patent was among multiple design and utility patents found to be infringed.

Apple's Impact on Design Patent Damages. Design patent infringement is determined based on whether the patented and accused designs are substantially the same, from the view of an *ordinary observer* giving such attention as a consumer generally would.

Design patent owners can seek damages under the general patent statute under Section 284 of *lost profits* or *reasonable royalties*.[228] However, they also have a remedy under an additional statute, which is unavailable for utility patent owners. Section 289 provides damages based on the *total profits* of the object on which the infringing design is applied.[229] This flexibility to obtain damages on the entire infringing device, not just a proportion for a copied feature, recognizes the importance of design in consumer purchasing decisions.

The lasting impact of Apple's design patent story is the potential of total profits as an advantage relative to utility patents, and a reason to elevate design patents within a thoughtful IP strategy. While design and utility types of patents share many provisions, the differences afford opportunities to consider protection using both.

Top-10 Takeaway 7

#ip2ip-7: Consider design patents for the visual look and feel of key commercial design features when you assess utility patents.

A design patent's estimated cost is less than $4,000 over 21.3 months, significantly cheaper than utility patents, and the likelihood of being granted a design patent is higher than a utility. The timing when a US patent is granted is comparable for both rights, at 21.3 and 25.9 months on average for design and utility, respectively.[230] However, an accelerated examination process targeting twelve months is available only for utility applications.

Design Patents for GUIs. Patents for designs have become more important for computer inventions because of the restrictions under Section 101 for utility grants. Design patents are available to protect GUIs and their features, such as icons and images.[231] However, like trade dress registration, the designs themselves still must be nonfunctional, even if the design is otherwise applied to useful articles.

Design Patent Protection against Counterfeits. Design patents can also combat unauthorized sales, counterfeits and knockoffs. They are especially useful in catching online infringement and restricting imports into the US.[232]

DESIGN PATENTS AND TRADE DRESS

Design Your Approach to Visual Identity IP Assets. After identifying and prioritizing the crown jewel visual identity of your company and its offerings, you are ready to consider the IP spectrum of trademarks (including trade dress), copyrights and design patents to protect brand elements. Patents for designs are commonly associated with trade dress, so that comparing them is instructive.

One difference is the test for infringement. Design patents use an objective standard of an ordinary observer giving such attention as a consumer generally would. Recall, in contrast, the subjective standard for trademark infringement of consumer perception. This generally makes it easier and less expensive to prove infringement of a design patent versus trade dress.

On the other hand, cost is another difference between design patents and trade dress, with an estimated $4,000 for patents for designs exceeding an estimated $1,250 for trademarks for a single-class federal trademark application with no Office Action, although trade dress applications prompt additional costs in proving acquired distinctiveness.[233] For some brand elements, optimal protection may start with these patents. In one example, they can provide secondary meaning to pave the way for trademark registration.

The Combination of Trademarks and Design Patents (and Even Copyrights). The synergies of these IP rights are part of an advanced strategy. Business strategy meetings focused on crown jewel commercial innovations or features provide touch points for professionals to assess and optimize the value of IP asset combinations and mutual reinforcement.

ANALYSIS

The process for protecting trademark rights varies. Some entrepreneurs will decide to pursue full trademark registrations for each potential mark, logo and design (plus design patents) at launch, but others may choose to pursue trademark registrations over time. There are pros and cons to each strategy.

Several customary considerations are:

1. *Domain names registrations.* Domain names are easy to register and ordinarily do not require attorney involvement, so registering a domain name should be your first move as an entrepreneur. Work with your website designers to ensure you acquire every domain needed and to ensure proper optimization of the names. Costs for domain name registrations can be under $10.

2. *Corporate identity reservations.* A good trademark might also be a formal corporate name as part of an overall strategy. Each state's corporate registries can be searched for name availability. Corporate name reservations vary in cost from state to state, but as part of the expense of incorporating itself, are not meaningfully additive.

3. *"Tradename" or d/b/a required state filings for doing business under an assumed name.* Most states require filing a tradename registration for a business operating under anything other than its official corporate name so that the public knows an entity behind any d/b/as in commerce. States usually do not examine tradename registrations, resulting in multiple registrations for the same or similar d/b/as. A pitfall is mistaking a tradename registration for a trademark registration, but they are different. A tradename registration is ministerial, but a trademark registration grants enforceable rights to stop others.

4. *State trademark application considerations.* Each state has a "state trademark registration" process. These are usually similar to the federal process, requiring an application and use of a mark in commerce in a state. State trademark regis-

trations are less expensive and quicker to issue than a federal trademark.

5. *Searching federal trademark applications for (a) wordmarks, (b) logos, (c) design and (d) other "devices."* Search for trademarks as part of selecting a mark. Formal attorney or service provider searches can extend beyond earlier registrations to common law uses, foreign uses and domain names, as well as provide formal opinions or only recommendations. Generally, basic costs for searching registrations can be under $1,000; add-on costs may apply, depending on the search landscape.

6. *Advertising and specimen creation.* All marketing and advertising materials should showcase trademarks, including the encircled ® for federally registered marks, to enable requesting money damages in litigation against an infringer.

RISKS

Risks abound in trademark law. Enforcement of trademarks is ultimately based on consumer perception, making it impossible for a mark owner to fully control its trademark destiny. Design patents with enforcement based on objective standards afford more control. The greatest risk is delay in addressing infringement.

Trademark Enforcement. Costs and processes to enforce a trademark vary widely depending on the mark and the market. The best companies have protocols for finding, investigating and terminating infringing uses. Others wait until the confusion is identified and expressed. The earlier you spot infringing uses, the easier they are to stop.

Cease-and-desist letters from counsel can cost under $1,500 and sometimes will work to end infringement without further action. Sometimes, a letter leads to negotiations and a written settlement, potentially adding costs. If litigation is needed, the costs to file and serve a trademark complaint and move for an injunction can exceed $10,000. Thus, early action to stop infringement before it is entrenched is best.

Additional trademark risks include these: "innocent" infringement, domain names and fair use, policing, abandonment and design patent termination.

"Innocent" infringement. Another primary risk is innocent infringement. Trademarks are enforced from the point of view of the consumer. "Innocent" adoption of a new mark can still invite a lawsuit and an injunction. This is a risk for both the owner and infringer, with the owner's thoughtful mark selection, registration and consistent showcasing of its marks theoretically reducing its occurrence. Some acts of innocent trademark infringement can be insured.

The otherwise innocent infringer reduces risk by searching, noting, however, that results might not reveal common law uses, trade dress rights or a geographic range of use by a senior user. All parties reduce risk by selecting marks in categories 4 or 5 as the least likely to overlap with the creative decisions of others.

Domain names and fair use. Trademarks require use, either actual use or a bona fide intent to use, to apply for registration (which will not issue until actual use is confirmed). By contrast, domain names use the "land rush" system where use is not required to obtain most top-level domains (e.g., .com, .net, .org, .us).

The domain name system does, however, have a global uniform dispute resolution policy (UDRP) that applies to any domain registration, requiring the domain owner to participate in disputes.

Policing. Erosion of goodwill can occur with failures to actively police against infringers. Trademark strength depends on that goodwill, and it is not entirely under the trademark owner's control. The paradox of success requires iconic trademarks to increase monitoring and enforcement to limit free riding as well as confusion. Even trademark licensing can risk goodwill erosion, requiring attention when licensing to maintain brand identity and adherence to quality control measures.

Abandonment. If a trademark is no longer in commercial use with no intent to revive it, the mark is abandoned and free to be adopted by others, with a default that any mark no longer in use for three years is presumed abandoned. Just as speculators attempt to leverage expiring domain names, they speculate on expiring trademarks.

Design Patent Termination. Design patent termination has the potential to impact traditional trade dress rights. Although the duration of trade secrets and trademarks can be infinite, patents and copyrights are limited in time by definition. So far, the law has seemed to allow the design of an expired patent to be enforced (and registered) as a trademark. However, legal scholars are not in agreement that this should be allowed.

Summary

Trademarks and patentable designs are fittingly the end of the substantive IP Chapters 2 through 7, aligned with the finishing brand touches for a company and its offerings. The face and energy of these assets are borne in the creative minds of your innovators and support the mutually reinforcing characteristic of visual identity IP rights.

Their selection is a critical business strategy to protect all that the consumer can see about the company and bolster their loyalty, which in turn uplifts your corporate brand. Trademarks and design patents enlist your customers to make your mark and succeed by design.

PART II

OBJECTIVE

CHAPTER 8

IP HONOR

HONOR THE INDIVIDUAL

ACTions

8.1 **Launch IP Honor to recognize inventors and creators.** *Top-10 Takeaway.*
8.2 Elevate IP Honorees with career opportunities to inspire tomorrow's inventors and creators.
8.3 Invest in your employees' potential through IP education and encouraging innovation from underrepresented groups.

While intellectual property is a product of the mind for protection of business assets, this chapter focuses on the heart of IP—inventors and creators. Those already in your ranks and those who can be inspired to join you in the future, based on the dream of invention reflecting our infinite potential.

What can you do as a company to cultivate and honor the contributions of originators of innovation? In the coming pages, three key steps are explored for launching and implementing IP Honor as a strategy to recognize inventors and creators and to elevate IP Honorees with new career paths.

I shouldn't play favorites, but I'm going to anyway. You're reading my most treasured #ip2ip chapter for a few reasons.

Firstly, IP Honor can transform an organization's culture and its bottom line. Writing that sentence brings me great joy. I earned a law degree thirty years ago. Back then, I never imagined that IP could serve as a catalyst of this magnitude.

This brings me to the second reason. The genesis of IP Honor came from my 2008 startup AOP to research patented technology, explored earlier in Chapter 2: Patents. The heart of my startup was 32,000 researchers in 170 countries, with my greeting for our researchers being, "I am honored to work with you."

The majority of them had no law background. Yet AOP researchers still earned more than $6 million in rewards on over five hundred patent studies and incentive programs during my tenure. The lessons I learned while growing our pioneering global community—the largest IP research community in the world when it was acquired in 2015—can also inspire the IP Honor strategy in your organization.

Inspiration in Action

My Inspiration for IP Honor Came from My Startup Journey

The company Article One Partners asked the public to contribute to valuing the quality of patents. One of the highlights was our discovery that anyone with an interest in technology had the ability to learn about patents and, in some cases, become IP professionals and even inventors and creators based on the education they received on our platform.

We also realized that we could direct projects to selected communities. For example, we identified US veterans based on members potentially being injured and therefore in some cases limited in performing physical labor but not online research. We hoped to inspire those with an interest to learn a new skill or career. We were thrilled that several who responded to the project did just that, with our official winner of one project continuing his career as a patent professional to this day. Another approached me years later at a United States Patent and Trademark Office event to inform me that he was a PTO Examiner, selecting the job path based on these defined AOP community projects.

We also have former researchers who went on to participate in the patent system as inventors and founders of startups. This list included a successful CEO who told me his story years after my leadership of AOP, when he asked me to assist in valuing his IP. He explained that his company pursued patents because of his history of researching them at AOP and being inspired to found his company as a result.

These are among the many outreaches and stories that I still learn about years later, derived from personal connections made with people globally for whom AOP funded education, health care and family needs. One of my most treasured occurred when a female researcher from the Southern US asked to speak with me. Her description of AOP was so poised and inspirational, I was unable to capture the magic of it in my notes. Fortunately, this remarkable woman sent me a follow-up email, providing this:

> Patent invention ideas have made our nation...as Americans, one of the most industrious and wealthiest nations on earth. Different and new innovations have provided a great sense of ease, comfort, and better quality of living in our society as consumers and as citizens which have made us a very strong economic nation... Thank you for having me on board as one of your most valued Article One Partners' researchers, and I do not take this position lightly. I am really well pleased with the patience, courtesy, and professionalism your firm has given me, and will always be honored to work with such a firm.

More than a decade after the founding of AOP, the platform still inspires its community. Members report that self-selecting the opportunities impacts lives, gives individuals purpose and prompts value and inspiration simply by taking a leap of faith and responding to opportunities.

I could not be more grateful and honored to have played a role in their growth, professionally and personally. Similarly, the gift at AOP of serving others by affording them meritorious work remains the highlight of my career.

Lastly, this subject allows me to brainstorm new ideas alongside you—that is, as long as we agree to suspend the usual rules of engagement. We cannot be in the same space as the traditional approach of counting patents and IP assets.

So instead, I am placing IP Honor ideas on today's paper. From there, you will read them, maybe in the same year and time zone that I typed them. Or perhaps it will be next year or the year after, in a language about inspiration that is not yet developed, and even in a locale I aspire to visit. In that case, may these IP Honor ideas transcend time and place. May you build upon the IP Honor steps set forth here, customizing them for your organization, and realize previously unimaginable employee and business growth.

STEP 1: LAUNCH IP HONOR TO RECOGNIZE INVENTORS AND CREATORS

How can your company express to inventors and creators that you are honored to work with them? Acknowledge their achievements by awarding the IP Honor title and showcasing the community, including traditional approaches such as patent office plaques, compensation and other incentive programs. However, this goes beyond patent basics to include inventors and creators across the IP spectrum for commercial inventions, trade secrets, visual identity IP assets and open source. This includes those developing products and services and reimagining the customer experience, and it even encompasses how you present your innovators both inside your company and to the market.

For example, when writing an article about the accomplishment and journey of an inventor, add an insert about the writer of the article. For an investor deck which traditionally lists a patent count, add the inventors' names, as well as the names of innovators for additional IP assets and open source. In addition to the IP Honor title, a professional listing or degree reflecting an innovator status can be added to the inventor's formal signature. For example, a degree of $US_{\#}$ can represent the number ("#")

of US patents granted to the inventor.[234] In this way, IP Honor supports innovators to succeed along with the company brand.

With the advent of generative artificial intelligence (AI), this recognition is more important now than ever. While AI promises benefits for society, rational concerns are the replacement of people by AI and the data used to train AI systems representing third-party IP used without compensation. You can answer that concern by elevating the recognition of your innovators.

For AI-related innovations, US IP law is clear that AI cannot be an inventor. That honor is reserved for humans, and some degree of human involvement is needed for copyright. Enlightened companies will expand beyond the race to value AI technology to valuing people.

Top-10 Takeaway 8

#ip2ip-8: Launch IP Honor to recognize inventors and creators.

Inventors on granted patents are easiest to recognize based on the rigorous assessment of patent applications equivalent to a professional degree, the subject being protecting your company's innovations. Set up inventors for patent success as part of the IP Honor program.

However, the US Patent Office grants only 57 percent of patent applications, leaving 43 percent rejected. Computer-implemented technologies are a particularly difficult subject matter to be granted as patents given the unevenness of the law.

As inventors participate in the patenting, awareness and education about these limitations are essential, as is assessing subject matter to select those inventions with the greatest chance of success. IP Honor should also promote the value of innovations even where a patent is not pursued or the PTO does not grant the patent. The PTO decision should not limit the company's high regard for its innovations and their source in its employees.

Trade secrets, copyrights and trademarks need not identify the originators in formal registrations for procuring government rights. Similarly, open-source contributions are based on corporate licenses, which generally name the corporate owner as the source of the innovations. As part of the process recommended in #ip2ip of formal registration for copyright (including covering trade secrets) and trademarks, the individual contributors can be identified internally. This same approach can be applied to open source. With the recordation of individuals comes the opportunity to then formalize recognition in a similar manner as for patent inventors. IP Honor can develop programs specifically to showcase these inventors and creators in high-profile ways, since trade secrets, copyrights and trademarks have the potential to contribute mightily to a company's innovations, brand and revenues.

Insider Lawball

Identifying the Originators of IP Assets and Open Source

One hurdle the IP Honor strategy will encounter is establishing policies and processes for identifying and celebrating the originators of IP assets and open source.

Patent Inventors. It is easiest to start with patents, as patent applications must include the names of the inventors as part of the patent process. The PTO records the company name and the inventor or group of inventors on patents, with inventors commonly assigning their patent rights to their company under their employment agreements. However, the requirement to assign does not diminish the inventors as the sources of inventions. Where a patent is granted based on the arduous US Patent Office examination process, a further level of recognition is warranted.

Inventors and Creators of Copyrights, Trademarks, Trade Secrets and Open Source. Additional IP assets, namely trade secrets, copyrights and trademarks, are not as easy to associate with individuals. This is because even where the owner chooses to register these rights, the United States Copyright Office (USCO, for copyrights and trade secrets) and US Patent and Trademark Office (for patents and trademarks) do not require creators or inventors to be named on applications filed on behalf of companies where registration is sought. Instead, that recognition is for a company as the owner of the subject matter (with an option in copyright registration to name the author). Since open source is founded on license agreements listing IP assets for source code, the same intention can be applied to credit those innovators who contribute the assets.

As a result, IP Honor must establish ways to capture the inventors and creators so that they may be formally associated with their IP assets and recognized for their achievements. Start with traditional recordation approaches from your HR department. IP Honor leaders then can apply their creativity to fully recognize and celebrate these innovators along with inventors on granted patents.

Identifying the optimal recognition of inventors and creators is not a simple task. Rather, it is a big problem to solve, making IP Honor tremendously valuable to your company, not only as an innovation culture changemaker but potentially attracting and retaining the brightest minds in inventors and creators. These employees, in turn, contribute to your revenue as well as to your company's rank and reputation in the IP and open-source ecosystems.

Simply put, when the *Honor the Individual* tenet is implemented within the inspiration of a business-aligned IP framework, employees are inspired to be IP stakeholders, creative decision-making flourishes and a company and its people soar.

STEP 2: ELEVATE IP HONOREES WITH CAREER OPPORTUNITIES TO INSPIRE TOMORROW'S INVENTORS AND CREATORS

The IP Honor community can empower the company to develop and deploy human-centered IP solutions at scale—as stewards of innovation and representing opportunity for all employees to tap their creative potential. Who better to lead efforts to inspire other inventors and creators than those who have experienced the act of inventing and creating and can be mentors to others?

Career opportunities can be launched for IP Honorees to formally build the inventors and creators of tomorrow. Even those who have not been involved in IP filings can learn about how IP protects innovation and provides unique opportunities for them and those they manage, as well as for the company. Creating personalized touch points, such as during career planning and advancement activities, and performance appraisals encourages employees to leverage those opportunities and receive coaching about how to do so. A dashboard can be designed to track IP Honor metrics such as first-time inventors and creators for patents and additional IP assets and open source. Over time, the impact of IP Honor to grow new innovators can be reflected in the dashboard.

The chief intellectual property officer (CIPO) is the traditional C-suite position responsible for the protection and performance of IP assets. IP Honor leaders may report to the CIPO, yet their purpose is decidedly innovator centric and committed to service and forging connections as their primary and recognized responsibility. They are virtuosos at discovering people's innovation passions and then helping them develop inventions and creations to benefit themselves and the company.

Given my experience with AOP, IP, startups and advising corporations, I have seen firsthand that IP fluency can be achieved through robust training and mentoring—by being the biggest fan of today's inventors and creators, and inspiring those of the future. You can read more about the biggest fan concept in the Conclusion: A Smile Goes a Mile.

STEP 3: INVEST IN YOUR EMPLOYEES' POTENTIAL THROUGH IP EDUCATION AND ENCOURAGING INNOVATION FROM UNDERREPRESENTED GROUPS

Most of your employees don't call themselves inventors or creators, and few likely consider themselves to be fluent in IP principles. IP Honor can change that through engaging curricula, intended to make all your employees aware of IP and the opportunities it affords.

Suggestions to access untapped IP potential: Employ best-in-class USPTO programs or partner with other top-tier institutions to craft IP courses. Enlist IP Honorees to serve in teaching or mentoring roles as their interest guides them. Teaching is the path to mastery of a subject. An IP Honor certification can be earned upon completion. It becomes a compelling innovation culture as the percentage of IP-certified employees builds.

For those in your ranks who want reskilling and upskilling, develop an advanced IP program that includes instructor-led courses and on-the-job training. Recruit visiting IP scholars to teach or conduct research for more immersive IP education. Employees can volunteer, apply or be nominated to participate. To earn this advanced IP Honor certification, participants can propose and implement a new IP initiative for the company. These employees could be your next IP Honor leaders.

Another intriguing approach is to host "Walk-In with Ideas, Walk-Out with Filed IP" sprint events. The aim is for employees to see their innovations come alive within a few hours rather than be saddled with what can be an intimidating and lengthy undertaking. IP Honor leaders can oversee the sprint events and preparation efforts, exalting the employee innovators while shepherding an efficient and productive initiative that benefits your company.

During the sprints, employees walk in and are partnered with the IP professionals to transform innovations into IP filings, such as provisional patent applications, copyright and trademark applications or guidance to pursue open source. The event culminates with a celebration of the accomplishments of each inventor and creator. From there, the IP professionals can respond to PTO correspondence in the months and years ahead, guiding the employees to the finish line of securing IP rights.

Inspiration for underrepresented groups. The most thrilling aspect of IP is that the legal rights represented by IP are open to anyone in the world with great ideas or creations. A culture founded upon broad thinking fosters this potential.

Based on Congressional efforts to improve inventorship among historic underrepresented groups, the PTO published a 2022 report focusing initially on women, with public data enabling analysis more readily than for other groups.[235] It found that women make up 13 percent of all inventor-patentees, which is significantly lower than other benchmarks of women's education and employment as scientists and engineers.[236]

How can IP Honor contribute to improving opportunities across society? Encouragement begins with data at your own company (provided that it is made available strictly on a voluntary basis and as part of your company's privacy policies). In addition to gender, race and military or veteran status, it is typical for corporate people reports to feature the following categories: people with disabilities, neurodiverse talent, ethnicity, LGBTQ+, education level and schools attended, number of years at your firm, divisions and regions represented, languages spoken and management levels.

The data insights can help IP Honor leaders determine how to encourage innovation from underrepresented groups. Solutions can include the IP Honor community as part of human resource approaches to welcome broad communities to the IP learning programs. IP Honorees from underrepresented people can then contribute to the diversity of innovators in your company—such as in senior management roles, the C-suite in an existing chief of intellectual property role, and even board of director representation.

A multifaceted approach to celebrating your inventors and creators can include inspiring new ones across the organization. Attention paid to underrepresented people who have less access to role models within their communities (based on the available statistics of historic lower numbers of inventors) will establish your organization as an incubator of IP talent and innovation.

Summary

IP Honor supports the practice of truly valuing people, listening deeply, being vulnerable, committing to learning about each other's lived experiences, nurturing a culture where all are comfortable addressing differences and ultimately trusting and supporting one another. A trusting environment is one where ideas flow freely, accelerating innovation and offering opportunities.

My excitement and good wishes for you on your IP Honor journey! I look forward to hearing how your stewards of innovation inspire colleagues to explore their abilities and potential to contribute—to your company, to innovation and to humankind.

PART III

SYSTEMS

CHAPTER 9

COST

$60 AND A DREAM

ACTions

9.1 **Use financial planning and budgets for IP strategy.** *Top-10 Takeaway.*
9.2 Set and meet IP procurement budgets.
9.3 Consider an iterative approach to patent applications to shift fees into the future and to conserve funding today.

BASIC FINANCIAL PLANNING AND BUDGETS ARE BASIC TO INTELLECTUAL PROPERTY TOO

Funding as part of business planning is driven by budgets. The same budget approaches can also support quantitative analytics about costs to file and maintain US patents and other forms of intellectual property. We begin by looking at traditional bottom-up and top-down budgeting approaches using publicly available financial data about IP.

Top-10 Takeaway 9

#ip2ip-9: Use financial planning and budgets for IP strategy.

Bottom-Up and Top-Down Budgets. Bottom-up budgets are based on publicly available data about IP procurement costs accumulating for the number of IP assets sought. We'll start with patents as the highest cost asset and then expand to additional IP, with comparatively lower costs.

The top-down approach will draw upon available data about corporate IP budgets. However, similar to a dearth of guidance on IP strategy, top-down budget data is limited.

Regardless of available data, budgets are subservient to available funding. For example, some startups have no budget for IP. The US Patent and Trademark Office provides tremendous free resources to get started on procuring patents with limited funds, hence this chapter's title, "$60 and a Dream."

We will touch on global filings for patents to provide a baseline for general costs, with global patent programs beyond the scope of this book.

BOTTOM-UP IP BUDGETS
BOTTOM-UP BUDGETS ARE BASED ON THE NUMBER OF IP ASSETS TO PURSUE

Cost estimates for procuring US IP assets are a gating item to budgeting.

Patent Applications Costs Can Be Lower than Publicly Reported. A commonly quoted statistic for "the cost of obtaining a [US] patent" is presented by law firms and in industry news. It is a range "from $5,000 to $20,000" including filing your patent applications (called *preparation*) and engaging with the USPTO for the Office's assessment of whether your invention is *patentable* and therefore warrants granting a patent (called *examination* or *prosecution*).[237] The minimum $5,000 outlay may cause an inventor to conclude that she cannot afford a patent filing.

COSTS FOR PROVISIONAL PATENT APPLICATIONS

$60 (Not $5,000) is the Minimum Price of Entry. The $5,000 figure omits an opportunity to get started in patents for $60, as the PTO fee for a *provisional* or preliminary patent application.[238] Importantly however, it does not include costs for the support of a professional in preparing the application.

The Cost of Obtaining a Patent is Iterative Over Two to Three Years. Significant additional costs are needed to receive a patent, including professional and PTO fees to prepare a follow-on *utility* patent application and to advocate before the Office. This accounts for the range of $5,000 to $20,000. However, the additional costs are spread out over two to three years or longer.[239] Once a patent is granted, there are fees to maintain it. However, provisional applications represent the optimism of patents in supporting inventors to realize their dreams.

$60 Reflects USPTO Support for New or Qualified Inventors. In its mission to help individuals and entities become part of the US patent system, the Office reduces fees based on new or qualified inventors under *small* or *micro entity* status of inventors.

Insider Lawball

**The US Patent and Trademark Office Service to the Public:
The $60 and a Dream Story**

The US patent system represents that an individual with limited funds can seek patent protection. It is an honor to pay tribute to this US institution for the optimism and opportunities it provides. These values are best represented by the $60 opportunity.

I was fortunate to qualify for this program in my early entrepreneurial years (with the added good fortune to be a patent attorney able to learn my profession by writing applications for my own inventions and continuing to help clients). My first patent application was a provisional filed at reduced rates.[240]

I put my entire heart and soul into that document. It was my first book—my story of technology. This is my second. The cost savings enabled me to invest funds in other startup needs. You can find more about my personal startup journey for Article One Partners (AOP) in Chapter 2: Patents and the Conclusion.

The same get-started fee is available for anyone globally who meets the USPTO criteria to be a *micro* or *small entity*, including individuals and entities with caps on inventor's income, the number of employees and patents filed.[241] A *micro entity* receives the highest discount and includes individuals, groups, nonprofits and universities which also qualify as a small entity. *Small entity* status applies to owners or inventors employed by a company which has up to five hundred employees and is not the subject of a transaction with an entity falling outside of the criteria. The $60 amount represents the largest fee reduction, resulting from an 80 percent overall reduction of all PTO fees. Small entities receive 60 percent off Office fees, or $120 for a provisional application.

This reduction continues throughout the patent life cycle, including utility application filing, processing and maintenance fees for granted patents. For example, in contrast to micro or small entities, the large entity filing fee for a provisional patent application is $300, and for a utility patent application, the filing fees are micro/small/large at $455/$910/$1,820.[242]

The history of our patent system rests on a belief that inventors should be able to pen written descriptions of their inventions for review by the Office (or appear pro se, without representation of a professional attorney or agent). The original intention and ongoing endorsement of individuals working independently continues with the PTO facilitating inventor free resources.[243] The reduced fee programs and resources endorse the entrepreneurial spirit and ingenuity which differentiates and highlights the US patent system as the source of the American dream, not only for US citizens but for the world.

With $60 as the Minimum Price of Entry, Patents Require Additional Investment and Advisedly, Patent Professionals. The $60 provisional does not start the PTO's formal consideration of whether to grant a patent. The purpose of a provisional application is merely to provide a placeholder for the filing date of the technology description presented in the application.

The provisional triggers a requirement to file a follow-on *utility* or formal application within one year. The provisional application must fully disclose the invention and satisfy the statutory terms required for the follow-on utility application. Importantly, the provisional must support claims which are eventually written and presented in the utility application. Failure to meet these requirements will cause the later utility application to fall short of relying on the provisional and, therefore, retaining the earlier provisional filing date.

With this understood, if the difference between not getting started in patents is a provisional or no filing, then $60 and a dream is the notion of filing a provisional patent application or forgoing access to US patents.

Another limitation of this $60 funding is that it does not account for hiring a professional to assist in writing the application. Where limited funding is available, I strongly advise working with a professional to, minimally, prepare exemplary claims and figures. You benefit by directing funds and your time to the patent's ultimate value—the claims section. When preparing provisionals, I commonly would rough out claims with clients to identify the invention's key elements and brainstorm claim elements, considering how competitors may try to *design around* them and *forward invent*, as described in Chapter 2: Patents. As a result, the commercial value can be enhanced beyond merely legal to business strategy and provide a default benefit of additional commercial features whether or not a patent is not granted.

Where the provisional is filed without professional input, then proceed to work with a professional as funds allow rather than waiting for the one-year deadline to file the utility. One also can file multiple provisionals for the utility application to rely on. Adding professionally prepared claims as early as possible, even in follow-on provisionals, optimizes quality.

Beyond the $60 Provisional Filing Fee, What Does a US Patent Cost? The activities and costs to obtain a patent come down to three key phases: *preparation* or filing, *prosecution* or examination at the PTO, and *post-grant maintenance*. The *preparation* phase involves preparing a utility application, which may be preceded by the provisional application described above at the $60 cost. The applicant has up to one year from the provisional submission to file the utility application.

With the utility, the *prosecution* phase includes a series of communications with the PTO, during which it determines whether to grant a patent. Prosecution generally includes two Office Actions from the PTO and two responses to advocate for the patent, accumulating to the high end of the $20,000 range. The Office reports on the time from a utility application filing to its final deposition of issued or rejected as 25.9 months.[244]

The Patent Grant. The US Patent and Trademark Office reports that 58.6 percent of US-originating applications through the PTO process are granted as patents.[245] Upon allowance, the owner pays fees to issue and maintain the patent over its twenty-year life cycle from the filing date.

An Invention but Not a Patent. The Office also rejects US-originating patent applications 41.4 percent of the time.[246] The outcome is dependent upon the complexity of the case, the prior art and the acuity of the applicant, patent professional and the PTO official who assesses the application (the Examiner). Consider the complexity of an improved clothes hanger versus an improvement to processing nuclear fission. Despite the greater complexity of nuclear fission, during prosecution, the PTO may locate extensive prior descriptions (recall, *prior art*) for the clothes hanger versus few for nuclear fusion. The clothes hanger therefore may result in greater cost than the nuclear fission subject. The second cost factor is based on the selection of patent professionals and their attendant fees as well as the administration of the formal docketing of patents.

Where the patent is rejected, the options are retrying, appealing or abandoning the case, with the selection between them requiring professional guidance.[247]

The Cost for Patenting. The cost to obtain a US patent can start with as little as $60 to between $17,500 and $20,000 over the 25.9-month process.[248] The table below presents estimated costs for a US patent grant with the following assumptions: the grant of an average complexity patent and timely communications with the PTO to avoid late filing fees. The table starts at year 0 with a provisional patent application and a utility application at year 1, completing the preparation (*Prep*) phase. The prosecution (*Pros and Examination*) phase is then presented, based on two rounds of PTO communications for the assessment process, called *Office Actions*. The patent grant prompts an issuance fee and additional maintenance fees at three, seven and eleven years.[249] The table also shows each USPTO fee level, including micro entity (80 percent) and small entity (60 percent) reductions from large entity fees.

Estimated Costs per US Patent[250]

Key:

- PTO = United States Patent and Trademark Office fees
- Atty = patent attorney, including costs to prepare formal drawings for the application
- Admin = administration or paralegal costs to assist attorneys with PTO filings, with an estimated flat fee of $150 per filing (a $60 provisional is assumed to be filed by the inventor without Admin support).

Year	Activity	Estimated Cost
	A patent attorney is presented for the patent professional; engaging a patent agent can reduce the costs shown.	**Common statistic: $5,000 to $20,000 to get a patent** PTO fees are based on an entity status of micro, small and large entities.
	Preparation Phase (Prep)	
0 (current)	Provisional application: the applicant can select the support for preparation of the application, from no cost preparation or an estimated $4,000 by a patent attorney (recommended)	$0–4,000 Preparation by applicant: $0 Preparation by a patent attorney: $4,000 Admin: $150
	PTO Provisional application filing fee	PTO: $60 / $120 / $300 (micro/small/large)
1	Utility application: preparation by patent attorney (recommended)	Atty: Minimum complexity: $8,000 Electrical/computer: $10,000–$14,000 Mechanical: $8,000–$12,000 *Average*: $10,000 Formal drawings: $500
	PTO Utility application filing fee, including filing and PTO search and examination fees	PTO: $455 / $910 / $1,820 (micro/small/large) Admin: $150

Key:

- PTO = United States Patent and Trademark Office fees
- Atty = patent attorney, including costs to prepare formal drawings for the application
- Admin = administration or paralegal costs to assist attorneys with PTO filings, with an estimated flat fee of $150 per filing (a $60 provisional is assumed to be filed by the inventor without Admin support).

Year	Activity	Estimated Cost
	A patent attorney is presented for the patent professional; engaging a patent agent can reduce the costs shown.	**Common statistic: $5,000 to $20,000 to get a patent** PTO fees are based on an entity status of micro, small and large entities.
Prosecution Phase (Pros and Examination)		
2	Response to Office Action (two on average)	Atty: • 1st Response: $3,000 • 2nd Response: $3,000 Admin: $150 for 2 filings (total $300)
25.9 months	PTO patent issuance fee	PTO: $240 / $480 / $1,200 (micro/small/large) Admin: $150
25.9 months	**Total for Issuance**	Based on an average utility application: $10,000 Utility (no provisional or a provisional filed without Atty/Admin): **$17,850 / $18,610 / $20,420** (micro/small/large) Utility based on a provisional filed by a patent attorney: **$22,005 / $22,760 / $24,570** (micro/small/large)

Key:

- PTO = United States Patent and Trademark Office fees
- Atty = patent attorney, including costs to prepare formal drawings for the application
- Admin = administration or paralegal costs to assist attorneys with PTO filings, with an estimated flat fee of $150 per filing (a $60 provisional is assumed to be filed by the inventor without Admin support).

Year	Activity	Estimated Cost
	A patent attorney is presented for the patent professional; engaging a patent agent can reduce the costs shown.	**Common statistic: $5,000 to $20,000 to get a patent** PTO fees are based on an entity status of micro, small and large entities.

Post Issuance

Where the USPTO grants a patent, it is issued when published and assigned a US Patent No.

	PTO Maintenance fees, with due dates from the issuance fee payment date.	Admin: $150 for three maintenance fee payments (total $450)
5	3–3.5 year	PTO: $400 / $800 / $2,000 (micro/small/large)
9	7–7.5 year	PTO: $752 / $1,504 / $3,760 (micro/small/large)
13	11–11.5 year	PTO: $1,540 / $3,080 / $7,700 (micro/small/large)
20	**Total for Patent Life Cycle**	Utility (no provisional or a provisional filed without a patent attorney): **$20,937 / $24,264 / $33,790** (micro/small/large) Provisional and utility prepared by a patent attorney: **$25,147 / $28,534 / $38,240** (micro/small/large)

Foreign Filing Overview of Costs. For an overview of foreign filings, focus on the one-year time requirement from the US filing date to foreign file. International patent filings require the guidance of specialized professionals and therefore will not be presented in detail. To get you started, here is a broad cost estimate for the common and cost-efficient approach of seeking worldwide patent protection under the Patent Cooperation Treaty (PCT). The PCT enables a single patent application as an entry point for up to 150 countries at a rough cost estimate of $4,000. Subsequently, patents in other countries can range in costs from $2,000 to $10,000 each. However, the PCT application delays deciding on countries and budgeting for about 2.5 years from the PCT application filing.[251]

There also is a patent highlight from June 2023 for the European Union (EU). After more than a decade of work by EU institutions supporting patents, a new court called the Unified Patent Court went live. With a single action, patent infringement can be enforced across seventeen EU member states. There is an expectation that the Court will support quality patents.[252]

BOTTOM-UP COSTS FOR PATENT PORTFOLIOS

From One to a Target Range of Three to Twelve US Patents. Getting started in patents means seeking your first patent. We can next accumulate sample budgets for multiple patent filings. This is done by applying costs for obtaining a single US patent to a range of patents, with a recommendation to start with a minimum of three patents, for example, applied to three key commercial innovations of a line of business. Three is selected because with a grant rate of 57 percent, filing three patent applications statistically has a 92.1 percent chance of resulting in at least one granted patent.[253]

Multiples of the range can support more aggressive strategies at the outset of building a portfolio. Additional sets of three can be filed initially or over time based on improvements or forward inventing for earlier filings, new innovations or new lines of business.

STARTER PATENT PROGRAM

An exemplary program is presented to guide a new inventor or company with minimal funding, called a *starter program*. It provides a range of one to three patent filings, based on the same approach as the table above for "Estimated Costs per US Patent" but adding two additional patent filings on consecutive years one and two, so that the timeframe is increased from a three-year period to a five-year period.

Starter Patent Program: Sample Bottom-Up Budget. The starter program spreads each of the three patent application filings over consecutive years zero, one and two, and relies on provisionals to minimize the initial filing fees. The first application is filed in year zero as a provisional during the preparation (Prep) phase, followed by the formal utility application in year one. Each utility filing corresponds to its provisionals filed the year before. In the prosecution (Pros) phase, this model assumes that after two communications with the PTO (as responses to Office Actions), the patents are granted over 25.9 months as the average PTO pendency for a patent grant.[254]

In the table below for the Starter Program, the individual and total costs are shown for years zero through four (or five) to account for the three granted patents. It assumes that for the initial applications, the applicant meets the criteria for a micro entity (applicable for up to four patents). Finally, maintenance fees are shown for each of three, seven and eleven years from the issuance dates.

Starter Program

Key (see Key above, Estimated Costs per US Patent):

- *Prov*: provisional patent application: followed by an application number, *Prov 1, Prov 2, Prov 3*
- *Util*: utility patent application: followed by an application number, *Util 1, Util 2, Util 3*

Actions	Year 0	Year 1	Year 2	Year 3	Year 4
Preparation Phase (Prep)					
Provisional (filed without a patent attorney)	*Prov 1*: PTO $60	*Prov 2*: PTO $60	*Prov 3*: PTO $60		
Utility (with a patent attorney)		*Util 1*: Atty $10,500 PTO $455	*Util 2*: Atty $10,500 PTO $455	*Util 3*: Atty $10,000 PTO $455	
Admin (provisional filed without an admin)		*Util 1*: Admin $150	*Util 2*: Admin $150	*Util 3*: Admin $150	
Prosecution Phase (Pros)					
Office Action 1			*Util 1*: Atty $3,000	*Util 2*: Atty $3,000	*Util 3*: Atty $3,000
Office Action 2			*Util 1*: Atty $3,000	*Util 2*: Atty $3,000	*Util 3*: Atty $3,000
Grant / Issuance			*Util 1*: PTO $240	*Util 2*: PTO $240	*Util 3*: PTO $240
Admin: one PTO filing for each application annually, for a total of three Admin fees			*Util 1* (3x): Admin $450	*Util 2* (3x): Admin $450	*Util 3* (3x): Admin $450

Key (see Key above, Estimated Costs per US Patent):

- *Prov*: provisional patent application: followed by an application number, *Prov 1, Prov 2, Prov 3*
- *Util*: utility patent application: followed by an application number, *Util 1, Util 2, Util 3*

		Aggregate view totals: Prep & Pros			
Prep	Prep:	Prep:	Prep:	Prep:	
		Util 1: $11,105	*Util 2*: $11,130	*Util 3*: $11,130	
	Prov 1: $60	*Prov 2*: $60	*Prov 3*: $60		
			Pros:	Pros:	Pros:
Pros			*Util 1*: $6,690	*Util 2*: $6,690	*Util 3*: $6,690

		TOTALS			
Actions	**Year 0**	**Year 1**	**Year 2**	**Year 3**	**Year 4**
1 utility + provisional (no attorney):	$60	$11,105	$6,690		
Total 3 years: $17,855					
3 patents + micro:	$60	$11,165	$17,855	$17,795	$6,690
Total 5 years: $53,565					

PTO Maintenance fees, with due dates from the issuance fee payment date for each patent (with an additional Admin fee of $150 for maintenance fee payment):

+ 3.5 years = $400/$800/$2,000 (micro/small/large)

+ 7.5 years = $752/$1,504/$3,760 (micro/small/large)

+ 11.5 years = $1,540/$3,080/$7,700 (micro/small/large)

A reader may glean from this table that for an investment of $60 in year zero, $11,105 in year one and $6,690 in year two, she can obtain a single US patent for a total three-year cost of $17,855. With three patent provisional and utilities over three years, assuming they issue, the total cost is shown for each year, with a total five-year cost of $53,565.

Getting started in patents with only $60 in year zero enables the same inventor to engage in startup activities, fundraising and due diligence to evaluate the commercial viability of her invention. She may then apply the results to determine whether to continue with the year-one costs to progress the application.

It should be noted that this is a baseline approach built upon the cost estimates presented to obtain a single US patent above. There can be a range of scenarios that impact the activities, costs or pendency for obtaining US patents. One example of a beneficial one is the USPTO One Track program. For an additional Office fee of $840 for a micro entity, the Office targets completing patent application examination within about twelve months from filing.[255]

BUDGETS FOR INTELLECTUAL PROPERTY PROGRAMS

With the basic costs for obtaining a US patent in hand, we can shift to introducing an equivalent cost exercise with other forms of intellectual property, US copyrights, trade secrets, trademarks and design patents.[256] At the outset, modeling costs for these IP assets are comparatively more straightforward than patents. Attorneys in these areas commonly offer flat-fee pricing, which includes legal analysis to optimize the quality of the assets (noting that professionals may recommend additional search costs prior to filing, particularly for trademarks). The flat fee is then applied generally within one year, so the budget for these assets is unlikely to stretch beyond year zero. If measured at the start of the year, fees can be incurred within the current annual budget.

Once owners have the basics and benefits of procuring additional forms of IP, pursuing those benefits makes (common) sense. I have counseled clients to simply execute these filings, as often hourly-rate discussions to determine whether to file are more expensive than applying the funding to IP filings (and clients can learn from the free DIY USPTO resources).

Below is a summary of estimated costs (including the data presented in Chapter 1: Mission Quality, with added details). The costs for additional IP can be added to patenting costs within the selected year to arrive at IP asset totals.

Copyrights (the Estimated Cost Is $750 to $1,500). For copyright, advertised attorneys' fees generally are less than $1,500 (and in some listings, $500 to $1,000) for registration with the USCO. Another $45 to $65 is required for online registration for a claim to an original work of authorship. There is a flat fee of $95 for recordation of documents.[257] In addition, there are perfunctory intake reviews for docketing the assets, resulting in minimal costs post-filing.

Trade Secrets (the Estimated Cost Equates to That for Copyright, Plus Fees for Redacting Evidence). The costs for trade secrets are incurred in setting up and managing the protection of confidential information included in employment and other agreements as part of HR or contracts executed anyway. Legal IP professionals are added in identifying and protecting trade secrets. However, when trade secrets are considered along with patents or copyright, IP protection costs are shared between the assets. While formal registration is not required, registering a copyright for a trade secret accesses copyright statutory benefits and creates evidence of key trade secrets (with additional fees for redacting materials in the copyright deposit).

Trademarks (the Estimated Cost Is Less Than $3,000 over 11.2 Months Where Registration Is Successful). Registration at the US Patent and Trademark Office is a nominal fee of $250, with trademark attorney estimated costs of less than $1,250, resulting in a total estimate of under $1,500. The next step is responding to an Office Action, with an estimated cost of $1,500. An optional search can be done to assess the availability of the trademark, called a *clearance opinion*, with an estimated cost of $1,250. Since the total pendency for trademarks is 11.2 months from filing to outcome, the necessary costs (without extended prosecution) generally are executed within the first year.

Design Patents (the Estimated Cost Is Less than $4,000 over 21.3 Months). For design patents, an easy rule of thumb for cost is less than $4,000 (including on estimate of $2,000 for attorney's fees and figure drafting preparation, $1,500 for straightforward prosecution and PTO costs of $255). Comparing design to utility patent costs is informative. The cost for a micro entity to procure one utility patent is $17,955 on average over 25.9 months, while a similar procurement cost for a design patent is $4,000 over 21.3 months. The twenty-year lifetime for utility patents adds maintenance fees, while the fifteen-year lifetime for design patents does not include additional fees.

Budget Add-Ons

IP Strategy Counseling. IP strategy counseling is an additional area to address in maximizing value for overall IP spending. Here are areas to consider as you embark on discussions with IP professionals.

First, IP strategy counseling is a precursor to filing for IP assets.

Strategy in this context generally includes due diligence to identify which IP assets to pursue, as well as the timing of filing. Specifics about the owner and innovation, however, strongly impact counseling, including industry, technology subject matter and development stage of innovations, relevant geographies for manufacturing and selling offerings, competitors, litigiousness of the industry, regulation, etc. For example, international manufacture or sale will weigh heavily on international IP protection. IP strategy therefore varies based on this range of factors.

Second, the largest cost for IP strategy is in counseling from IP professionals. My goal in #ip2ip is to provide stepwise execution, objectives and systems to advance IP strategy significantly, thereby reducing cost. Identify professionals who share your values. For example, an ideal IP strategist will introduce IP strategy and budgets to you, instead of your having to ask.

Third, the costs presented are estimated figures. Professional fees also need to be evaluated for the best fit with your business objectives, not simply based on the lowest cost. Attention to budget is optimally the responsibility of your professional, to assist in both setting and achieving.

Fourth, cost and quality go hand in hand. Quality in yields quality out. I also humbly add that I historically have included a quality review with at least one of my colleagues for patent applications, especially claim drafting, along with many high-quality professionals and firms. In doing so, we acknowledge that in this complex intersection of technology and law, collaboration with skilled colleagues is the best path to quality. This quality review should be factored into budgets.

TOP-DOWN IP BUDGETS

Exploring industry norms for top-down IP budgeting is instructive as another check for optimizing cost. I draw upon public surveys of corporate technology owners to present available data about corporate IP budgets. Interestingly, unlike the public availability of data about the costs to obtain a patent and additional IP, top-down budget data detailed enough for decision-making is hard to come by. Why? Top-down budgeting is a limit on spending. One can hypothesize that data about how to cap spending is limited because IP industry resources benefit from spending.

Companies Spend between 0.15 and 3 Percent per $1 Billion in Revenue on IP. For larger companies, as reported in 2016, there was a range of investment in IP compared to gross revenues of 0.15 to 3 percent of every $1 billion in gross revenues, with the number likely to drive to the low end.[258] However, what can be covered involves not just IP costs for procurement and maintenance, but likely also litigation. Another qualification is that research is often directed to companies earning over $billion with sophisticated IP departments. While providing insights for smaller enterprises, there is simply a lack of data for companies earning less than $1 billion, such as SMEs.

Sample Top-Down Budgets by the Available Numbers. A simpler assessment is to select top-down budgets based on available funds. This is inherently provided in the bottom-up sample budgets by looking at the totals for the starter patent program and adding fees for additional IP and counseling. The total that is the closest match to your available funds for patenting is your top-down patent budget number.

Then, where applicable, add about $1,000 to get started on IP strategy with each of your selected copyrights, trade secrets and trademarks assets to pursue. Finally, add the cost for IP professional counseling as best gauged for your individual company by your leadership.

$60 (or $0) Top-Down Patent Program: $60 and a Dream. One instructive example, of course derived from this chapter's title, "$60 and a Dream," is the inventor with no money, period.

Good on you for pursuing a business dream with a lack of immediate access to funds. The story of the immigrant who arrived in America without a penny in her pocket and still rose to financial heights is a source of inspiration. However, there is no dream if the inventor or owner cannot find $60 to invest in getting started in filing for his first US patent. It is among additional entry costs in starting a business, and therefore should not be the cause of thwarting planting the seed of a startup and nurturing its growth.

Similar to the inventor starting in her garage, an inventor interested in pursuing an idea to profit must be scrappy enough to gather this minimal fee as a proxy for her ability to withstand the continuing and steeper financial hills on the road to success.

Ideas at an early stage of conception are difficult for the market to act upon. On the other hand, once reduced to a tangible form available to be distributed and contemplated by others, such as investors, a connection is formed. That description is then ready for use in the first step on the journey to the American dream. The provisional patent application described above can derive from this tangible description a path to getting started in patents.

A RETURN TO MISSION QUALITY
USE BUDGETS TO DRIVE CROWN JEWEL IP ASSETS

Crown jewel IP assets have been presented based on aligning IP with business objectives. Budgets are about a target number of patents and other IP assets. The next step is then selecting the subject matter for future crown jewel IP assets, either based on existing or follow-on filings. How do technology owners determine which subject matter warrants filing to meet budget, IP strategy and crown jewel objectives?

Next Level Use of Historic Patent Tools. Fortunately, historic IP tools have you covered. They can be used as input in selecting the subject matter. Let's look at these historic tools and a next-level use of them.

Laboratory Notebooks. Long before intellectual property rights, inventors and creators wrote down their inventions, creations, imaginings and all forms of art in notebooks, such as the famous drawing by Leonardo da Vinci, the *Vitruvian Man*.[259]

When it comes to patents, one approach to capturing inventions as stories of technology is utilizing special-purpose notebooks used by scientists and researchers, called *laboratory notebooks*. They are designed to document and authenticate invention using bound, page-numbered notebooks, complete with inventor and witness signatures and date fields. Their systematic use creates a formal record of the technology story and information to support it, often including figures and other data.

Despite amendments to US patent laws that have reduced the need for evidence about how and when an invention came about, the use of laboratory notebooks is still a valuable and commonly used tool for inventions. There are digital laboratory notebooks of course, and blockchain technologies are sure to play a role in this area for documenting provenance in the future. The lab notebook entries also can document trade secrets for inventions considered for patenting, or in the alternative, trade secret protection.

Invention Disclosure Forms. Another traditional tool is an Invention Disclosure Form (or IDF, as described in Chapter 6: Trade Secrets).[260] Similar to lab notebooks, IDFs traditionally document inventions and can be prepared as input for leadership (such as patent committees) charged with deciding whether to pursue patents or trade secrets. They enable the inventors to describe how and when the invention came about, assess public disclosure and provide information about known prior art.

Some IDFs go further by enabling an assessment of the invention's value to the business. It can be completed in part by the inventor, but business factors can also be integrated by collaborating can be integrated by collaborating with business stakeholders for the related line of business. The focus then is shifted from documenting the invention to aligning it with business strategies. In addition to evaluating individual inventions, IDFs ideally are introduced within regularly held business meetings as part of objectives, strategies, R & D timing and planning, with participants including inventors, business stakeholders and IP professionals (in order to guide the discussion and protect the analysis as privileged).

The table below, or Patent Filing Prioritization Tool, is an example of this assessment, presenting ten questions with which to standardize decision-making. The questions are directed to legal considerations, as well as specific business assessments and financial impact on the related line of business. Each question has three alternative answers carrying a different score, with a maximum score of 10 per question, yielding a potential total score of 100. IDFs then are converted from a patent strategy to true business alignment in enabling technology owners to prioritize inventions for filing.

This approach can facilitate prioritization by setting a necessary score to be considered for filing. Additional predetermined scores can trigger either immediate utility filings or provisional filings which delay decision-making (thereby preserving funding) about follow-on utility filings, so the most deserving applications receive priority. The tool enables owners to select and prioritize a predetermined number of patents per line of business—identifying patent crown jewels for filing. Inventions withheld for later decisions about utility filings can be further assessed relative to each other and prioritized inventions.

IDF PATENT FILING PRIORITIZATION TOOL

CRITERIA	POINTS	SCORE
	Answer A is 10 points; B is 5 points; C is 0 points	
1. Is the invention critical to the line of business (LOB) it supports?	A. It's critical (e.g., it will be in all lines of the LOB or will drive customers to purchase the offerings in the LOB).	
	B. It's important to the LOB.	
	C. It's relevant to the LOB.	
2. Is the invention likely to increase net profit by either increasing revenue or reducing costs?	A. It's likely to significantly increase net profit (e.g., comprise over 15 percent of profits; be a branded feature/product/service).	
	B. It's likely to moderately increase net profit (e.g., comprise over 3 percent of profits).	
	C. It's not likely to affect net profit.	
3. Can infringement of the invention be easily detected?	A. Infringement can be easily detected (e.g., a user interface invention or public product/service).	
	B. Infringement can be detected by reverse engineering.	
	C. Infringement will be difficult to detect and, by extension, reverse engineering by others will be difficult if we elect to keep the invention as a trade secret.	
4. Are competitors currently using, or will they use, the invention or similar technology?	A. Competitors will likely use the invention (e.g., customers have asked for it, competitors have announced that it will be in future offerings, etc.).	
	B. Competitors may use it or similar technology.	
	C. Competitors are unlikely to use it or similar technology.	
5. Is the invention likely to have a significant market life?	A. It's likely to have a relatively long market life (e.g., it will be in future releases over the next ten years).	
	B. It's likely to have a moderately long market life.	
	C. It's likely to have a relatively short market life (less than five years).	

CRITERIA	POINTS	SCORE
	Answer A is 10 points; B is 5 points; C is 0 points	
6. Is the invention potentially broad, in light of related art?	A. It's potentially very broad (e.g., related inventions are not known).	
	B. It's likely to be moderately broad (e.g., similar solutions exist in other fields).	
	C. It's likely to be very narrow (e.g., it improves on existing solutions in this field).	
7. Is the invention difficult to design around?	A. It's difficult to design around while maintaining essential functionality (e.g., it's the only solution to the problem—no alternative solutions exist).	
	B. It can be designed around but doing so requires significant costs.	
	C. It's relatively easy to design around (e.g., equally functional alternative solutions exist).	
8. Is the invention currently in use or ready for implementation?	A. It's currently in use or is fully developed and implementation is imminent. However, it is before or within one year of public disclosure or sale.	
	B. It's within one year of either first public disclosure, offer for sale or sale date.	
	C. It's in an R & D phase with commercialization expected within one year.	
9. Is the invention relatively simple to describe?	A. It's relatively simple (e.g., it's a simple mechanical, user interface or industrial design).	
	B. It's moderately complex (e.g., it's an electro/mechanical system).	
	C. It's very complex (e.g., it's an electrical/computer hardware system).	
10. Does the invention have broad applications outside the current market?	A. It potentially has very broad applications outside of the current market (and could be licensed to others).	
	B. It may have some applications outside the current market.	
	C. It's not likely to have any commercial significance outside the current market (e.g., used only internally).	

TOTAL SCORE FOR THIS INVENTION
(Maximum possible score = 100)

Some technology owners also can apply an advanced IP strategy by revisiting this filing decision upon the USPTO's decision about whether to grant the patent. Individual patents are anchored in time to their technology description for twenty years from their filing date. It is not surprising that during that twenty-year pendency, the offerings and market supported by the invention will change, as will the law. Revisiting the patent application prior to the patent grant for new developments is productive to optimize business value. The technology owner can update the IDF assessment to determine whether to file a follow-on application (called a *child* of a *parent* application).

Where a patented innovation is a crown jewel, more frequent reviews are warranted, such as timed to business, R & D and product management activities over the life cycle of the line of business the patent supports. Crown jewel innovations often are improved upon, and follow-on applications can reflect their dynamic business value.

Finally, we have approached the spectrum of IP assets to be considered holistically based on the timing to consider patents. Laboratory notebooks and IDFs also can trigger the consideration of other forms of IP. Dusting off these historic patent tools and adding business strategy makes them not only exponentially more valuable for patents, but for other IP as well.

Summary

Chapter 1: Mission Quality shares costs including estimated attorney and administrative costs and USPTO formal fees, with a thesis that IP investments are cost efficient. This chapter provides foundational data for annual budgets, average time frames for US patent grants and added maintenance fees for the lifetime of the US patent assets. A starter program also makes actionable a target of one to three US-granted patents for those new to patenting, making them potentially eligible for 80 percent off PTO filing fees. Allowing the data to speak for itself, this information supports your excellence in not just procuring these assets but also for budgeting for them.

CHAPTER 10

#IP2IP CHECKLIST

DO BUSINESS IN THE BULLSEYE
CO-AUTHOR, J. CHRISTOPHER LYNCH

ACTion

10.1 Apply the #ip2ip checklist within the ordinary course of business planning.

Hopefully, you are arriving here with a sense of expectation of being able to apply what #ip2ip has offered in a productive and organized manner. Checklists are empowering because you can spend time executing rather than assessing what needs to be done, allowing you to *Do Business in the Bullseye*.

The #ip2ip checklist presents the offensive and defensive give and take, or opportunities and risks of legal rights. In patent litigation, the gravamen for the patent owner is the strength of the patent (or its validity) and infringement by a third party.

Issues outside of those core areas add costs and distractions. For example, adjudicating whether a patent is invalid because the owner made the invention public before filing for a patent is a non-substantive distraction and can result in a patent being held invalid and *all rights being lost.*

Employing best-in-class planning, and in this case prevention, to avoid outright errors that destroy value in the future, is arguably within management's responsibility. When viewed in the broader context of competition, you are subject to the obligations of others who will leverage all legal, business and competitive strategies, regardless of whether you do. Your reading #ip2ip demonstrates your interest in gaining this competitive advantage and defense for your innovation.

THE USE OF THE #IP2IP CHECKLIST

The use and value of the checklist, once embraced, is straightforward. Initiate IP strategy based on it and then reassess systematically at the most productive timing for your company. Here are suggestions to jump-start its use: employ it at least twice (such as in the first and second half of the fiscal year) and build the checklist into the business cycle of product planning and budgeting. This invites business-focused executives to be an integral part of IP strategy as part of an ordinary course of business, further establishing and ideally building a view of IP as a tool for business strategy.

Use of the #ip2ip checklist also should include flexibility for unplanned events or changes to the business or legal environments, and be managed to optimize its use as business and legal trends warrant. IP strategy based on the checklist is inherently about monitoring and anticipating shifts, then planning for actions to take should they occur. A next-level strategy is to create your own trends and then leverage them.

Let's pause here though and not get ahead of the simplicity and immediacy of incorporating the #ip2ip checklist into your work. It presents IP Strategy, Patents and Intellectual Property, including topics for Execution, Objective and Systems which are applicable across the IP Spectrum. Individual IP assets are then introduced with topics unique to each of the assets: copyrights, trade secrets and trademarks. The ACTions and Top-10 Takeaways are included.

IP Strategy, Patents and Intellectual Property

☐ ACTions

☐ Chapter 1: **Mission Quality**

1.1 Prioritize quality over quantity.

1.2 Think beyond patents and across the intellectual property spectrum.

1.3 Showcase crown jewel IP assets aligned with their line of business (LOB).

1.4 Be intentional about IP strategy to optimize patent value and reduce risk.

☐ Chapters 2–4: **Patents**

2.1 Apply for patent rights before an innovation is made available to anyone outside of the company. Top-10 Takeaway.

2.2 Apply as early as possible upon creation of an invention. Top-10 Takeaway.

3.1 Apply intentional strategies for computer-implemented inventions, given the downward pressure on patents.

3.2 Generate a litigation playbook for bringing and defending against litigation, including corporate policies which demonstrate good IP citizenship. Top-10 Takeaway.

4.1 Be a guest author. Write your ACTions for Your Future Success along with your guest authors. Visit cherylmilone.com.

☐ Part I: Execution (Patent/IP Program, Chapters 1–4)

☐ *Patent Assets*: Total number of US and related foreign utility patents (provisional, issued, pending, planned); organization of patent portfolio based on lines of business (LOB); curation of patent/IP data for leadership to demonstrate return on investment, including business alignment, value and risk reduction.

☐ Identification of crown jewel patents (list the top three per LOB):

_____

_____

_____

☐ *Offerings*: For each LOB: baseline financial data, market, percentage of the market captured, key commercial innovations and features, end or intermediate offering, phase of development (R & D, preproduction, production, versions/generations, expansion strategy, mature offering, replacement strategy); geographies for R & D, manufacture, sales, assembly export/import; business strategy; global IP. Consideration of global reach of offerings; prioritize countries and regions; timing of applications globally within twelve months of US applications.

☐ *Customers/Suppliers*: Geographies; patent/IP asset drivers or risks; agreements (licensing, indemnification, know-how).

- ☐ *Financials and ROI for Patents/IP Assets*: Financial statements; identify portion of R&D budget for IP asset expenses; budget for R & D; approach to preparing patent/IP budget; comparison of patent/IP budget to other business operations; cost/benefit analysis; ROI analytics; audit of past budgets.

- ☐ *Cost*: Implement annual budgets (see samples in Chapter 9: Cost) collaboratively with IP professionals, formalize and meet budgets within business planning and timing

- ☐ *Business Industry*: For each LOB, identify market and percentage of the market captured; IP strategy and business strategy one, three and five-year-plus, and alignment; audit of past strategies; portfolio growth, forward patenting, organic or acquisition; competitor analytics and planning; M & A planning, financing, acquirers and a market view of the company's innovation and IP.

- ☐ *Corporate Legal Support*: Foundational corporate programs/policies/agreements to protect IP; employment agreements, including corporate IP ownership (work made for hire), trade secret/confidentiality and procedures and reconfirmation at annual meetings; third-party agreements, including nondisclosure agreements, assignments, licensing, indemnification, know-how and management of filing for patents before activities outside of the company; "license on transfer" (LOT) considerations.

- ☐ *Corporate Sponsorship*: C-suite and LOB leadership recognition of IP and inventors.

- ☐ *Business Alignment*: Patents/IP aligned with business strategy; protect offerings and reduce risks as a basis for profits.

- ☐ *Litigation Readiness*: patent marking; trade secret/confidentiality marking; document retention; insurance; patent/IP-driven offensive and defensive strategies, including identifying potential litigation sources; third-party risk management; activities and results of competitors and NPEs, adjudication fora (judicial, USPTO, ITC, international).

- ☐ *Industry-Specific Considerations/Factors*: computer technology, electrical/mechanical technology, software, mechanical, biochemistry/life sciences, digital health; standards; export regulations.

- ☐ *Timing to File for Patents*: management of statutory bar dates (do not rely on NDAs to avoid sales or offers for sale) in the era of "first inventor to file," requiring coordination between public use and patent filing in order not to limit patent rights.

- ☐ *Monetization* (see Litigation Enforcement below): Explore nonenforcement models.

☐ **ACTions**

☐ Chapter 8: **IP Honor**

8.1 Launch IP Honor to recognize inventors and creators. *Top-10 Takeaway.*

8.2 Elevate IP Honorees with career opportunities to inspire tomorrow's inventors and creators.

8.3 Invest in your employees' potential through IP education and encouraging innovation from underrepresented groups.

☐ **Part II: Objective**

☐ *IP Honor:* incentives to file for patents, IP assets and open source for inventors and creators and identify and honor the sources of innovations across the IP spectrum.

☐ **ACTions**

☐ Chapter 9: **Cost**

9.1 Use financial planning and budgets for IP strategy. *Top-10 Takeaway.*

9.2 Set and meet IP procurement budgets.

9.3 Consider an iterative approach to patent applications to shift fees into the future and to conserve funding today.

☐ Chapter 10: **#ip2ip Checklist**

10.1 Apply the #ip2ip checklist within the ordinary course of business planning.

☐ Conclusion:

"We are what we repeatedly do. Excellence then is not an act but a habit." *Top-10 Takeaway.*

☐ **Part III: Systems (Chapters 9-10)**

☐ **Operations**

☐ *Docket Management*: Maintain due dates for all registered IP and bar dates for IP not yet filed.

☐ *#ip2ip Strategy Planning*: Implement systematically by date (quarterly, annually) and add to business activities in the ordinary course of business of innovation development (for example, during R & D, product planning, quality control and before a launch of new or improved offerings), corporate legal activities and risk management.

☐ *Contract Management*: Coordinate all IP and license contract obligations and deadlines; implement IP strategy through contract negotiation and management.

- ☐ *Enforcement*: coordinate reporting of suspected misappropriation or infringement by employees, workers, customers, vendors, supply or distribution chain sources or third parties.

- ☐ *Tools*: #ip2ip checklist; lab notebooks; Invention Disclosure Form (IDF) (documenting patents and trade secret identification); IDF Patent Prioritization Tool; coordination of patents with other IP assets (trade secrets, copyrights).

☐ **Benchmarking Data**

- ☐ *Historic Data*: Historic accuracy of patent/IP budgets and alignment with business and ROI strategies.

- ☐ *Competition*: Competitive patents/IP strategy; identify key competitors for benchmarking and litigation readiness.

- ☐ *Market*: Primary markets, industry economic characteristics; current and potential customers, competitors, geographies, trends one, three and five years–plus; patent/IP drivers/differentiators in the market; industry patent/IP drivers reporting; identify companies acquired by potential acquirers/investors for benchmarking.

- ☐ *Comparables*: Potential acquirers and investors and patent/IP drivers for comparable companies acquired or invested in.

- ☐ *Patent Analytics*: Artificial intelligence and big data analytics, patent value, landscape and white space for technology, competitors and market.

☐ **Third-Party and Industry Data**

- ☐ *Competitors*: Patent-driven offensive and defensive strategies; competitors' view of company innovation based on patents/other IP drivers, innovation leadership; risks, market expansion strategies.

- ☐ *Legal and Regulatory Market*: Standards; geography considerations; trade, export/import controls, military offerings; antitrust.

- ☐ *US Government*: Executive, legislative and judicial considerations.

- ☐ *Foreign*: Law and jurisdiction considerations.

- ☐ *Industry Opportunities*: IPwe, IP support companies, Licensing Executives Society (LES), Unified Patents, License on Transfer (LOT—consider LOT concepts carefully for any startup with expectations of license revenue), Allied Security, RPX.

Each of the Patents/IP checklist items above can apply to each intellectual property right—copyrights, trademarks and trade secrets, as well as design patents. But each of the four areas has a few unique considerations. Here are the unique Execution/Objective/Systems checklist items for each of the additional IP assets.

Copyrights

☐ ACTions

☐ Chapter 5: **#ip2ip Copyrights**

5.1 Register copyrights to receive statutory benefits as or before a work is published. *Top-10 Takeaway*.

5.2 Use a copyright wrap technique to protect trade secrets, particularly for computer-software businesses.

- ☐ *Employment and Independent Contractor Agreements*: Coordinate and aggregate ownership of all newly created work under work made for hire—employees and contractors are different under copyright.

- ☐ *Licenses-In*: Review and understand in-bound licenses; negotiate commercial licenses strategically.

- ☐ *Licenses-Out*: Prepare a comprehensive strategy to monetize copyrights; consider exclusive and nonexclusive strategies.

- ☐ *Content Management*: Ensure ownership or license rights before publication; ensure the use of copyright notice; obtain DMCA safe harbor certification if third-party content will be published.

- ☐ *Preparation to Enforce*: Register works promptly at or before publication; be ready to enforce a copyright quickly, with all of the available benefits of registration.

- ☐ *Building a Portfolio*: identify copyrights in the context of other business transactions, be aware of any third-party content use.

- ☐ *Archiving*: Document dates of creation and publication.

Trade Secrets

☐ ACTions

☐ Chapter 6: **#ip2ip Trade Secrets**

6.1 Formalize a list of trade secrets as part of your patent and copyright strategies. *Top-10 Takeaway*.

6.2 Document trade secrets as they are created.

6.3 Leverage a trade secret program as a tool against espionage and everyday employee movement.

- ☐ *Strategy*: Balance trade secret versus patent issues; consider all implications of collaboration; be realistic about the potential for reverse engineering or legitimate independent development.

- ☐ *Licenses-In*: Have strategies to avoid "pollution" of employees or systems with third-party secrecy obligations.

- ☐ *Licenses-Out*: Create a tight chain of custody for trade secrets that are shared with any third parties; consider the misappropriation scenarios and account for the protection of the trade secrets from those scenarios in the documentation.

- ☐ *Maintaining the Secret*: Reasonable measures may change over time, so implement changes as necessary and audit periodically.

- ☐ *Preparation to Enforce*: Align documentation in preparation of foreseeable misappropriation scenarios, including the use of the Information Disclosure Form to jump-start identifying trade secrets.

- ☐ *Employees and Contractors*: Manage contracts with each to maintain secrets; consider "chain of custody" issues and who in the chain should have standing to enforce trade secrets against misappropriation.

- ☐ *Technological Measures*: Build systems to maintain secrecy and refresh as needed.

Trademark

☐ ACTions

☐ Chapter 7: **#ip2ip Trademarks and Design Patents**

7.1 Create marks—names and logos—as crown jewel assets to showcase your company and its offerings.

7.2 Prioritize a strong mark which minimizes your investment over its lifetime. *Top-10 Takeaway.*

7.3 File for US federal trademark protection upon selecting your mark, with an option to register before you use your mark.

- ☐ *Branding Strategy*: Build branding themes; recognize differing marks from these themes—words, logos, slogans, design themes; ensure any agency paperwork provides IP ownership and appropriate warranties; coordinate URL strategy with brand strategy.

- ☐ *Priority Documentation*: Train employees on date of first use issues and document those for trademark application and priority purposes; coordinate marketing.

- ☐ *Application Strategy*: Consider USPTO and state registrations; URL acquisition and maintenance; consider global strategy and timing of filings; consider marks for common law protection only; utilize marking for all registrations; consider abandonment and trademark life-support issues for discontinued marks.

☐ *License Strategy*: Ensure quality control in all trademark licenses (in-bound or out-bound)—this can affect the practicality of certain licensing strategies; all trademark transactions require support for goodwill being associated with the mark.

☐ *Documenting Priority*: Document the date of the first use in commerce; most trademark disputes arise over the priority of use—who was first, with what mark, on what offerings, sold where and how.

☐ *Brand Awareness*: Keep track of events relating to the brand as they relate to increasing the value of goodwill; intangible goodwill is important in enforcement because it enhances trademark strength.

☐ *Avoiding Abandonment*: Never cease trademark use without considering the implications; trademark nonuse of three years is presumed abandonment.

☐ *Docket Management*: Coordinate all trademark filings, renewals and required documents for each of those obligations.

☐ *Contract Management*: Coordinate and document license obligations plus quality control obligations.

Design Patents

☐ ACTions

☐ Chapter 7 (continued): **#ip2ip Trademarks and Design Patents**

7.4 Consider design patents for the visual look and feel of key commercial design features when you assess utility patents. *Top-10 Takeaway.*

☐ *Subject Matter*: Observe your product or the customer face of your service; design patents cover the ornamental design, not the functional features, of a product.

☐ *Timing*: Note your public sale dates—design patents must be filed within one year; consider design patent versus trade dress protection for any new designs; only brand-new designs can be patented; but in use, designs can have protectable trade dress; consider the commercial life span of the product.

☐ *Documenting Profitability*: Very important for design patent enforcement, track your profitability; design patent includes a unique profit disgorgement remedy; be prepared to show margins to adjudge the competitor's profits.

☐ *Documenting Goodwill*: Track consumer recognition of your design; designs can qualify for trade dress protection with acquired distinctiveness, presenting a potential for protection under both schemes.

☐ *Protect Identity*: Monitor the market for infringers; design patents can ensure some limited exclusivity in a crowded field, where knockoffs might be common.

- ☐ *Build Margins*: Track relative success of differing designs; in certain industries, customers will pay more for an attractively designed product.

- ☐ *Allocate IP Resources*: Ensure that design protection in some form is part of your intellectual property budget; design patents are less expensive than utility patents.

- ☐ *Documenting Priority/Docket:* Build systems for documenting priority and meeting filing deadlines.

- ☐ *Licensing*: Build licenses to recognize goodwill issues and to leverage design patent attributes and trade dress.

☐ Litigation Enforcement

- ☐ *Monitor for Infringers*: Consider how infringers might misappropriate or infringe, and then monitor that activity directly or as appropriate; document any instances of infringement, confusion in the marketplace, or potential misappropriation.

- ☐ *Document Profitability*: Track profits; each IP asset allows for lost profits for lost sales due to infringement (be prepared to prove the value of IP in this manner).

- ☐ *Priority*: Track priority of invention and use (not all IP disputes are about priority, but many are); be prepared to prove priority—original evidence is very important here, such as lab notebooks.

- ☐ *License Strategies*: Consider who is best positioned to identify and pursue infringers or those who misappropriate trade secrets; sometimes, the licensee is best equipped—but the licensor must be informed and involved; or else, the licensor must be prepared to enforce and consider how that affects terms with licensees.

- ☐ *Monitor IP Infringement*: Monitor the market for infringers for early action to enforce the exclusive rights of IP.

- ☐ *Monetize IP*: Consider options for third parties to make and sell your ideas; licensing and litigation are used in concert to aid in monetizing IP.

- ☐ *Build Goodwill*: Track your goodwill events; a track record of successful IP enforcement builds goodwill, establishes royalty rates and makes future enforcement easier.

- ☐ *Watch Services*: Monitor the marketplace for infringers; use third-party services to watch for infringement or objectionable IP of third parties.

- ☐ *Document Monitoring*: Document and investigate claims of infringement, confusion, suspicious activity and competitor movements.

- ☐ *Cease-and-Desist Programs*: See available takedown programs; third-party sellers have notice and takedown programs; DMCA has a notice and takedown program; WIPO has a program to address copying of URLs; traditional cease-and-desist letters work but carry a risk of a declaratory relief action in response.

CONCLUSION

A SMILE GOES A MILE

ACTion

"We are what we repeatedly do. Excellence then is not an act but a habit." Top-10 Takeaway.
—WILLIAM DURANT, AN AMERICAN WRITER, BASED ON HIS INTERPRETATION OF ARISTOTLE'S WORK[261]

As you're reading this, I hope that #ip2ip is next to a stack of papers representing initial intellectual property (IP) filings.

ACTion. That's my goal.

If not, then ideally these final pages are your inspirational launchpad. I'm excited for you and for how you will honor our US IP law's original intention of promoting innovation and advancing society.

Allow me humbly to add another tool for your efforts: a positive attitude.

I have been fortunate to be taught this by my parents. As far as my father is concerned, complaints are a foreign language that he has never understood nor entertained. His view of his career (and family) has always been to approach each with positivity. My mother in turn was the biggest fan of her children, with a running commentary on being able to learn and to do anything. As I grew to a young adult, on occasion, I lightheartedly asked Mom for constructive criticism, but to no avail; Mom found only praise. My parents inspired me to be my best self, represented by a smile.

This optimism gave me the confidence to strive for success. Did it substitute for performance? Not at all. I didn't mention work ethic above. Neither did my parents. It was taught by habitual examples. A positive attitude also enabled me to overcome inevitable setbacks encountered in striving to better myself. This always returned me to a confident foundation, knowing that I could persevere.

Positivity can be a catalyst for execution and inspiration to conduct yourself at your highest quality. This of course is easiest on the success side. When impediments come, you can move into action more quickly with a positive attitude than a negative or defeated perspective. A reservoir of positiveness can be both an inspiration and solace.

This is borne out in research, research which for me was an epiphany. I knew inherently how fortunate I was with the values, attitudes and support I received growing up. But it was not until

I happened upon a presentation about leadership long after I mirrored my parents' approach for my own family and my team at my startup Article One Partners that I realized I had been coached by my parents as world-class leaders. Here's how.

The authors of the leadership presentation identified traits of twelve thousand world-renowned leaders by interviewing the subjects and those they led. The study uncovered that there is a universal tenet for how leaders motivate and inspire others— one that "works with everybody all the time, irrespective of their age, their generation, their experience, their organizations, their cultures."[262] With excitement built and an exemplary real-world story or two, the answer was revealed.

The universal tenet is "being a fan of those you lead." Study respondents reported that when someone they respect and admire is their fan, they are compelled to action and perform at their highest level. When you as a leader demonstrate to people that you would do anything for them to succeed, that you are always rooting for them, you can impact their ability to meet their goals.

This described my parents, who also demonstrated being a fan of others and that a positive attitude could be taught and learned, consistently. This book's epigraph—and the one ACTion for this chapter—represents these teachings for me. It is a magnificent directive which has guided me, which I now pass to you for inspiration (and possibly to gift to others).

For the earlier years of my family, part of our bedtime routine with my children was to ask, "What are you most proud of today?" I wanted them to retire for the day with positive thoughts. Those talks are still some of my most cherished moments as a parent. I commend this to you to pass it along to your family in a manner of honoring them—honor the individual—and their infinite potential.

You can also imbue your work teams with this positive attitude, consistently. A colleague once responded to my written outreach with, "I can read your smile." We also employed these concepts in the startup days at AOP, developing a tradition for finding and celebrating success. It started with exclaiming that someone "hit it out of the park," shortened to HOOP (yes, another one of my acronyms) when someone achieved a milestone or objective.

We then established a consistent place to look for praise. Concluding our weekly review meetings, we took turns saying what we were most proud of. We didn't stop there though. Next, we picked our favorite answer and its operational area for the point of pride. For example, one week it might be in community building of our crowdsourced platform, labeled as a C for community (or another week, an S for sales). We then combined the C for community with HOOP to produce a shout-out—CHOOP. With our favorite accomplishment at the ready, we proceeded to the highlight.

One of our employees, David DiGammarino, had a resounding announcer's voice and announced the shout-out. To use CHOOP as an example, David would proceed with the weekly ritual: "This week we're celebrating community, so on the count of three, let's all say CHOOP!" Shouts of an elongated cchh-hooooooppp followed, along with belly laughs and a room (and conference call) full of smiles. That ritual became a defining part of our culture, so much so that when David was on holiday, he prerecorded a version of our cherished HOOP shout-out for our weekly meeting.

This optimism went beyond the weekly accomplishment and shout-out. It bonded us in a shared positivity about our work and enabled us not only to strive for results but to manage the challenges that accompany startups. It also honored the team, and in looking for praise, reinforced our individual and collective potential.

For my family, the lessons of being positive continue. While Dad's surgery is long past, my mother has needed all of my family's love and care with a long-term cognitive decline. Throughout this time of Mom's illness, Dad's optimism and absence of complaints have never wavered. He cares for Mom as an act of love; it's his role at this time in their life together. My father's positive attitude has enabled him to maintain his energy to help my mother, and even to create moments of happiness through these difficult times. Dad still makes Mom smile.

Positivity also counters business challenges, such as implementing IP strategy. I commend you for being here, reading through these pages. With the demands on business owners, I appreciate your limited time to optimize IP strategy and realize its value.

Let me offer you my own biggest fan moment!

Here's a lighthearted suggestion to prompt action. The Top-10 Takeaways are a summary of the chapter ACTions to simplify execution. While we don't have an announcer for a resounding encouragement, let's imagine your IP strategy team together building up to this shout-out: "Annndddd...the Top-10 Takeaway accomplished this week is—(pick from the full list below, or shorten it like we did at AOP, picking up the Ts in the Top-10 Takeaways to shout out ttthhoooopppp)—THOOP!"

It has been such an honor to spend this time with you, and your attention already bodes well for your success.

Top-10 Takeaways in reverse order:

Top-10 Takeaways

#ip2ip-10: "We are what we repeatedly do. Excellence then is not an act but a habit."

#ip2ip-9: Use financial planning and budgets for IP strategy.

#ip2ip-8: Launch IP Honor to recognize inventors and creators.

#ip2ip-7: Consider design patents for the visual look and feel of key commercial design features when you assess utility patents.

#ip2ip-6: Prioritize a strong mark which minimizes your investment over its lifetime.

#ip2ip-5: Formalize a list of trade secrets as part of your patent and copyright strategies.

#ip2ip-4: Register copyrights to receive statutory benefits as or before a work is published.

#ip2ip-3: Generate a litigation playbook for bringing and defending against litigation, including corporate policies which demonstrate good IP citizenship.

#ip2ip-2: Apply as early as possible upon creation of an invention.

#ip2ip-1: Apply for patent rights before an innovation is made available to anyone outside of the company.

ACKNOWLEDGMENTS

To my parents, whose inspiration for this book and my career are described in the Introduction and Conclusion. The strongest lessons are learned by example and with a certainty of one's potential. To my children, with so much love for giving me the marvel of watching you grow into the astounding adults you are as service members in the US Military Marines, with the honor of being in your company and sharing in your journeys, and with appreciation for your encouragement and patience with a mom who always is working. I hope my work and this book memorialize the why and what of my career and reflect what I hope I have exemplified for you both, and that whether its business or as inventors and creators, I'll continue to be a guide to you in your own careers.

To Cynthia, my twin sister, in whom I have a better half, whose joy and sorrow at my successes and challenges bring me hope and resilience. Thank you for improving this writing at every one of the many turns, and thanks to Armins for his constant brilliant coaching as one of the most impressive business executives I have the blessing to know.

To my broader family, Jeff and Linda—we are so fortunate to give each other and all of the family constant support and encouragement. Thanks to the full Italian family of "MilBaRu" with my nephew Alex providing one of my favorite mottos: "Dreams are what you work for." My nieces and nephews all inspire me as well, even if they must accept my love of business and focus on entrepreneurship in almost every discussion: Jessica, Lily, Jacob, Andrew and Zachary. Adding with joy my newest daughter in Jason's wife Emily, who keeps a love of history front and center to inspire our family as a history teacher.

Co-Author and Contributors. I also have been fortunate to work with leading IP experts and to have their contributions to this book.

As my co-author on copyrights, trademark and design patents, **J. Christopher Lynch** is an outstanding intellectual property attorney, corporate executive, professor and colleague, leading him to influence his students to a record-making showing in a national moot court competition. He is a licensed patent attorney and intellectual property generalist, with decades in private law practice and as an adjunct professor teaching intellectual property. Chris is currently General Counsel of Silica-X, a materials science company. His mantra for entrepreneurs is "Get it. Keep it. Enforce it" as part of a holistic and robust IP strategy. You and I are fortunate to have his insights in Chapters 5: Copyrights, 7: Trademarks and Design Patents and related sections of 10: Checklist.

Other global experts who make guest appearances with industry-leading insights are the following, in order of appearance:

Julie Mar-Spinola, as a top litigator and monetizer of IP assets, is a Vice President of Legal Operations and Chief IP Officer for Finjan Holdings and a manager and board director of three of its subsidiaries, and oversaw the companies' revenue-based operations, securing nearly $300 million in licensing revenues and jury awards. She also led the defeat of securities-related litigations resulting from the acquisition of Finjan by Fortress Investments. Julie also is an inventor in cybersecurity, a former executive and director at numerous cutting-edge technology companies, and a former Chair of the prestigious US Patent and Trademark Office's Patent Public Advisory Committee (PPAC), where she successfully advocated in 2020 and 2021 for Congress and the Biden Administration to release to the USPTO $4.058 billion held in its treasury account to modernize its administration of patent law. In addition, Julie founded in 2005 a groundbreaking five thousand–plus member nonprofit women's organization known as ChIPs. Julie's unwavering belief that US innovation is the strength behind the US economy and her mentorship to women and men to align IP with business has had a singular shining impact on successes of companies, inventors and our precious US patent system.

Ruud Peters, formerly the Chief Intellectual Property Officer and Executive Vice President of Koninklijke Philips NV® for more than thirty-five years, was part of global leaders and visionaries who leveraged IP assets to support their global brand. In developing new methods for determining profits through IP for product sales and licensing transactions, Ruud converted the IP organization from a cost center into a successful profit-and-loss operation, commemorated in his 2010 induction into the IP Hall of Fame. Ruud graciously offers his insights on designing IP strategy with a profit mindset from the start in Chapter 4: Patents: Your Future Success.

Robert Rando is a partner in the Intellectual Property and Litigation practice groups and at Greenspoon Marder LLP and is the 2023 President of the prestigious New York IP Law Association. He has substantial experience in federal civil litigation, serving as lead counsel before numerous New York and national district courts, and in appellate courts as counsel/co-counsel of record on widely reported amicus brief filings before the United States Supreme Court and Federal Circuit since 2006.

Erich Spangenberg has the distinction of being one of the most successful patent litigators in history. After his litigation focus, Erich founded IPwe® in 2019 with a vision for the future of patents that commercializes patents outside of litigation models to drive innovation. IPwe has partnered with IBM® to use blockchain-enabled technologies in realizing patent value. I was proud to be the Chief Intellectual Property Officer (CIPO) to mind the store of the company's IP assets, and also to act as a consulting CIPO for our SME clients. This book brings that role and its guidance alive. We are fortunate to have CEO Erich, assisted by IPwe's Chief Product Officer **Jonas Block** (and an accomplished EU patent litigator), make guest appearances to introduce monetization—how to profit from patents in Chapter 4: Patents: Your Future Success.

Vincent Violago and his team at Parola Analytics, Inc., a leading analytics company, provide accessible, actionable intelligence for patents and IP strategy. Parola is the company behind the book from supporting research to editing, and of course with Vince offering his insights and experience along the way. Vince also led operations and community for Article One Partners as one of its key employees and champions for its researchers and culture. With appreciation Vince, Jenny, Naomi and team.

A special thanks as well to Susan Joy Paul who is a wonderful colleague as part of the team at Scribe, the publisher of this book. Susan inspired and illuminated this journey with her tremendous encouragement to follow the process, with the eventual result being holding your book in your hands. I have had a visualization of sitting next to my family and sharing #ip2ip, and I appreciate Susan and Scribe's approach to making it a reality.

ABOUT THE AUTHOR

CHERYL MILONE is an intellectual property attorney, electrical engineer, inventor, IP visionary and fierce champion of inventors and creators. Currently a Managing Director of Global IP Strategy at a leading global investment bank, Cheryl has contributed to the IP portfolios of companies from startups and SMEs to Fortune 50 companies, and she has been recognized as a Top 300 World's Leading IP Strategist by *IAM* magazine. Article One Partners, Cheryl's first venture, was named 2009 Startup of the Year by *Insider*, and she was honored at the White House as one of the top 50 most innovative CEOs in the US. Cheryl's career is devoted to honoring and valuing inventors and creators and innovating IP strategy. Visit Cheryl's website, cherylmilone.com, for more information.

REFERENCED INDIVIDUALS (LINKEDIN)

Co-Author: J. Christopher Lynch, Esq.:
https://www.linkedin.com/in/christopher-lynch-030b9b4/

***CONTRIBUTORS* (IN ORDER OF APPEARANCE):**

I am honored to have the contributions of global visionaries in intellectual property. For these contributors and for every individual referenced in this book, here are their LinkedIn® profiles to showcase them.

Julie Mar-Spinola, Esq.:
https://www.linkedin.com/in/jmarspinola2023/

Ruud Peters, Esq.:
https://www.linkedin.com/in/ruud-peters-489b741/

Robert Rando, Esq.:
https://www.linkedin.com/in/robert-rando-4696851/

Erich Spangenberg, Esq.:
https://www.linkedin.com/in/erichspangenberg/

Jonas Block, Esq.:
https://www.linkedin.com/in/jonas-block-25769658/

REFERENCES (IN ORDER OF APPEARANCE):

Joshua Malone:
https://www.linkedin.com/in/malonejosh/

Dr. Gary Michelson:
https://www.linkedin.com/in/gary-michelson/

David DiGiammarino:
https://www.linkedin.com/in/daviddigi/

Vincent Violago:
https://www.linkedin.com/in/vincentviolago/

For endnotes citations, my approach is informal, providing internet links for access to references and leaning more toward secondary resources to provide both source data, plus analysis and guidance by patent experts for additional learning. Where cases are cited, unless there is a specific quote from a case, I reference the full case for your review and context.

NOTES

1. *Thryv v. Click-to-Call*, No. 18-916 (US April 20, 2020) (Gorsuch, J., Sotomayor, J., dissenting), https://www.supremecourt.gov/opinions/19pdf/18-916_f2ah.pdf. And so it begins, even with this fundamental descriptor of patents as "real property," there is debate. Like any owner of property, patent owners seek governmental checks and balances to ensure their rights are protected. I defer to the eloquent analysis of United States Supreme Court justices in a 2020 dissenting opinion in *Thryv v. Click-to-Call*.

2. United States Patent and Trademark Office, "Remarks by USPTO Director Kathi Vidal at the 2022 SelectUSA Investment Summit," June 29, 2022, https://www.uspto.gov/about-us/news-updates/remarks-uspto-director-kathi-vidal-2022-selectusa-investment-summit.

3. Gene Quinn, "Iancu Weighs in on IP Waiver, Critical Role of Patents for SMEs at World IP Day Event," IPWatchdog, April 27, 2021, https://www.ipwatchdog.com/2021/04/27/iancu-weighs-ip-waiver-critical-role-patents-smes-world-ip-day/id=132816/.

4. US Patent Act, 35 U.S.C. §§ 1–351, https://www.govinfo.gov/content/pkg/USCODE-2011-title35/html/USCODE-2011-title35.htm.

5. Quinn, "Iancu Weighs in on IP Waiver."

6. United States Patent and Trademark Office, "Remarks by USPTO Director."

7. United States Patent and Trademark Office, "Remarks by Director Iancu at the State of Technology Conference," December 3, 2018, https://www.uspto.gov/about-us/news-updates/remarks-director-iancu-state-technology-conference.

8. Aisha Al-Muslim, "Intellectual-Property Assets are Getting More Valuable," *Wall Street Journal*, August 19, 2020, https://www.wsj.com/articles/intellectual-property-assets-are-getting-more-valuable-11597829401.

9. Irving Wladawsky-Berger, "The Intangible Asset Revolution," *Irving Wladawsky-Berger* (blog), January 16, 2021, https://blog.irvingwb.com/blog/2021/01/the-intangible-asset-revolutino.html.

10. Reprinted by permission from Aon PLC, "Tangible Assets vs. Intangible Assets for S&P 500 Companies, 1975–2018," in *2019 Intangible Assets Financial Statement Impact Comparison Report* (Ponemon Institute LLC, April 2019), https://www.aon.com/getmedia/60fbb49a-c7a5-4027-ba98-0553b29dc89f/Ponemon-Report-V24.aspx.

11   European Commission, "Action Plan on Intellectual Property—Questions and Answers," November 25, 2020, https://ec.europa.eu/commission/presscorner/detail/en/qanda_20_2188.

12   Randa Kriss, "14 Business Startup Costs Business Owners Need to Know," NerdWallet, December 16, 2020, https://www.nerdwallet.com/article/small-business/business-startup-costs.

13   Jonathan H. Ashtor, Michael J. Mazzeo, and Samantha Zyontz, "Patents at Issue: The Data Behind the Patent Troll Debate," *George Mason Law Review* 21 (2014): 957, https://www.kellogg.northwestern.edu/faculty/mazzeo/htm/patents_at_issue.pdf.

14   Jason Crotty, "Limiting the Number of Asserted Claims in Patent Cases," Mauriel Kapouytian Woods LLP, July 20, 2019, https://www.mkwllp.com/from-the-field/limiting-the-number-of-asserted-claims-in-patent-cases/.

15   IPWatchdog, "The Invent + Patent System"—Do It Yourself Provisional Patent Drafting Made Easy—Just $199*," https://ipwatchdog.com/patent/invent-patent-system/. IPWatchdog, a leading source of news and analysis on IP, and a team which I view as best-in-class, launched a program to assist with patent application preparation. I recommend you explore it as you evaluate patent agent and professional resources.

16   Counterfeit Goods Seizure Act of 2019, S. 2987, 116th Cong. (2019), https://www.congress.gov/bill/116th-congress/senate-bill/2987; Law360, "Design Patents Prove Successful on Enforcement, Defense," Sterne Kessler, May 2020, https://www.sternekessler.com/news-insights/publications/design-patents-prove-successful-enforcement-defense; United States Patent and Trademark Office, "USPTO Fee Schedule," last modified July 7, 2023, https://www.uspto.gov/learning-and-resources/fees-and-payment/uspto-fee-schedule; 15 U.S.C. § 638, https://docs.uscode.justia.com/2001/title15/USCODE-2001-title15/pdf/USCODE-2001-title15-chap14A-sec638.pdf; SBIR, STTR, "Timeline and Costs for Patent Filings," SBA, September 2017, https://www.sbir.gov/sites/all/themes/sbir/dawnbreaker/img/documents/Course16-Tutorial2.pdf ("Cost estimates…vary widely, but numerous surveys…have indicated…$5,000 to $15,000 for a US utility application depending upon the complexity of the technology."); American Intellectual Property Law Association, "2021 Report of the Economic Survey," September 2021, https://www.aipla.org/detail/journal-issue/2021-report-of-the-economic-survey (the American Intellectual Property Law Association produces a definitive source based on US attorney surveys, which can be ordered); UpCounsel, "How Much Does an International Patent Cost: Everything You Need to Know," accessed August 22, 2023, https://www.upcounsel.com/how-much-does-an-international-patent-cost. However, "[t]he total investment to prepare, prosecute, and maintain a patent for its life in four or five countries can easily exceed $200,000."

17   Johanna Dwyer, "Why IP Strategy Matters," LOT Network, accessed August 17, 2023, https://lotnet.com/why-ip-strategy-matters/.

18   Samuel Stebbins, "The World's 50 Most Innovative Companies," *USA Today*, January 12, 2018, https://www.usatoday.com/story/money/business/2018/01/12/worlds-50-most-innovative-companies/1023095001/.

19   *Merriam-Webster*, s.v. "quality (n.)," accessed August 17, 2023, https://www.merriam-webster.com/dictionary/quality.

20   Ashtor, Mazzeo, and Zyontz, "Patents at Issue."

21   John R. Allison and Ronald J. Mann, "The Disputed Quality of Software Patents," Columbia Law School Scholarship Archive, 2007, https://scholarship.law.columbia.edu/cgi/viewcontent.cgi?article=1272&context=faculty_scholarship.

22   Computer Software Copyright Act of 1980, H.R. 6934, 96th Cong. (1980), https://www.congress.gov/bill/96th-congress/house-bill/6934. The 1960s' and '70s' volleys focused on whether software should be copyrighted, with the USCO leading the way on registering copyrights, followed by court battles and finally a resolution by the Computer Software Copyright Act of 1980.

23   *Diamond v. Diehr*, 450 US 175 (1981), https://supreme.justia.com/cases/federal/us/450/175/.

24 David Kline and David Kappos, "America's Uniquely Democratic Patent System," in *Intellectual Property* (2021), https://openstax.org/books/introduction-intellectual-property/pages/1-3-americas-uniquely-democratic-patent-system.

25 RogerKay, "Where Did the Patent Troll Narrative Come From?," *Medium*, February 12, 2018, https://rogerkay.medium.com/where-did-the-patent-troll-narrative-come-from-301b20072dac.

26 Cheryl Milone, "Stopping Abusive Patent Litigants," *The Federal Lawyer* (October/November 2013): 38–45, https://www.fedbar.org/wp-content/uploads/2013/10/feature3-octnov13-pdf-1.pdf.

27 Allison and Mann, "The Disputed Quality of Software Patents."

28 Adam Mossoff, "A Brief History of Software Patents (and Why They're Valid)," George Mason University Law and Economics Research Paper Series, *Arizona Law Review Syllabus* 56 (2014): 62–77, https://papers.ssrn.com/sol3/papers.cfm?abstract_id=2477462. I commend you to a trenchant history of this innovation and the vacillations of the stakeholders pressing their positions.

29 Quinn, "Iancu Weighs in on IP Waiver."

30 Both patents and trade secrets can be sought for different facets of key innovations using sophisticated strategies too.

31 Alfonso Borello, *War of the Currents: Nikola Tesla*, second ed. (Villaggio Publishing Ltd., 2018), https://www.amazon.com/War-Currents-Nikola-Tesla-Edtion/dp/B0848P32JL.

32 Elizabeth Nix, "How Edison, Tesla and Westinghouse Battled to Electrify America," History, May 2, 2023, https://www.history.com/news/what-was-the-war-of-the-currents.

33 Elon Musk, "All Our Patent Are Belong to You," Tesla, June 12, 2014, https://www.tesla.com/blog/all-our-patent-are-belong-you. Elon Musk also directed Tesla in 2014 to formally donate the company's patents to the industry, as a form of open-source contribution.

34 The Michaelson Institute for Intellectual Property, home page, accessed August 17, 2023, https://michelsonip.com.

35 The name of my startup commemorated the source of patent law in Article 1 of the US Constitution.

36 Zuru, "Bunch O Balloons," brand page, accessed August 17, 2023, https://www.bunchoballoons.com/.

37 Ruth Simon, "Four-Year Water Balloon Fight Ends with $31 Million Truce," *Wall Street Journal*, May 20, 2019, https://www.wsj.com/articles/four-year-water-balloon-fight-ends-with-31-million-truce-11558388873.

38 Gene Quinn, "The Most Iconic (and Patented) Toys and Games of All Time," IPWatchdog, December 23, 2018, https://ipwatchdog.com/2018/12/23/iconic-patented-toys-games/id=91631/; Toy Building Brick (LEGO), US Patent No. 3,005,282 (issued Oct. 24, 1961), https://image-ppubs.uspto.gov/dirsearch-public/print/downloadPdf/3005282; Spatial Logical Toy (Rubik's Cube), US Patent No. 4,378,116 (issued March 29, 1983), https://image-ppubs.uspto.gov/dirsearch-public/print/downloadPdf/4378116; Board Game Apparatus (Monopoly), US Patent No. 2,026,082 (issued December 31, 1935), https://image-ppubs.uspto.gov/dirsearch-public/print/downloadPdf/2026082; Game Board (Battleship), US Patent No. 1,988,301 (issued January 15, 1935), https://image-ppubs.uspto.gov/dirsearch-public/print/downloadPdf/1988301. These chess patents are showcased in a leading IP blog, founded by Gene Quinn, a great supporter of strong US patent rights.

39 The specification technically includes the claims and excludes the front page and the drawings.

40 A formal analysis of claim scope requires an assessment of the patent's history at the USPTO (contained in a compilation of communications about the patent with the Office called a file wrapper) and the technology at the time of filing.

41 Patent validity is determined as of a point in time. Were this patent litigated today, it likely would be challenged as invalid under 35 U.S.C. § 101.

42 US Patent No. 19,783 (issued March 30, 1858), https://patentimages.storage.googleapis.com/1a/4b/36/54189f6c3675fa/US19783.pdf.

43 This spark and its date classically were called the date of conception. Conception was followed by developing the invention enough to have a working product or service, or describing it in a patent application filing to meet the statutory requirements, called a "reduction to practice."

44 America Invents Act, S. Res. 23, 112th Cong. (2011), https://www.congress.gov/bill/112th-congress/senate-bill/23.

45 Adriana L. Burgy et al., "Record-Keeping and Proving Inventorship," *Prosecution First Blog*, Finnegan, February 12, 2021, https://www.finnegan.com/en/insights/blogs/prosecution-first/record-keeping-and-proving-inventorship.html.

46 Fenn Mathew, *Understanding Prior Art and its Use in Determining Patentability* (Alexandria, VA: United States Patent and Trademark Office, Office of Innovation, accessed August 18, 2023), https://www.uspto.gov/sites/default/files/documents/May%20Info%20Chat%20slides%20%28003%29.pdf. Additional examples of prior art include published, printed, audio or handwritten documents which are publicly available or other evidence of publicly known technology, such as testimonial evidence of prior use, and commercially available products or services and their advertisements.

47 Matthew Kitces and Angelo Christopher, "Understanding Global Grace Periods to Avoid Missing Patent Opportunities," Nixon Peabody, September 29, 2021, https://www.nixonpeabody.com/insights/alerts/2021/09/29/worldwide-patent-grace-periods.

48 Dennis Crouch, "On Sale Bar—Sales Require Consideration, Not Necessarily Money Payment," Patently-O, May 2, 2022, https://patentlyo.com/patent/2022/05/require-consideration-necessarily.html.

49 Karen Sutton, "Secret Sales Sink Patents: Why You Cannot Rely on an NDA to Fully Protect Your Invention," LinkedIn, January 22, 2019, https://www.linkedin.com/pulse/secret-sales-sink-patents-why-you-cannot-rely-nda-karen/.

50 Daniel G. Shanley and Steven L. Wood, "An Absolute Novelty Design Patent Trap for the Unwary," The National Law Review, December 23, 2021, https://www.natlawreview.com/article/absolute-novelty-design-patent-trap-unwary.

51 I have presented it in lighter font because my strong guidance is for you to ignore it and instead follow Top-10 Takeaway 1.

52 US Patent Act, 35 U.S.C. § 101.

53 US Patent Act, 35 U.S.C. §§ 102, 103, 112.

54 US Patent Act, 35 U.S.C. § 282.

55 Daniel Vojcak, "Proving a Patent Invalid: The Burden Is on the Challenger," IPWatchdog, November 18, 2017, https://ipwatchdog.com/2017/11/18/proving-patent-invalid/id=89780/.

56 RPX, "*Alice* Invalidation Rate Stands at 60% Overall Despite Berkheimer Dip," April 1, 2020, https://www.rpxcorp.com/data-byte/alice-invalidation-rate-stands-at-60-overall-despite-berkheimer-dip/.

57 Dennis Crouch, "What is Required for Willful Infringement and Enhanced Damages?," Patently-O, March 20, 2022, https://patentlyo.com/patent/2022/03/required-infringement-enhanced.html.

58 Eric Rogers and Young Jeon, "Inhibiting Patent Trolling: A New Approach for Applying Rule 11," *Journal of Technology and Intellectual Property* 12, no. 4 (2014), https://scholarlycommons.law.northwestern.edu/njtip/vol12/iss4/2/.

59 Joff Wild, "A Comeback for Injunctions Would Help to Revive US Patent Leadership," IAM, March 2, 2023, https://www.iam-media.com/article/jw-column-2nd-march-2023-us-patent-leadership-sacrificed.

60 Gene Quinn, "Why *eBay v. MercExchange* Should, But Won't, Be Overruled," IPWatchdog, February 16, 2020, https://ipwatchdog.com/2020/02/16/ebay-v-mercexchange-wont-overruled/id=118929/.

61 Dharshini David, "COVID: Germany Rejects US-Backed Proposal to Waive Vaccine Patents," *BBC News*, May 6, 2021, https://www.bbc.com/news/world-europe-57013096.

62 Andrei Iancu, "World Leaders Should Acknowledge That IP Protections Facilitate Vaccine Access," Center for Strategic and International Studies, January 6, 2022, https://www.csis.org/analysis/world-leaders-should-acknowledge-ip-protections-facilitate-vaccine-access.

63 US Patent Act, 35 U.S.C. § 111(b); Kimberlee Leonard, Jane Haskins, and Cassie Bottorff, "How to File a Provisional Patent in 2023," *Forbes Advisor*, August 6, 2022, https://www.forbes.com/advisor/business/how-to-file-provisional-patent/.

64 United States Patent and Trademark Office, "U.S. Patent Statistics Chart Calendar Years 1963–2020," last modified August 18, 2023, https://www.uspto.gov/web/offices/ac/ido/oeip/taf/us_stat.htm.

65 Inventors Digest, "Your USPTO: Rejected Again. Now What?," March 1, 2023, https://www.inventorsdigest.com/articles/your-uspto-rejected-again-now-what/. When an owner wants to continue to pursue patent rights, patents are most often refiled with the PTO in order to present new arguments to the Examiner, under a request for examination (or RCE). Other options are to file an appeal or abandon the application. Failure to take action results in abandonment.

66 *Alice v. CLS Bank*, 573 US 208 (2014) (interpreted key prior case law, including another US case, *Mayo v. Prometheus*), https://casetext.com/case/alice-corp-v-cls-bank-intl; *Mayo v. Prometheus*, 566 US 66 (2012), https://casetext.com/case/mayo-collaborative-servs-v-prometheus-labs-inc-3.

67 RPX, "Alice Invalidation Rate Stands at 60%."

68 Gaston Kroub, "3 Takeaways from the Lex Machina 2023 Patent Report," Above the Law, February 21, 2023, https://abovethelaw.com/2023/02/3-takeaways-from-the-lex-machina-2023-patent-report/; Lex Machina, "Lex Machina Releases 2023 Patent Litigation Report," Cision, February 15, 2023, https://www.prnewswire.com/news-releases/lex-machina-releases-2023-patent-litigation-report-301743487. Represented by 2020 damage awards.

69 Unified Patents, "2022 Patent Dispute Report: First Half in Review," July 1, 2022, https://www.unifiedpatents.com/insights/2022/7/1/2022-patent-dispute-report-first-half-in-review/; Steve Brachmann and Gene Quinn, "Are More Than 90 Percent of Patents Challenged at the PTAB Defective?," IPWatchdog, June 14, 2017, https://ipwatchdog.com/2017/06/14/90-percent-patents-challenged-ptab-defective/id=84343/. About 39.5 percent of disputes in district court prompt a challenge at the PTAB. While the statistics provided by the USPTO on a claim count basis present that only 10 percent of challenged claims are invalidated, patent owners are often subject to multiple petitions on the same claims, resulting in only 4 percent to 16 percent of all PTAB petitions concluding with all claims being upheld as patentable. Importantly, fifty-five or so patent owners targeted by PTAB challenges account for 20 percent of petitions total.

70 Raymond Millien and Yi Chen, "In First Half of 2021, 63 Percent of US Patents, 48.9 percent at EPO and 40.1 Percent in China Were Software-Related," IPWatchdog, August 26, 2021, https://ipwatchdog.com/2021/08/26/first-half-2021-63-u-s-patents-48-9-epo-40-1-china-software-related/id=137100/.

71 Raymond Millien, "Seven Years after *Alice*, 63.2 Percent of the US Patents Issued in 2020 Were Software-Related," IPWatchdog, March 17, 2021, https://www.ipwatchdog.com/2021/03/17/seven-years-after-alice-63-2-of-the-u-s-patents-issued-in-2020-were-software-related/id=130978/. Sixty-three percent of patents issued in 2020 are "software-related."

72 *Diamond v. Chakrabarty*, 447 US 303, 309 (1980) (citing S. Rep. No. 1979, 82d Cong. at 5 [1952]), https://casetext.com/case/diamond-v-chakrabarty.

73 *Alice v. CLS Bank*, 573 US 208 at 235.

74 *Alice v. CLS Bank*, 573 US 208 at 235.

75 *Mirror Imaging v. PNC Bank*, No. 6:21-cv-00518-ADA (W.D. Tex.) at 7 (2022), https://law.justia.com/cases/federal/district-courts/texas/txwdce/6:2021cv00518/1134951/31/.

76 *State Street Bank & Trust v. Signature Financial Group*, 149 F.3d 1368 (Fed. Cir. 1998), https://law.justia.com/cases/federal/appellate-courts/F3/149/1368/560460/.

77 *Bilski v. Kappos*, 561 US 593 (2010), https://supreme.justia.com/cases/federal/us/561/593/.

78 Leahy-Smith America Invents Act, Pub. L. 112-29, 125 Stat. 284 (2011), https://www.uspto.gov/sites/default/files/aia_implementation/20110916-pub-l112-29.pdf.

79 United States Patent and Trademark Office, "2019 Revised Patent Subject Matter Eligibility Guidance," *Federal Register* 84, no. 4 (January 7, 2019), https://www.govinfo.gov/content/pkg/FR-2019-01-07/pdf/2018-28282.pdf.

80 *Cleveland Clinic Foundation v. True Health Diagnostics*, 760 Fed. App'x. 1013 (Fed. Cir. 2019), http://cafc.uscourts.gov/sites/default/files/opinions-orders/18-1218.Opinion.4-1-2019.pdf; Bookoff McAndrews, "Federal Courts Not Bound by USPTO § 101 Guidance," *Bookoff McAndrews* (blog), June 11, 2019, https://www.bomcip.com/blog/federal-courts-not-bound-uspto-%C2%A7-101-guidance/.

81 United States Patent and Trademark Office, "Remarks by USPTO Director Kathi Vidal" (see SME statistics). Kathi Vidal has been an active director to date, authoring numerous precedential decisions.

82 *Alice v. CLS Bank*, 573 US 208 at 217.

83 *Yu v. Apple*, 1 F.4th 1040 (Fed. Cir. 2021) (Newman, J., dissenting), https://casetext.com/case/yu-v-apple-inc-2.

84 *The State of Patent Eligibility in America: Part I: Hearing Before the United States Senate Subcomm. on Intellectual Property, Comm. on the Judiciary*, 116th Cong. (2019) (testimony from Paul R. Michel, J., ret., Fed. Cir.), https://www.judiciary.senate.gov/committee-activity/hearings/the-state-of-patent-eligibility-in-america-part-i.

85 *American Axle & Manufacturing v. Neapco Holdings*, 939 F.3d 1355 (Fed. Cir. 2019), cert. denied, WL 2347622 (US June 30, 2022), https://casetext.com/case/am-axle-mfg-v-neapco-holdings-llc; Foley Hoag, "Déjà Vu: The Supreme Court Ignores the Solicitor General's Invitation to Revisit Section 101…Again," May 19, 2023, https://foleyhoag.com/news-and-insights/publications/alerts-and-updates/2023/may/deja-vu-the-supreme-court-ignores-the-solicitor-generals-invitation-to-revisit-section-101/.

86 Patent Eligibility Restoration Act of 2023, S. Res. 2140, 118th Cong. (2023) (introduced by Reps. Coons and Tillis, using the narrow language that they "cannot practically be performed without the use of a machine or manufacture"), https://www.congress.gov/bill/118th-congress/senate-bill/2140/cosponsors?s=1&r=29.

87 Judge Paul Michel, "Senators' Patent Reform Bills Offer a Strong Way Forward for the U.S. Patent System," IPWatchdog, June 26, 2023, https://ipwatchdog.com/2023/06/26/senators-patent-reform-bills-offer-strong-way-forward-us-patent-system/id=162686/.

88 *American Axle & Manufacturing v. Neapco Holdings*, "Brief Amicus Curiae of United States Senator Thom Tillis, Honorable Paul R. Michel and Honorable David J. Kappos," March 1, 2021, https://www.supremecourt.gov/search.aspx?filename=/docket/docketfiles/html/public/20-891.html.

89 *Alice v. CLS Bank*, 573 US 208 at 219; *Uniloc v. LG Electronics*, 957 F.3d 1303, 1306–07 (Fed. Cir. 2020) ("In cases involving software innovations, this inquiry often turns on whether the claims focus on specific asserted improvements in computer capabilities or instead on a process or system that qualifies an abstract idea for which computers are invoked merely as a tool."), https://casetext.com/case/uniloc-usa-inc-v-lg-elecs-usa-inc-3.

90 United States Patent and Trademark Office, "2019 Revised Patent Subject Matter Eligibility Guidance."

91 *Enfish v. Microsoft*, 822 F.3d 1327 (Fed. Cir. 2016), https://casetext.com/case/enfish-llc-v-microsoft-corp-4.

92 While the Court generally considers improving the functionality of a computer under Step 2B, the *Enfish* Court went further, holding that the claim recitation of improved computer functionality satisfied Step 2A.

93 *DDR Holdings v. Hotels.com*, 773 F.3d 1245 (Fed. Cir. 2014), https://casetext.com/case/ddr-holdings-llc-v-hotelscom-lp.

94 *CosmoKey Solutions v. Duo Security*, Case No. 20-2043 (Fed. Cir. 2021), https://cafc.uscourts.gov/opinions-orders/20-2043.opinion.10-4-2021_1843694.pdf. In addition to the favorable and unusual holding, a concurrence by Judge Jimmie V. Reyna presented that the analysis should have been undertaken under the Mayo/Alice framework step one rather than step two. *Enfish v. Microsoft*, 822 F.3d 1327; *DDR Holdings v. Hotels.com*, 773 F.3d 1245; *Trading Techs v. IBG*, 921 F.3d 1084 (Fed. Cir. 2019), https://casetext.com/case/trading-techs-intl-inc-v-ibg-llc.

95 *Koninklijke KPN v. Gemalto M2M*, 942 F.3d 1143, 1150 (Fed. Cir. 2019) ("Absent sufficient recitation of how the purported invention improved the functionality of a computer, the 'improvement' captured by those claims was recited at such a level of result-oriented generality that those claims amounted to a mere implementation of an abstract idea on a computer, not the specific way to improve the functionality of a computer."), https://casetext.com/case/koninklijke-kpn-nv-v-gemalto-m2m-gmbh.

96 *Amdocs (Israel) v. Openet Telecom*, 841 F.3d 1288 (Fed. Cir. 2016), https://casetext.com/case/amdocs-israel-ltd-v-openet-telecom-inc-2; *Enfish v. Microsoft*, 822 F.3d 1327.

97 *Amdocs (Israel) v. Openet Telecom*, 841 F.3d 1288; *Enfish v. Microsoft*, 822 F.3d 1327. *Bascom Global Internet Services v. AT&T*, 827 F.3d 1341 (Fed. Cir. 2016), https://foiadocuments.uspto.gov/federal/15-1763_1.pdf; *Thales Visionix v. U.S.*, 850 F.3d 1343 (Fed. Cir. 2017), https://foiadocuments.uspto.gov/federal/15-5150_1.pdf.

98 *Diamond v. Diehr*, 450 U.S. 175; *Bilski v. Kappos*, 561 U.S. 593. In *Bilski* (2010), the SCOTUS presented that the machine or transformation test is not definitive or the sole test for patent eligibility; it is only an important and useful clue.

99 United States Patent and Trademark Office, "2019 Revised Patent Subject Matter Eligibility Guidance."

100 *Classen Immunotherapies v. Biogen Idec*, 659 F.3d 1057 (Fed. Cir. 2011) (on remand from the Supreme Court after Bilski [2010]), https://casetext.com/case/classen-immunotherapies-inc-v-idec; Courtenay C. Brinckerhoff, "Federal Circuit Reverses Course on *Classen*, Finds that Many Method Claims Satisfy 35 USC § 101, Safe Harbor of 35 USC § 271(e)(1) Does Not Shelter Many Defendants," Foley, August 31, 2011, https://www.foley.com/en/insights/publications/2011/08/federal-circuit-reverses-course-on-iclasseni-finds.

101 In addition, the timing of an invalidity finding in the Court and the USPTO may conflict, resulting in different appellate tracks and further complexity and delays in ultimate outcomes.

102 United States Patent and Trademark Office, "Inter Partes Review," October 10, 2022, https://www.uspto.gov/patents/ptab/trials/inter-partes-review; *Uniloc 2017 v. Hulu*, 966 F.3d 1295 (Fed. Cir. 2020), https://casetext.com/case/uniloc-2017-llc-v-hulu-llc; Charles R. Macedo and Christopher Lisiewski, "ARE PTAB Alert: Two Recent Federal Circuit and PTAB Decisions Have Expanded the Role of the PTAB in Motions to Amend," Amster, Rothstein & Ebenstein LLP, July 24, 2020, https://www.arelaw.com/publications/view/alert07242020/.

103 Leahy-Smith America Invents Act, Pub. L. 112-29; The National Law Review, "IPR and CBM Statistics for Final Written Decisions Issued in December 2020 and January 2021," March 10, 2021, https://www.natlawreview.com/article/ipr-and-cbm-statistics-final-written-decisions-issued-december-2020-and-january-2021.

104 Law360, "Stays Pending IPR in Del. District Courts are Here to Stay," accessed August 21, 2023, https://www.law360.com/articles/1472447/stays-pending-ipr-in-del-district-courts-are-here-to-stay. District courts decide to stay their cases where an IPR is filed about 65 percent of the time nationwide, with 80 percent for the District of Delaware (as a primary litigation jurisdiction).

105 Georgianna Witt Braden, *USPTO Administrative Tribunal: Patent Trial and Appeal Board* (Alexandria, VA: United States Patent and Trademark Office, 2023), https://www.uspto.gov/sites/default/files/documents/ptab_stadium_tour_20230223_.pdf. Post-AIA, a historic PTAB approach to interpreting claims was also changed so both fora are now aligned in using the ordinary and customary meaning of the claims. Additional issues are the use of the same or "substantially the same" prior art in multiple IPRs and court.

106 Braden, *USPTO Administrative Tribunal.*

107 Steve Brachmann, "PTAB Precedential Decision Nomination Form Could Lead to More Controversial Decision-Making Outside of Informal Rulemaking," IPWatchdog, October 15, 2020, https://ipwatchdog.com/2020/10/15/ptab-precedential-decision-nomination-form-could-lead-to-more-controversial-decision-making-outside-of-informal-rulemaking/id=126239/. Courts have provided that they do not recognize the USPTO decisions, such as those designated as POP, as precedential.

108 US Patent Act, 35 U.S.C. § 284.

109 In re Seagate Tech., 497 F.3d 1360, 1365 (Fed. Cir. 2007) ("to establish willful infringement, a patentee must show by clear and convincing evidence that the infringer acted despite an objectively high likelihood that its actions constituted infringement of a valid patent." Once this threshold was satisfied, it was required to establish that "the risk of infringement was "either known or so obvious that it should have been known to the accused infringer."), https://casetext.com/case/in-re-seagate-technology-llc.

110 *Halo Elecs. v. Pulse Elecs.*, 136 S. Ct. 1923 (2016), https://casetext.com/case/halo-elecs-inc-v-pulse-elecs-inc-5.

111 *Halo Elecs. v. Pulse Elecs.*, 136 S. Ct. 1923 at 1934–1935.

112 *SRI Int'l v. Cisco Sys.*, 14 F.4th 1323 (Fed. Cir. 2021) (Fed. Cir. denied rehearing, Jan. 4, 2022) ("To eliminate the confusion created by our reference to the language 'wanton, malicious, and bad-faith' in Halo, we clarify that it was not our intent to create a heightened requirement for willful infringement."), https://casetext.com/case/sri-intl-v-cisco-sys.

113 Vivek Krishnan, "Insights From Judges From Panel on Willfulness, FRAND, & Patentability," Winston & Strawn LLP, August 14, 2020, https://www.winston.com/en/federal-circuit-update-intellectual-property-decisions/insights-from-judges-from-panel-on-willfulness,-frand,-and-patentability.html.

114 Eric Siegel, "The AI Hype Cycle is Distracting Companies," *Harvard Business Review*, June 2, 2023, https://hbr.org/2023/06/the-ai-hype-cycle-is-distracting-companies.

115 *Thaler v. Vidal*, No. 21-2347, 43 F.4th 1207 (Fed. Cir. 2022), https://cafc.uscourts.gov/opinions-orders/21-2347.OPINION.8-5-2022_1988142.pdf; United States Patent and Trademark Office, *Public Views on Artificial Intelligence and Intellectual Property Policy* (Alexandria, VA: United States Patent and Trademark Office, 2020), https://www.uspto.gov/sites/default/files/documents/USPTO_AI-Report_2020-10-07.pdf; https://www.wipo.int/wipo_magazine/en/2019/01/article_0001.html#:~:text=The%20fields%20showing%20the%20highest,government%3B%20law%3B%20and%20transportation; United States Copyright Office, "Copyright Office Launches New Artificial Intelligence Initiative," Copyright.gov, March 16, 2023, https://www.copyright.gov/newsnet/2023/1004.html; https://www.foxnews.com/us/copyright-board-delivers-blow-terminator-tech-photo-protections.

116 Blake Brittain, "Judge Pares Down Artists' AI Copyright Lawsuit against Midjourney, Stability AI," *Reuters*, October 30, 2023, https://www.reuters.com/legal/litigation/judge-pares-down-artists-ai-copyright-lawsuit-against-midjourney-stability-ai-2023-10-30/; Marty Swant, "U.S. Lawmakers Focus on Copyright Issues around AI's Impact on Intellectual Property," *Digiday*, July 13, 2023, https://digiday.com/media/u-s-lawmakers-focus-on-copyright-issues-around-ais-impact-on-intellectual-property/; Scott Nover, "A.I. May Not Get a Chance to Kill Us If This Kills It First," *Slate*, October 17, 2023, https://slate.com/technology/2023/10/artificial-intelligence-copyright-thomson-reuters-ross-intelligence-westlaw-lawsuit.html; Bobby Allyn, "*New York Times* Considers Legal Action Against OpenAI as Copyright Tensions Swirl," *NPR*, August 16, 2023, https://www.npr.org/2023/08/16/1194202562/new-york-times-considers-legal-action-against-openai-as-copyright-tensions-swirl; John Kell, "AI is about to Face Many More Legal Risks. Here's How Businesses Can Prepare," *Fortune*, November 8, 2023, https://fortune.com/2023/11/08/ai-playbook-legality/; Winston Cho, "As AI Battle Lines are Drawn, Studios Align with Big Tech in a Risky Bet," *The Hollywood Reporter*, November 7, 2023, https://www.hollywoodreporter.com/business/business-news/ai-copyright-law-studios-tech-actors-writers-1235638242/; Toby Headdon, Anneke Pol, and Toby Crick, "Copyright Infringement Class Action Against Microsoft, Open AI and GitHub Concerning Co-Pilot AI Tool," Bristows, November 10, 2022, https://www.lexology.com/library/detail.aspx?g=de8ac9fe-53d8-4a05-8b66-096bdaa2f6fb.

117 *Andy Warhol Found. for Visual Arts v. Goldsmith*, No. 21-869 (US May 18, 2023), https://www.supremecourt.gov/opinions/22pdf/21-869_87ad.pdf; *Jack Daniel's Properties v. VIP Products*, No. 22-148 (US June 8, 2023), https://www.supremecourt.gov/opinions/22pdf/22-148_3e04.pdf. These cases are discussed in Chapters 5 and 7, Copyrights and Trademarks.

118 Kell, "AI Is about to Face Many More Legal Risks"; Tate Ryan-Mosley and Melissa Heikkilä, "Three Things to Know about the White House's Executive Order on AI," MIT Technology Review, October 30, 2023, https://www.technologyreview.com/2023/10/30/1082678/three-things-to-know-about-the-white-houses-executive-order-on-ai/; BCLP, "U.S. State Legislative Bills on AI: A Mid-Year Update," June 22, 2023, https://www.bclplaw.com/en-US/events-insights-news/overview-of-us-state-legislative-bills-on-ai-in-2023.html.

119 Spencer Feingold, "The European Union's Artificial Intelligence Act—Explained," World Economic Forum, June 30, 2023, https://www.weforum.org/agenda/2023/06/european-union-ai-act-explained/.

120 Ana Nicenko, "Goldman Sachs Ranks Bitcoin as the Best-Performing Asset of 2023," *Finbold*, January 25, 2023, https://finbold.com/goldman-sachs-ranks-bitcoin-as-the-best-performing-asset-of-2023/.

121 Bernard Marr, "Web3, NFTs, and the Future of Art," *Forbes*, August 19, 2022, https://www.forbes.com/sites/bernardmarr/2022/08/19/web3-nfts-and-the-future-of-art/?sh=4c395ffa1e05.

122 The Linux Foundation, "Why the Future of Web3 Needs Open Source, Sustainable Blockchains," February 28, 2023, https://www.linuxfoundation.org/blog/why-the-future-of-web3-needs-open-source-sustainable-blockchains.

123 Arun Chandrasekaran, "What IT Leaders Need to Know about Open Source Software," InformationWeek, March 23, 2021, https://www.informationweek.com/devops/what-it-leaders-need-to-know-about-open-source-software.

124 Finjan Cybersecurity, "Finjan Holdings Commits to Licensing Best Practices," press release, March 20, 2014, https://www.finjan.com/news-media/press-releases/detail/204/finjan-holdings-commits-to-licensing-best-practices.

125 Nathan Wajsman et al., *High-Growth Firms and Intellectual Property Rights* (Alicante, Spain: European Union Intellectual Property Office, 2019), https://euipo.europa.eu/tunnel-web/secure/webdav/guest/document_library/observatory/documents/reports/2019_High-growth_firms_and_intellectual_property_rights/2019_High-growth_firms_and_intellectual_property_rights.pdf.

126 Patent Effect, "How Patents Affect VCs' Funding Decisions?—Case of Early Stage Ventures," August 28, 2019, https://www.patenteffect.com/post/how-patents-affect-vcs-funding-decisions.

127 17 U.S.C. § 102, https://www.law.cornell.edu/uscode/text/17/102; United States Copyright Office, "Copyrightable Authorship: What Can Be Registered," in *Compendium of U.S. Copyright Office Practices*, third ed. (2021), https://www.copyright.gov/comp3/chap300/ch300-copyrightable-authorship.pdf; *Feist Publications v. Rural Tel. Serv.*, 499 US 340 (1991) ("Factual compilations...may possess the requisite originality. The compilation author typically chooses which facts to include, what order to place them, and how to arrange the collected data so that they may be used effectively by readers. These choices as to selection and arrangement, so long as they are made independently by the compiler and entail a minimal degree of creativity, are sufficiently original that Congress may protect such compilations through the copyright laws."), https://supreme.justia.com/cases/federal/us/499/340/. Regarding digital content, copyright is available for a sufficiently creative or original selection or arrangement of data as a compilation, but not the underlying data or factual content itself.

128 United States Copyright Office, "Register Your Work: Registration Portal," Copyright.gov, accessed August 21, 2023, https://www.copyright.gov/registration/.

129 17 U.S.C. § 102; United States Copyright Office, "Copyrightable Authorship"; *Feist Publications v. Rural Tel. Serv.*, 499 US 340.

130 University Copyright Office, "Copyright Infringement Penalties," Purdue University, https://www.lib.purdue.edu/uco/infringement. Some copyright litigation, however, is anything but quiet. Notoriety can accompany expression, especially for celebrity artists and musicians. This legal question is focused on whether the expression itself is copied as a more narrow or quiet analysis identifying the boundaries for ideas before assessing copying in patent litigation.

131 17 U.S.C. § 101; *SAS Inst. v. World Programming*, No. 21-1542 (Fed. Cir. 2023), https://casetext.com/case/sas-inst-v-world-programming-ltd; Google v. Oracle, 141 S. Ct. 1183 (2021), https://casetext.com/case/google-llc-v-oracle-am-inc. The House Report for the Act explicitly includes computer programs in the definition of "literary works."

132 *SAS Inst. v. World Programming*, No. 21-1542; *Google v. Oracle*, 141 S. Ct. 1183.

133 17 U.S.C. § 107; *Andy Warhol Found. for Visual Arts v. Goldsmith*, No. 21-869.

134 United States Copyright Office, "Register Your Work."

135 17 U.S.C. § 504.

136 As with statutory damages, attorneys' fees are only available to timely registered copyright owners. If the registration comes after the commencement of the infringement (and outside the ninety-day grace period after publication) then no attorneys' fees can be had for the infringement, making most copyright litigation impractical without a timely registration unless the actual damages are significant.

137 Neil Turkewitz, "In Honor of Constitution Day: Article 1, Section 8, Clause 8 and the Pursuit of Happiness," *Medium*, September 17, 2018, https://medium.com/@@nturkewitz_56674/in-honor-of-constitution-day-article-1-section-8-clause-8-and-the-pursuit-of-happiness-8bd46ac608.

138 The sentence is protectable, but reuse might be fair use.

139 17 U.S.C. § 102.

140 The application includes an indication of whether or not the deposit includes trade secret material. The USCO provides two options for a representative portion, either the first and last ten pages of the code (for a total of twenty pages) or the first and last twenty-five pages of the code (for a total of fifty pages). Selecting which option to use depends upon whether the code contains trade secrets. The pages of the deposit should include a copyright notice and notification of trade secrets.

141 World Intellectual Property Organization, "Berne Convention for the Protection of Literary and Artistic Works," accessed August 21, 2023, https://www.wipo.int/treaties/en/ip/berne/; Copyright Term Extension, H.R. 2589, 105th Cong., 2d Sess. (1998), https://www.congress.gov/105/bills/hr2589/BILLS-105hr2589eh.pdf. The 1989 Berne Convention Implementation Act enabled the US to join the international copyright community. Then, the 1998 enactment of the Sonny Bono Copyright Term Extension Act extended the duration of copyright protection to life plus seventy for individuals, and ninety-five years for corporate works.

142 17 U.S.C. § 102.

143 17 U.S.C. § 410.

144 17 U.S.C. § 101.

145 17 U.S.C. §§ 411, 412.

146 17 U.S.C. §§ 101, 201.

147 17 U.S.C. § 102, and all subsequent amendments to copyright law and other related statutes.

148 17 U.S.C. §§ 101, 201.

149 17 U.S.C. § 101.

150 Brownstein Client Alert, "The Importance of a Work Made For Hire Agreement," Brownstein, August 15, 2022, https://www.bhfs.com/insights/alerts-articles/2022/the-importance-of-a-work-made-for-hire-agreement; US Department of Labor, "US Department of Labor Announces Proposes Rule on Classifying Employees, Independent Contractors; Seeks to Return to Longstanding Interpretation," news release no. 22-1526-NAT, October 11, 2022, https://www.dol.gov/newsroom/releases/WHD/WHD20221011-0. With 2023 proposed rule changes, follow the developments as you are finalizing independent contractor agreements.

151 United States Copyright Office, "What Is Publication and Why Is It Important?," in *Copyright Basics*, Copyright.gov, September 2021, https://www.copyright.gov/circs/circ01.pdf#page=7; 17 U.S.C. § 412.

152 *SAS Inst. v. World Programming*, No. 21-1542; *Google v. Oracle*, 141 S. Ct. 1183.

153 17 U.S.C. § 107.

154 *SAS Inst. v. World Programming*, No. 21-1542; *Google v. Oracle*, 141 S. Ct. 1183.

155 17 U.S.C. § 102.

156 *Andy Warhol Found. for Visual Arts v. Goldsmith*, No. 21-869.

157 United States Copyright Office, "Registration Processing Times," accessed August 21, 2023, https://www.copyright.gov/registration/docs/processing-times-faqs.pdf.

158 United States Copyright Office, "Chapter 1900: Publication," in *Compendium of U.S. Copyright Office Practices*, third ed. (2021), https://www.copyright.gov/comp3/chap1900/ch1900-publication.pdf.

159 17 U.S.C. § 410.

160 17 U.S.C. § 203.

161 17 U.S.C. § 106.

162 17 U.S.C. § 101.

163 17 U.S.C. § 102.

164 18 U.S.C § 1836, https://www.law.cornell.edu/uscode/text/18/1839#.

165 The DTSA enacted the first federal civil cause of action in the US, providing a single uniform cause of action for trade secret misappropriation across states. It also established "federal question" jurisdiction for claims under the DTSA in federal courts. Previously, state causes of action were brought in federal court based on hurdles such as diversity or pendent jurisdiction.

166 18 U.S.C § 1839(3).

167 Suzanne Barto Hill, "Top Secret: How to Successfully Build a Trade Secrets Case," IPWatchdog, October 1, 2019, https://www.ipwatchdog.com/2019/10/01/top-secret-successfully-build-trade-secrets-case/id=114009/.

168 The Coca-Cola Company, "Coca-Cola's Formula Is At the World of Coca-Cola," accessed August 21, 2023, https://www.coca-colacompany.com/about-us/history/coca-cola-formula-is-at-the-world-of-coca-cola#.

169 Nick Statt, "Self-Driving Car Engineer Anthony Levandowski Pleads Guilty to Stealing Google Trade Secrets," *The Verge*, March 19, 2020, https://www.theverge.com/2020/3/19/21187651/anthony-levandowski-pleads-guilty-google-waymo-uber-trade-secret-theft-lawsuit.

170 Statt, "Self-Driving Car Engineer Anthony Levandowski Pleads Guilty."

171 Peter S. Menell et al., *Trade Secret Case Management Judicial Guide* (Washington, DC: Federal Judicial Center, 2023), https://papers.ssrn.com/sol3/papers.cfm?abstract_id=4360102.

172 Anna Majestro, "Preparing for and Obtaining Preliminary Injunctive Relief," American Bar Association, June 4, 2018, https://www.americanbar.org/groups/litigation/committees/woman-advocate/practice/2018/preliminary-injuction-relief/. A temporary restraining order provides the potential of an ex parte decision and is for a shortened defined period, such as fourteen days. The DTSA also added a new form of relief of an ex parte seizure. However, it has rarely been granted.

173 One purpose was that the new statute would reduce variable outcomes based on a patchwork of sometimes inconsistent state laws.

174 Protecting American Intellectual Property Act of 2022, Pub. L. 117–336, 117th Cong., S.1294 (2023), https://www.congress.gov/bill/117th-congress/senate-bill/1294/text.

175 18 U.S.C. § 1839(3)

176 *Turret Labs US v. CargoSprint*, No. 21-952, 2022 WL 701161 (2d Cir. Mar. 9, 2022), https://casetext.com/case/turret-labs-us-v-cargosprint-llc; The Sedona Conference, accessed August 21, 2023, https://thesedonaconference.org/publication/Commentary_on_Governance_and_Management_of_Trade_Secrets; James Pooley, "'Reasonable Efforts' Require Care and Consistency," IPWatchdog, June 27, 2022, https://ipwatchdog.com/2022/06/27/reasonable-efforts-require-care-consistency/id=149835/.

177 18 U.S.C § 1836.

178 Experienced litigators generally agree that the DTSA provisions are interpreted with their overlap in state and federal civil procedure laws. As a result, areas of relief such as injunctions, monetary damages, and attorneys' fees are little changed from Federal Rules of Civil Procedure and state laws predating the DTSA.

179 David Bohrer, "Threatened Misappropriation of Trade Secrets: Making a Federal (DTSA) Case Out of It," *Santa Clara High Technology Law Journal* 33, no. 4 (April 22, 2017): 533 ("Central Valley, through these 'variants,' essentially distinguishes threatened misappropriation as requiring evidence of *bad behavior* by the departing employee, separate and additional to anything they may *know*."), https://digitalcommons.law.scu.edu/cgi/viewcontent.cgi?article=1620&context=chtlj; *Cent. Valley Gen. Hosp. v. Smith*, 162 Cal. App.4th 501, 527–28 (Cal. Ct. App. 2008), https://casetext.com/case/central-valley-gen-hosp-v-smith.

180 Bohrer, "Threatened Misappropriation of Trade Secrets," 537–38. The facts generally are from California litigations, noting that California laws and court opinions represent the ceiling for pro-employee mobility.

181 R. Mark Halligan, "Trade Secrets: The Inevitable Disclosure Doctrine," *Reuters*, November 9, 2021, https://www.reuters.com/legal/legalindustry/trade-secrets-inevitable-disclosure-doctrine-2021-11-09/.

182 Fair Competition Law, "Inevitable Disclosure Doctrine," June 5, 2019, https://faircompetitionlaw.com/2019/06/05/inevitable-disclosure-doctrine-a-brief-history-and-summary/. As a nod to the importance of the Coke and, as it turns out, beverage formula trade secrets generally, here is an excellent assessment of IDD.

183 Editorial Board, "Does the Inevitable Disclosure Doctrine Apply Under the DTSA? It Depends on the State," Orrick, April 1, 2020, https://blogs.orrick.com/trade-secrets-watch/2020/04/01/does-the-inevitable-disclosure-doctrine-apply-under-the-dtsa-it-depends-on-the-state/.

184 Oliver F. Ennis, Nicholas W. Armington, and Adam P. Samansky, "An Emerging Split on the Applicability of the Inevitable Disclosure Doctrine Under the DTSA," Mintz, October 10, 2022, https://www.mintz.com/insights-center/viewpoints/2231/2022-10-10-emerging-split-applicability-inevitable-disclosure.

185 Federal Trade Commission, "Protecting Personal Information: A Guide for Business," October 2016, https://www.ftc.gov/business-guidance/resources/protecting-personal-information-guide-business; *Turret Labs U.S. v. CargoSprint*, No. 21-952; Sedona Conference, accessed August 21, 2023; Pooley, "'Reasonable Efforts' Require Care and Consistency."

186 Confidentiality/nondisclosure terms or agreements are referred to as confidentiality terms to encompass confidentiality terms within employment agreements or standalone confidentiality agreements.

187 The Michelson Institute for Intellectual Property, "How to Protect Your Intellectual Property with a Non-Disclosure Agreement," *The Michelson Institute for Intellectual Property* (blog), August 25, 2020, https://michelsonip.com/intellectual-property-non-disclosure-agreement/.

188 David Atallah and Alessandro Spina, "Fostering a Corporate Culture That Embraces Trade Secret Protection," *Landslide* 15, no. 2 (December/January 2023), https://www.americanbar.org/groups/intellectual_property_law/publications/landslide/2022-23/december-january/fostering-corporate-culture-embraces-trade-secret-protection/.

189 Steven E. Jedlinski, "Summary Judgment of No Misappropriation Due to Failure to Follow Confidentiality Marking Requirements," *Holland & Knight Trade Secrets Blog*, July 10, 2019, https://www.hklaw.com/en/insights/publications/2019/07/summary-judgment-of-no-misappropriation-due-to-failure.

190 Phelps, "Alternative Ways to Protect Trade Secrets Given the Uncertainty Surrounding Noncompete Agreements," March 6, 2023, https://www.phelps.com/insights/alternative-ways-to-protect-trade-secrets-given-the-uncertainty-surrounding-noncompete-agreements.html; Krista M. Cabrera and Mikle S. Jew, "Protecting Trade Secrets in States that Disfavor Noncompetes," Foley & Lardner LLP, December 20, 2022, https://www.foley.com/en/insights/publications/2022/12/protecting-trade-secrets-states-noncompetes.

191 Federal Trade Commission, "FTC Proposes Rule to Ban Noncompete Clauses, Which Hurt Workers and Harm Competition," press release, January 5, 2023, https://www.ftc.gov/news-events/news/press-releases/2023/01/ftc-proposes-rule-ban-noncompete-clauses-which-hurt-workers-harm-competition.

192 A practical takeaway is to place noncompete terms in a separate agreement to reduce the risk of voiding or impacting related rights within the same agreement.

193 This includes being aware of personal values such as integrity, honesty and respect for colleagues and the company, with these traits evaluated in making a hiring decision and throughout employment being bellwethers for a similar treatment of corporate assets.

194 The actual trade secret must, therefore, be filed under seal as part of a protective order evidentiary approach, further adding to the complexity of the evidence in trade secret cases.

195 The list itself, just like trade secrets, generally should be maintained as secret except for those with a need to know based on individual secrets and legal professionals.

196 A ubiquitous defense in trade secret litigation is that the misappropriating defendant doesn't know what trade secrets she is accused of misappropriating. Formal filings for patents and copyrights ameliorate this factual argument because the assets are identified. Copyright filings of trade secrets, as well as documenting acknowledgment of trade secret lists during annual reviews, limit the lack of knowledge defense.

197 Yumiko Hamano, *Invention Disclosure: Form, Reporting Mechanism, Receipt and Processing* (Geneva, Switzerland: World Intellectual Property Organization, 2017), https://www.wipo.int/edocs/mdocs/aspac/en/wipo_ip_bkk_17/wipo_ip_bkk_17_8.pdf.

198 *Oakwood Labs. v. Thanoo*, 999 F.3d 892 (3d Cir. 2021), https://casetext.com/case/oakwood-labs-llc-v-thanoo-4; *Mallet v. Lacayo*, 16 F.4th 364 (3d Cir. 2021), https://casetext.com/case/mallet-co-v-lacayo-3.

199 Not being a soda drinker, I cannot attest to this personally.

200 United States Patent and Trademark Office, "What Is a Trademark?," July 18, 2023, https://www.uspto.gov/trademarks/basics/what-trademark; Lanham Act, 15 U.S.C. § § 1051–1127, 1946, https://uscode.house.gov/view.xhtml?path=/prelim@@title15/chapter22&edition=prelim. Formally, the term "trademark" applies to marks or identifications related both to goods (trademarks) and services (service marks). We will adopt trademarks and refer to goods and services as products for ease of reference.

201 United States Patent and Trademark Office, "Design Patent Application Guide," April 23, 2023, https://www.uspto.gov/patents/basics/types-patent-applications/design-patent-application-guide.

202 Many logos and designs can be subject to copyright protection as well as trademark and design patent, so copyright remains an important consideration.

203 International Trademark Association, "Assignments, Licensing, and Valuation of Trademarks," last modified November 9, 2020, https://www.inta.org/fact-sheets/assignments-licensing-and-valuation-of-trademarks/.

204 Gregory P. Gulia and Vanessa C. Hew, "Trademark Litigation: Likelihood of Confusion," *Practical Law: The Journal, Reuters*, March 1, 2023, https://www.reuters.com/practical-law-the-journal/litigation/trademark-litigation-likelihood-confusion-2023-03-01/.

205 Steven M. Auvil and Michael Gonzalez, "In Assessing Design Patent Infringement, the Devil Is in the Details," The National Law Review, July 17, 2020, https://www.natlawreview.com/article/assessing-design-patent-infringement-devil-details.

206 *Jack Daniel's Properties v. VIP Products*, No. 22-148.

207 Alina Cohen, "How Tiffany & Co. Monopolized a Shade of Blue," Artsy, April 16, 2019, https://www.artsy.net/article/artsy-editorial-tiffany-monopolized-shade-blue. A related turquoise hue was first used by Tiffany & Co. in the 1889 Paris World's Fair. The color was trademarked in 1998 and then formalized as "1837 Blue," commemorating its founding year.

208 Chauncey Crail, Jane Haskins, and Rob Watts, "How to Trademark a Name (2023 Guide)," *Forbes Advisor*, October 13, 2022, https://www.forbes.com/advisor/business/how-to-trademark-your-businesss-name/.

209 *USPTO v. Booking.com*, No. 19-46 (US June 30, 2020), https://www.supremecourt.gov/opinions/19pdf/19-46_8n59.pdf.

210 *USPTO v. Booking.com*, No. 19-46.

211 *USPTO v. Booking.com*, No. 19-46 at 11.

212 *USPTO v. Booking.com*, No. 19-46 at 3.

213 *USPTO v. Booking.com*, No. 19-46.

214 *USPTO v. Booking.com*, No. 19-46 at 13.

215 Pfizer, "What's in a Brand Name? How Drugs Get Their Names," accessed August 22, 2023, https://www.pfizer.com/news/articles/part_2_what_s_in_a_brand_name_how_drugs_get_their_names.

216 Thomas J. Daly and Alek Emery, "Branding Pharmaceuticals: Drug Naming and Non-Traditional Trademarks," *World Trademark Review*, July 17, 2019, https://www.worldtrademarkreview.com/article/branding-pharmaceuticals-drug-naming-and-non-traditional-trademarks.

217 Annie Crawford, "What's in a Brand? How to Define Your Visual Identity," *Adobe Experience Cloud Blog*, October 1, 2017, https://business.adobe.com/blog/how-to/whats-in-a-brand-how-to-define-your-visual-identity.

218 United States Patent and Trademark Office, *Protecting Your Trademark: Enhancing Your Rights through Federal Registration* (Alexandria, VA: United States Patent and Trademark Office, 2016), https://www.uspto.gov/sites/default/files/BasicFacts_1.pdf.

219 For convenience, trademarks cover both. However, for detail-oriented owners, the semantics reflect an appreciation that services businesses are in many cases more valuable than product businesses.

220 Manon Burns and Lisa Holubar, "Is It Functional or Is It Functional? Trade Dress vs. Design Patent 'Functionality,'" American Bar Association, February 8, 2021, https://www.americanbar.org/groups/intellectual_property_law/publications/landslide/2020-21/january-february/is-it-functional-trade-dress-vs-design-patent-functionality/.

221 Guankai, "New Approach with Intellectual Property as Marketing Strategy," *Nabcore* (blog), July 11, 2021, https://nabcore.com/marketing-strategy-with-intellectual-property/.

222 US Patent Act, 35 U.S.C. § 171.

223 *LKQ v. GM Global Tech.*, No. 22-1253 (Fed. Cir. Jan. 20, 2023), https://casetext.com/case/lkq-corp-v-gm-glob-tech-operations-1; *LKQ v. GM Global Tech.*, No. 21-2348 (Fed. Cir. June 30, 2023) (based on the utility patent validity analysis overturning rigid tests for assessing obviousness of utility patents, in *KSR Int'l v. Teleflex*, 550 US 398), https://casetext.com/case/lkq-corp-v-gm-glob-tech-operations-2; *KSR Int'l v. Teleflex*, 550 US 398 (2007), https://casetext.com/case/ksr-intl-co-v-teleflex-inc.

224 Electronic device, US Patent No. US-D593087-S (issued April 26, 2009), https://image-ppubs.uspto.gov/dirsearch-public/print/downloadPdf/D593087.

225 Greenfield Wolf and P. C. Sacks, "United States: $533 Million Apple v. Samsung Verdict Highlights Importance of Design Patents," *Mondaq*, May 18, 2018, https://www.mondaq.com/unitedstates/patent/706348/533-million-apple-v-samsung-verdict-highlights-importance-of-design-patents; Apple v. Samsung Electronics, 678 F.3d 1314 at 8–9 (Fed. Cir. 2012), No. 11-CV-01846-LHK (N.D. Cal. Oct. 22, 2017), https://casetext.com/case/apple-inc-v-samsung-elecs-co-152; Shara Tibken, "Apple and Samsung Finally Settle Their Patent Dispute," CNET, June 27, 2018, https://www.cnet.com/tech/mobile/apple-and-samsung-finally-settle-their-patent-dispute/.

226 United States Patent and Trademark Office, "Design Patent Application Guide."

227 United States Patent and Trademark Office, "Design Patent Application Guide."

228 US Patent Act, 35 U.S.C. § 284.

229 "Total profits" for designs generally means the amount the infringer made. "Lost profits for utility" means the amount the patent owner would have made, which generally is lower than the infringer's profits. The evidence is complex, but overall total profits are easier to prove because the calculation involves evidence about the business of the infringer. Lost profits add evidence about the patent owner, and therefore additional complexity.

230 United States Patent and Trademark Office, "Design Data June 2023," April 30, 2023, https://www.uspto.gov/dashboard/patents/design.html; United States Innovation and Competition Act of 2021, S. 1260, 117th Cong. (2021), https://www.congress.gov/bill/117th-congress/senate-bill/1260; CHIPS and Science Act, H.R. 4346, 117th Cong. (2022), https://www.congress.gov/bill/117th-congress/house-bill/4346; Emily G. Blevins, "Equity in Innovation: Trends in U.S. Patenting and Inventor Diversity," Congressional Research Service, November 30, 2022, https://sgp.fas.org/crs/misc/IF12259.pdf.

231 Vic Lin, "GUI Design Patents: How to Protect Graphical User Interfaces," *PatentTrademarkBlog*, accessed August 22, 2023, https://www.patenttrademarkblog.com/gui-design-patent/.

232 Counterfeit Goods Seizure Act of 2019, S. 2987; Law360, "Design Patents Prove Successful on Enforcement, Defense."

233 United States Patent and Trademark Office, "USPTO Fee Schedule"; 15 U.S.C. § 638; SBIR, STTR, "Timeline and Costs for Patent Filings ("Cost estimates...vary widely, but numerous surveys...have indicated...$5,000 to $15,000 for a US utility application depending upon the complexity of the technology."); American Intellectual Property Law Association, "2021 Report of the Economic Survey" (the American Intellectual Property Law Association produces a definitive source based on US attorney surveys, which can be ordered); Chapter 9: Costs.

234 United States Innovation and Competition Act of 2021, S. 1260; CHIPS and Science Act, H.R. 4346; Blevins, "Equity in Innovation." The proposal was contained in the US Innovation and Competition Act of 2021, which along with a companion House bill was superseded by the CHIPS and Science Act. CHIPS focused on broader areas of semiconductor innovation and national security, but also including an investment for R & D programs. A November 2022 research study also presents trends in patenting and inventor diversity.

235 Michelle Saksena, Nicholas Rada, and Lisa Cook, *Where are U.S. Women Patentees? Assessing Three Decades of Growth* (Alexandria, VA: United States Patent and Trademark Office, October 2022), https://www.uspto.gov/sites/default/files/documents/oce-women-patentees-report.pdf.

236 Similar monikers with a numbering reference can be used for global geographies or treaty regions, such as under the new EU Unitary Patent, starting June 1, 2023.

237 Baker Botts, "Patent Prosecution for Lean Startups: Seven Steps for Protecting Your Early-Stage Ideas," August 1, 2022, https://www.bakerbotts.com/thought-leadership/publications/2022/august/patent-prosecution-for-lean-startups; UpCounsel, "How to File a Provisional Patent: Everything You Need to Know," last modified July 10, 2020, https://www.upcounsel.com/how-to-file-a-provisional-patent; MaRS Startup Toolkit, "Patent Strategy for Tech Startups: Protecting Intellectual Property," MaRS, accessed August 22, 2023, https://learn.marsdd.com/article/patent-strategy/; Oceanport, NJ, "Starting a Sports League with a Unique Format. Can Intellectual Property Help Protect the Format from Being Copied?," r/Copyright, Entertainment/Sports, Justia Ask a Lawyer, 2017, https://answers.justia.com/question/2017/05/15/starting-a-sports-league-with-a-unique-f-271689; Vic Lin, "What Should a Startup IP Checklist Include?," *PatentTrademarkBlog*, accessed August 22, 2023, https://www.patenttrademarkblog.com/startup-ip-checklist/.

238 Leonard, Haskins, and Bottorff, "How to File a Provisional Patent in 2023"; Chapter 2: Patents.

239 United States Patent and Trademark Office, "Patents Pendency Data June 2023," July 31, 2023, https://www.uspto.gov/dashboard/patents/pendency.html. This is referred to as the activities for Traditional Total Pendency by the USPTO, which as of December 2022 was 25.9 months.

240 US Patent No. 8,527,355 (filed Mar. 28, 2007) (based on a provisional application No. 60/920,395), https://image-ppubs.uspto.gov/dirsearch-public/print/downloadPdf/8527355.

241 United States Patent and Trademark Office, "USPTO Fee Schedule"; United States Patent and Trademark Office, "Inventor & Entrepreneur Resources," last modified July 27, 2023, https://www.uspto.gov/learning-and-resources/inventors-entrepreneurs-resources; United States Patent and Trademark Office, "Micro Entity Status," June 30, 2023, https://www.uspto.gov/patents/laws/micro-entity-status#:~:text.

242 In contrast, the fee levels of at maximum $1,820 for larger corporations do not limit participation in the patent system to the same extent as for SMEs or individuals with limited funding resources.

243 United States Patent and Trademark Office, "Filing a Patent Application on Your Own," March 15, 2023, https://www.uspto.gov/patents/basics/using-legal-services/pro-se-assistance-program.

244 United States Patent and Trademark Office, "Patents Pendency Data June 2023."

245 Patent Technology Monitoring Team, "U.S. Patent Statistics Chart Calendar Years 1963–2020," United States Patent and Trademark Office, last modified August 22, 2023, https://www.uspto.gov/web/offices/ac/ido/oeip/taf/us_stat.htm. The USPTO reports on the counts of patent applications and grants annually. The percentage of US originating grants is higher than internationally sourced filings, with US originating patents having a 57 percent grant rate.

246 Patent Technology Monitoring Team, "U.S. Patent Statistics Chart."

247 Gene Quinn, "Patent Prosecution 101: Understanding Patent Examiner Rejections," IPWatchdog, February 11, 2017, https://ipwatchdog.com/2017/02/11/patent-prosecution-patent-examiner-rejections/id=78211/.

248 Baker Botts, "Patent Prosecution for Lean Startups"; UpCounsel, "How to File a Provisional Patent"; MaRS Startup Toolkit, "Patent Strategy for Tech Startups"; Oceanport, NJ, "Starting a Sports League with a Unique Format"; Vic Lin, "What Should a Startup IP Checklist Include?"; United States Patent and Trademark Office, "Patents Pendency Data June 2023."

249 United States Patent and Trademark Office, "2506 Times for Submitting Maintenance Fee Payments," USPTO.gov, last modified February 16, 2023, https://www.uspto.gov/web/offices/pac/mpep/s2506.html. The maintenance fee timing can be paid over a range of six months; where a maintenance fee is missed, the patent goes abandoned.

250 United States Patent and Trademark Office, "USPTO Fee Schedule"; 15 U.S.C. § 638; SBIR, STTR, "Timeline and Costs for Patent Filings ("Cost estimates…vary widely, but numerous surveys…have indicated…$5,000 to $15,000 for a US utility application depending upon the complexity of the technology."); American Intellectual Property Law Association, "2021 Report of the Economic Survey" (the American Intellectual Property Law Association produces a definitive source based on US attorney surveys, which can be ordered). The estimated patent attorney utility filing fee is the average of $10,000 for the $5,000 to $15,000 range presented by the Small Business Association, the Small Business Innovation Research (SBIR) program authorized by 15 US Code § 638, in 2017. The patent attorney utility and provisional filing fees, and administrative fees (including formal notice and docketing of patenting activity), also are based on advertised fees on law firm websites, my personal experience and alignment with the common statistic of up to $20,000 for the cost to obtain a patent. While the SBIR statistic is five years old, competition for flat fee patent preparation is strong and where the applicant also files a provisional at the estimated patent attorney fee of $4,000 (as recommended), the total patent preparation fee is $14,000.

251 UpCounsel, "How Much Does an International Patent Cost"; SBIR, STTR, "Timeline and Costs for Patent Filings." However, "[t]he total investment to prepare, prosecute, and maintain a patent for its life in four or five countries can easily exceed $200,000."

252 Eileen McDermott, "New EPO Unitary Patent Dashboard Show 5,000+ Requests Since Launch," IPWatchdog, July 24, 2023, https://ipwatchdog.com/2023/07/24/epo-launches-unitary-patent-dashboard-5000-requests/id=163984/.

253 United States Patent and Trademark Office, "U.S. Patent Statistics Chart."

254 United States Patent and Trademark Office, "Patents Pendency Data June 2023."

255 United States Patent and Trademark Office, "USPTO's Prioritized Patent Examination Program," March 4, 2020, https://www.uspto.gov/patents/initiatives/usptos-prioritized-patent-examination-program; United States Patent and Trademark Office, "USPTO Fee Schedule."

256 United States Copyright Office, "Fees," accessed August 22, 2023, https://www.copyright.gov/about/fees.html; United States Patent and Trademark Office, "USPTO Fee Schedule" (trademark and design fees); United States Patent and Trademark Office, "Trademarks Data Q3 2023 at a Glance," July 21, 2023, https://www.uspto.gov/dashboard/trademarks/. For each IP asset, estimated attorneys' fees are based on advertised fees on law firm websites and the personal experience of my co-author, J. Christopher Lynch.

257 United States Copyright Office, "Fees"; United States Patent and Trademark Office, "USPTO Fee Schedule"; United States Patent and Trademark Office, "Trademarks Data Q3 2023 at a Glance"; United States Patent and Trademark Office, "Patents Pendency Data June 2023."

258 Casey C. Sullivan, "How Does Your IP Legal Budget Measure Up?," FindLaw, last modified March 21, 2019, https://www.findlaw.com/legalblogs/in-house/how-does-your-ip-legal-budget-measure-up/v; HBR Consulting, "Annual HBR Law Department Survey Finds Only Moderate Increase in Total Legal Spending Worldwide Despite Major Increase in Organizations' Legal Needs," Business Wire, October 8, 2015, https://www.businesswire.com/news/home/20151008005223/en/Annual-HBR-Law-Department-Survey-Finds-Only-Moderate-Increase-in-Total-Legal-Spending-Worldwide-Despite-Major-Increase-in-Organizations.

259 Victoria and Albert Museum, "Leonardo da Vinci's Notebooks," accessed August 22, 2023, https://www.vam.ac.uk/articles/leonardo-da-vincis-notebooks; Leonardo da Vinci, "Vitruvian Man," drawing, c. 1490, http://home.ubalt.edu/NTYGFIT/ai_04_distinguishing_perspective/ai_04_see/ren_art/renpers0101_l_.htm.

260 Hamano, *Invention Disclosure*; Chapter 6: Trade Secrets.

261 Will Durant, *The Story of Philosophy* (New York: Pocket Books, 1926), https://www.simonandschuster.com/books/Story-of-Philosophy/Will-Durant/9780671201593. Will Durant was an American writer who interpreted Aristotle's philosophy in his book *The Story of Philosophy*.

262 "'Fanness'—An Idea that Will Change the Way You Motivate and Inspire Others," Admired Leadership, June 4, 2020, YouTube video, 21:58, https://www.youtube.com/watch?v=W05S07wIU78.

Milton Keynes UK
Ingram Content Group UK Ltd.
UKHW010759100324
439213UK00009B/92/J